# Identity, Culture and Belonging

*Educating Young Children for a Changing World*

Also available from Bloomsbury

*Developing the Expertise of Primary and Elementary Classroom Teachers,*
Tony Eaude
*Social and Learning Relationships in the Primary School,*
Alison Kington and Karen Blackmore
*New Perspectives on Young Children's Moral Education,*
Tony Eaude

# Identity, Culture and Belonging

*Educating Young Children for a Changing World*

Tony Eaude

BLOOMSBURY ACADEMIC
LONDON • NEW YORK • OXFORD • NEW DELHI • SYDNEY

BLOOMSBURY ACADEMIC
Bloomsbury Publishing Plc
50 Bedford Square, London, WC1B 3DP, UK
1385 Broadway, New York, NY 10018, USA
29 Earlsfort Terrace, Dublin 2, Ireland

BLOOMSBURY, BLOOMSBURY ACADEMIC and the Diana logo
are trademarks of Bloomsbury Publishing Plc

First published in Great Britain 2020
Paperback edition first published 2021

Copyright © Tony Eaude, 2020

Tony Eaude has asserted his right under the Copyright,
Designs and Patents Act, 1988, to be identified as Author of this work.

For legal purposes the Acknowledgements on p. vi constitute an
extension of this copyright page.

Cover image © FatCamera/iStock

All rights reserved. No part of this publication may be reproduced or
transmitted in any form or by any means, electronic or mechanical,
including photocopying, recording, or any information storage or retrieval
system, without prior permission in writing from the publishers.

Bloomsbury Publishing Plc does not have any control over, or responsibility for,
any third-party websites referred to or in this book. All internet addresses given
in this book were correct at the time of going to press. The author and publisher
regret any inconvenience caused if addresses have changed or sites have
ceased to exist, but can accept no responsibility for any such changes.

A catalogue record for this book is available from the British Library.

A catalog record for this book is available from the Library of Congress.

ISBN: HB: 978-1-3500-9780-3
PB: 978-1-3502-0669-4
ePDF: 978-1-3500-9781-0
eBook: 978-1-3500-9782-7

Typeset by Deanta Global Publishing Services, Chennai, India

To find out more about our authors and books visit
www.bloomsbury.com and sign up for our newsletters.

# Contents

Acknowledgements — vi

Introduction — 1

## Part I  Identity and Culture in a World of Uncertainty

1  Exploring identity and culture — 17
2  Thinking through the intersections of identity and culture — 34
3  Understanding the changing social, cultural and educational landscape — 52

## Part II  How Young Children's Identities Are Shaped

4  Constructing identities — 75
5  Exercising agency, creativity and imagination — 93
6  Belonging and participating in inclusive environments — 111

## Part III  The Implications for Adults

7  Working towards a holistic approach — 133
8  Considering the implications for adults outside schools — 151
9  Reviewing the implications for schools and teachers — 169

Conclusion — 187

Glossary — 203
Bibliography — 204
Index — 215

# Acknowledgements

It is impossible to acknowledge adequately all the many people who have influenced my thinking and the writing of this book. I wish to recognize the contribution of many people who have helped shape my thinking. Among those writers whom I do not know personally but whose work has been influential are Clifford Geertz, Margaret Donaldson, Phillida Salmon and Jerome Bruner, whom I did have the privilege of hearing. Richard Pring, Mark Halstead, Robin Alexander, Andrew Pollard, Brendan Hyde, Marian de Souza and Karen-Marie Yust are among those academics I know whose work has enriched my understanding about the complex issues discussed.

I wish to celebrate the many inspirational and caring teachers and head teachers, too many to name, with whom I have worked, as colleagues in primary schools. They have helped to shape their children's identities as confident and compassionate young people, often in the face of policies which have encouraged a narrow and restrictive curriculum. Such teachers, and I, have also learned a great deal from the children we have taught and in many cases their parents.

I am grateful to two anonymous reviewers for their thoughtful comments and to all those at Bloomsbury who have offered guidance and helped to bring the book to publication.

I wish to thank these publishers for permission to use quotations as epigraphs as follows:

- Harvard University Press for those at the start of Chapters 1 and 8;
- Chalice Press for the one at the start of Chapter 2;
- Routledge for the one at the start of Chapter 3;
- Bloomsbury Publishing plc for those at the start of Chapters 4 and 9;
- Faber and Faber for the one at the start of Chapter 6; and
- SAGE for the one at the start of Chapter 7.

The epigraph at the start of Chapter 5 has been reproduced under the UK Open Government Licence.

More specifically, I am grateful to friends and colleagues who have discussed the ideas and read and commented on drafts of the chapters. One group who did so on several occasions consisted of Geerthi Ahilan, Liz Burton, Jane Godby, Clare Whyles and Chris Williams. Simon Godby and Christian Panzer also helped me to understand more about the role of technology in children's lives. A conversation with Mary Fountain was valuable especially in relation to gender and class identity. Daryn and Jessica Egan-Simon and Caroline and Joe Egan provided insightful comments on the milestones in their own children's development in relation to identity. My thanks to them all.

I wish to mark the roles that my late father, my mother and my brother, Philip, Margaret and Michael Eaude, played in how my own identity was shaped and reshaped, as a child and subsequently. I have been fortunate for their support in ways not available to many less privileged children.

Finally, and most importantly, I want to thank Jude Egan for her love and support for more than thirty-two years. Her quiet but persistent emphasis on how relationships and environments shape how young children's identities are constructed and are central to how adults should relate to and nurture young children have exerted a profound influence on my own thinking and, I hope, my actions. More specifically, her patience, willingness to listen to and discuss my ideas and her wise words throughout the gestation of this book have been invaluable in helping me to keep going and maintain some sense of perspective.

Tony Eaude
Oxford
tony@edperspectives.org.uk
www.edperspectives.org.uk

# Introduction

This book explores the interaction between identity and culture and how culture – in various ways – helps to shape young children's identities, and why children from an early age require a robust but flexible sense of identity to thrive in a diverse, changing and uncertain world. From this, it aims to present a radical, inclusive, culturally sensitive vision of how young children should be educated for such a world.

It is not based on a particular research project, but draws on research about identity and culture and factors such as gender, race and class from historical, sociological and anthropological sources, and about how young children learn, mainly from neuroscientific and psychological research. I also consider my own experience and interests, and the cultural influences on me, as a person and an educator, trying not to give these too much prominence but to use these as illustrations. This approach has led me to reflect on, and challenge, many current, and my own long-held, assumptions about identity, culture, childhood and education.

One distinctive feature is the exploration of questions of identity, culture and belonging through the lens of childhood, with education seen more broadly than as formal schooling. The focus is on young children and on how their identities are shaped by the cultures in which they live and by the range of experiences which they encounter. Adolescence is often seen as the key period when identity is formed; and much of the research on identity relates to adolescents rather than younger children. This book argues that the roots of identity are established in early childhood, without suggesting that identities cannot change, as they do in many respects, notably in adolescence. Adolescence is a time of challenge to, and rejection of, adult norms, for instance through music, fashion and experimenting with sex and drugs, to shock and question the assumptions of their parents' generation. For younger children, such challenges are usually less extreme, but many of the pressures and influences associated with adolescence are increasingly affecting younger children, especially those in the seven- to eleven-year-old age group.

My main focus is on children up to about eleven years old. I make a broad distinction between those younger than about seven and those who are older. I adopt Adler and Adler's (1998) use of the term 'pre-adolescence' to cover the age group roughly between seven and eleven, called by psychoanalysts 'the latency period'. For those children between about three and seven years old, I use the term 'early childhood' and for those under three 'babies and toddlers'. However, ideas about what a child is, and how adults should relate to children and the latter be expected to respond, vary significantly between cultures, as discussed in Chapter 3. And in Chapter 4, I argue that the idea of linear, age-related stages of development is of limited use when discussing complex constructs such as identity. Therefore, such distinctions should be treated with some caution.

Ideas such as identity and culture are extremely complex and contested, with meanings and connotations which vary significantly between societies and cultures. What these terms mean and how they are related and intersect are discussed in Chapters 1 and 2, but introduced here.

In discussing identity, Jenkins (2014: 41–2) suggests that the world as experienced by humans can be best understood as three linked orders

- the individual one;
- the interactional one; and
- the institutional one.

Therefore, any individual's attitudes, beliefs and actions are affected by the relationships she or he experiences and the cultures and groups to which she or he belongs. However, in simple terms, identity refers to who one is, and becomes – with each of us having multiple identities, which go to make up, and define, the whole person. But individual identity must be seen in the context of the different groups of which any individual is part, so that one may talk of personal, group and national identities, though these may frequently be intertwined. For example, religious, linguistic and cultural identities may be related to national identities, but how national identities are expressed by some people may not fit with how these are understood by other groups and individuals.

Gilroy (1997: 301–2) suggests that 'identity is always particular, as much about difference as about shared identity ... identities depend on the marking of difference'. We all belong to many different groups, of varying levels of significance and permanence and have multiple identities, some of which may clash with each other. Identities are sources of both belonging and conflict. A seven-year-old may have a sense of belonging not only to her family, class, school and perhaps a faith community but also to a friendship group, a geographical neighbourhood, a sports club and other groups. These may vary in importance, but all are micro-cultures, with their own, often-implicit, assumptions, ways of working and beliefs. As we shall see, the peer group, and its markers of identity, both visible and invisible, has become increasingly important for children, particularly as they approach adolescence.

Some – mostly superficial – aspects of identity are voluntary and can be changed, while others are not and must be accepted and incorporated into one's emerging sense of identity. Some are profoundly affected by factors such as gender, race, physical ability, social background, language and religion, as discussed in Chapter 2. Others are more individual and shaped by experience. I shall argue that a sense of identity and who one is seen to be, and may become, matters more, especially for young children, than who one 'is' in terms of background, but that the latter cannot, and should not, be ignored.

An individual's identity is like a constantly changing narrative which involves the whole person – influenced by the many people with whom she or he interacts, for good or ill. Chapter 4 suggests that the processes of primary and, to a lesser extent, secondary socialization, to use Berger and Luckmann's (1967) terms, exert profound influences on individuals' identities. Identities are affected by cultural influences much broader than what happens at home or at school, though socialization influences, rather than determines, who children become, as identities are constantly reshaped and re-negotiated.

In Chapter 1, I explore different ways in which the term 'culture' is understood and how it operates, highlighting three related, overlapping meanings, referring to

- the norms, values and beliefs of a group;
- the idea of a 'cultured person'; and
- the space(s) in which nurture and growth takes place.

Culture deals with, and can enhance our understanding of, many of the most central questions in life, such as what it is to be human and how we, and other people, think, act and interact. Culture is like the lens through which everyone interprets, understands and makes sense of experience, even when we do not recognize this, a filter which is always there, even though we may not be aware of it, exerting a powerful influence on people's identities, but in ways that are hard to pin down.

Young (1994: 14) highlights that

- culture is learned and depends on being brought up within a framework of beliefs and assumptions – a cultural space;

- a large component of culture operates below the level of conscious awareness; and
- cultural patterns structure both thought and perception.

In other words, how we think and how we see, interpret and understand the world and other people depends to a large extent on culture. Culture transmits messages, often implicitly, about actions, activities and beliefs to be encouraged or discouraged. For instance, we may have strong views on whether one should be allowed to carry guns or whether people like ourselves are superior (or inferior) to others, and may believe that such views are rational or even obvious. However, our early experiences, and the company we keep, have a much stronger influence on our beliefs – and the behaviours which follow from those – than we imagine.

Culture binds groups of individuals together, and in doing so separates them to some extent from others. Culture both shapes and reflects how individuals think about and understand experience. For instance, what one reads, the TV programmes one watches and the people one mixes with tend to be aligned with one's beliefs and to reinforce these. For young children, culture tends to act more as a shaping influence, whereas it increasingly reflects existing beliefs as people get older and, usually, more set in their ways. Culture helps to express and mould who we are and become, as individuals and groups, and is closely linked to personal and group identity. The links with identity are explored in Chapter 2 and thereafter, especially in relation to gender, race, class and religion, highlighting that, especially when manifested in specific practices, such factors raise controversial, strongly contested and often uncomfortable issues.

As Bronfenbrenner (1979) suggests, culture operates at different levels simultaneously, with varying layers of influence. He identifies up to six layers in which the individual child, or adult, is nested. However, in this book, I refer mainly to macro- and micro-cultures. A macro-culture is the culture of society, whether national or increasingly international, manifested for instance in the expectations and the language used and expressed through, and shaped by, many types of media. Chapter 3 considers how the macro-culture has changed considerably over the last fifty years, leading to greater fragmentation and diversity. As a result, the context has become more complex, providing considerable challenges for all children, especially those from disadvantaged and/or disrupted backgrounds, and the adults who nurture and educate them. Many children find it hard to achieve a sense of belonging or do so in ways which may be harmful to them and other people, increasingly so as they approach adolescence.

Micro-cultures are more local and intimate. For young children, influential micro-cultures are those of the small groups to which they belong, whether formal ones such as the family, a nursery, a faith-based or scout group or school or informal ones such as a group or friends or supporters of a football team. Micro-cultures have hidden aspects, and often a set of practices and assumptions, known to insiders and not to others. For instance, the children at the school where I was head teacher knew which toilets were, and were to be, used by boys or by girls, without adults knowing this or their injunctions making much difference. Such aspects may be relatively fixed over time or change frequently, helping both to include and to exclude.

Each individual inhabits not just one culture but an amalgam of micro-cultures within a macro-culture which is increasingly global in its reach. We all live within many intersecting and overlapping micro-cultures and subcultures. The influence of different cultures varies and is individually experienced, but culture reflects, often implicitly, what individuals value and societies and communities hold dear.

Each of us is part of, and belongs to, many groups, some more distant, such as a nation or a religion, others more immediate and intimate, such as a family, community or a group of friends. So, personal identities are nested within a range of collective identities of differing levels of significance, with identities fitting, sometimes uneasily, with each other. The groups to which we belong help to shape behaviours, values and beliefs. We are all socialized (often tacitly) into cultural norms, many of which are deep-seated, so that we may not be aware of them – what is often called 'second nature', even though they have been learned. Individuals are 'encultured' into particular ways of acting and interacting, often implicitly and unconsciously, though the effect on any individual varies.

Culture, both the immediate micro-cultures of family, community and school and the wider macro-culture, exerts strong, often subtle and invisible, influences, which affect how young children act and see themselves. For instance, young children tend to absorb their parents' views from the toys chosen, the books read, the questions asked, the language used and the example set. And attitudes and stereotypes based on gender, race and class are learned very early – and hard to change. But such micro-cultures also provide spaces for exploration of what being a member of such a group entails and of how to act appropriately.

Macro-cultural messages are transmitted by the media, such as TV, the internet and magazines, which provide powerful messages about what constitutes success and leads to happiness, often targeted particularly at young children in sophisticated ways, as considered in more depth in Chapter 3. While formal settings, such as schools, exert considerable influence, this is perhaps less than the adults involved may think and wish.

Cultures are inherently normative, and regulatory, in that they indicate how people should act and think, as well as descriptive, that is, how people do act and think. For instance, the culture of a group, such as one defined by religious faith or gender, or a nursery, a choir or a sports club, indicates how one should conduct oneself and discourages those who may be inclined to deviate from doing so.

Culture can act as a tradition which encapsulates beliefs and practice passed from one generation to the next. Traditions tend to be associated with an unchanging, even ossified, view, taking little account of changing circumstances, though they influence the beliefs and actions of individuals and groups and are changed by them, albeit slowly and in small ways. In this sense, culture operates like a framework which can be, or seem, restrictive, but also provides boundaries which can help provide predictability.

I do not believe that one can think or write authentically about identity and culture without recognizing the legacy of patriarchy and colonialism, the marginalization of the poor and religious intolerance – and the extent to which this legacy still continues. One's own, or at least one's own culture's, superiority is frequently assumed even if not actually asserted; and we become so used to our cultural assumptions that we often fail to see them, or even believe that they exist. Henrich's idea (see Lancy, 2015) of WEIRDs (Western, educated, industrialized, rich democracies) is useful as a reminder that what members of such societies, like me, may see as normal is not universal. It is not only other people who inhabit a culture; and one must be wary of believing that other cultures, and the people who belong to them, are a bit odd and involve strange, even exotic, assumptions and practices, usually seen as inferior to one's own.

This book suggests that there may be much to learn from other cultures, more concerning adults' underlying attitudes towards children than adopting specific practices. For example, most 'Western', industrialized societies are obsessed with milestones of cognitive development, whereas many other societies are more interested in children becoming socially adept and in their acquiring practical skills through engaging in meaningful, useful activities.

I believe that societies are usually enriched by social and cultural diversity, though I recognize that such a view is disputed. The rapid pace of change may make some groups and individuals who have previously felt relatively secure, fearful of the consequences, especially those who are, or feel, excluded.

I shall suggest that all children – and the societies they live in – benefit from opportunities and encouragement to create what Putnam (2000) calls bridging, as well as bonding, capital. The latter refers to what binds those who are similar, and the former, which is much harder to create, leads to a greater understanding of, and respect and empathy for, those who are different.

All individuals, by definition, have identities. I shall suggest that, in a world of constant change, children's identities must be robust but flexible enough – more like rubber than glass – to enable them to cope with change and adversity and the turbulence of adolescence. To achieve this, children from a young age need to know about, experience and welcome cultural diversity and must explore both similarity and difference – and, where appropriate, question and challenge cultural norms, including their own family's and community's.

The view of schooling for young children which I advocate differs substantially from that currently adopted in most systems, where the main focus is on knowledge and skills, especially those related to literacy and numeracy, which can be easily tested. I shall suggest that one main purpose of education is to enrich children's experience and so to extend their cultural horizons. By this, I do not just mean providing and enabling a wide experience of activities often associated with the term 'culture' – such as drama, art, music and literature – or visiting theatres, museums and places of worship. Rather, schools must enable all children to understand themselves and their own society and other people, and their cultures and societies; and to become the sorts of people who will help to create a more just, inclusive and sustainable society.

As we shall see, broadening young children's cultural horizons and ensuring high levels of achievement are not opposed to each other, as is often thought, but meeting these aims presents many paradoxes, puzzles and dilemmas. Some individuals and groups may benefit from particular approaches which this book cannot address in detail. The complexity of children's lives and families, and how children's experiences, responses and life trajectories vary, means that specific considerations apply, for instance in how the identities of children with complex disabilities are strengthened.

Inevitably, we all bring our own assumptions in discussing complex and contested issues. To explain some of mine, let me say a little about my own background, identities and the cultures in which I grew up. I was born in 1953, the younger of two brothers, in a family where my father and mother married and remained so until my father's death, when my brother and I were both adults. I define myself as white and have been able-bodied and in good physical and mental health throughout my life. I have not had children of my own, though helped to some extent in bringing up my partner's daughter and son and acting as a grandparent to their four young children.

When I was a child, we lived in a middle-class suburb near London, UK. Both there and in the wider society – the macro-culture – there was little diversity of religious affiliation, obedience was expected and deference to authority was common and disparaging comments about women, black people, foreigners, homosexuals and those with disabilities were rife. Many of these are now rightly seen as so offensive that it is inappropriate to put them in writing here. Religion did not figure very strongly in my upbringing, at home, though the boys-only boarding schools to which I went from the age of nine had a broadly Christian ethos. While corporal punishment in schools was allowed, it was becoming less prevalent, but smacking children was common, though not in our family. We did not have a television until I was about ten years old – and of course computers and mobile phones had not been invented.

My schooling was academic, with more emphasis on English, the classics and the humanities than science, mathematics, music, art or practical activities. I learned to read easily, though I found writing difficult since I was left-handed and had poor fine motor skills. I was interested in reading, history and sport from a young age. As a result I became a voracious reader, keen on participating in drama and sport, less so music and art.

I had a high level of self-esteem and confidence academically, though was small and emotionally cautious. I was quite anxious and well-behaved, though untidy and not very concerned about my appearance. As with most boys of my generation, I was not encouraged to express my emotions. Though competitive, I was quite a solitary, serious and self-contained child, who made a lot of acquaintances rather than close friendships. Many of these traits have continued into adulthood, suggesting that they are deep-seated, whether because of temperament or early socialization.

After three years studying history at the University of Oxford, UK, I became a primary school teacher, not having wanted to teach just one subject. I was a classroom teacher for thirteen years, then the head teacher, for nine years, of a socially and ethnically diverse school. Since studying for a doctorate, I have spent about fifteen years as an independent researcher and writer. I have written a range of articles and books about young children, especially in relation to spiritual and moral development, and the implications for teachers.

This brief – and necessarily selective – personal narrative is intended to indicate that everyone has multiple, intersecting, identities from an early age and the background to some of my own beliefs and assumptions. While a thumbnail sketch only hints at some of these, I write as someone who has lived through a period of considerable social and cultural change and is fascinated by the challenges and opportunities of how children and adults can be enabled to live harmoniously and respectfully as global citizens in a diverse society.

You may think it inappropriate for someone, like me, as a member of most groups which have been historically advantaged, to write, and suggest what should be done, about issues such as gender, race, class and physical ability. However, I suggest that discrimination on such grounds damages those who are discriminated against and those who do the discriminating and the societies within which they live. While those who are disadvantaged have more personal experience of, and insight into, discrimination, those who are advantaged bear the main responsibility for trying to put historic injustices right. The messages are therefore often directed most forcefully to those from advantaged groups.

There are four fundamental problems in writing – and reading – about complex concepts such as identity and culture, gender, ethnicity/race and class. The first is that we tend to be trapped within the language, and the assumptions, of our own culture. Language, especially the written word, is a somewhat inadequate tool to describe and discuss the most complex aspects of human experience. For instance, an apparently simple idea such as cultural development is problematic in that the whole educational process is so dependent on culture that cultural development is arguably integral to education. Moreover, the idea of development tends to imply improvement – and we tend to believe that our own culture and its practices are, mostly, superior to others. How an action is understood and may be interpreted is not universally agreed. For example, shaking hands with, or kissing, someone one knows may be usual in one culture, but taboo in another. Similarly, for a child to look an adult in the eye may be expected in some cultures and seen as a mark of disrespect in others. Therefore, children have to learn what such actions may signify, and how to act, in different contexts; and adults must be sensitive to such differences if they are to be inclusive. This said, the idea of cultural development can be useful as an overarching term to refer to how children learn to understand their own culture and that of other individuals and groups, often with differing norms and expectations.

A second difficulty, highlighted by anthropology, is that members of one culture, especially a dominant one, cannot really understand another culture and how its members think and feel. There is an acute danger of outsiders making facile and possibly inaccurate judgements. However much I, as a man, may try to inhabit, or describe, the experience of a woman, or as a white person that of a person of colour, my efforts will always fall short – and vice versa. The more barriers – of gender, race, class, religion, sexuality, (dis)ability and age – exist, and exert their influence, the more cautious one should be of believing that one understands, or can empathize with, other people fully. Moreover, the connotations of terms such as 'minority ethnic' or 'persons of colour' can be a source of contention depending on whether such terms are used by members of such groups or others. It is easy to cause offence without meaning to do so. The complexity and contestability of issues related to identity and culture should make one cautious about generalization, but should not, in my view, preclude one from making some statements confidently and recognizing that some are so culturally specific that one must be more tentative. For reasons to be discussed, this does not mean that one should not stand up for one's own beliefs, but must do so carefully and sensitively, with some hesitation.

The third problem follows from the previous one: that of trivializing what really matters to other people or overstating the importance of what does not. We shall see that signifiers, or markers, of culture come in many guises, including the way one talks; the food one eats; the clothes one wears; the jewellery or tattoos one has; the music and books one values; the attitudes one has to relationships between men and women, or between adults and children; or the artefacts and texts which one deems to be sacred. I am not suggesting that these are all of equal significance, but rather that other people may not realize how much importance an individual ascribes to these – and that an individual, especially a child, may not really know.

The fourth problem is that of being seen to preach – a danger to which I am prone. None of us can escape, entirely, our own cultural assumptions. The complexity and diversity of these, and the changing context, suggest that one should try to avoid parochialism and the belief that one's own assumptions are necessarily correct or appropriate for their children. Those who are privileged must try to recognize the challenges for those who are not; and should be wary of imposing their own views on other people. These are dangers to which those from dominant cultural groups, like me, should strive particularly to avoid. However, this does not mean that 'anything goes', in the name of a particular culture or tradition, either for children or for the adults who nurture and educate them.

Such considerations make it extremely difficult to write about identity and culture without giving too much prominence or credence to one's own culture and beliefs. As a result, thinking about these ideas requires humility and tentativeness, without losing sight of one's principles and beliefs, both from me, writing as a white, male, middle-class, English academic, and from you as a reader, whatever your background.

This book has been written primarily for academics and professionals, internationally, but the ideas will be of interest to parents/carers and others concerned with how young children's identities are shaped and nurtured. I try to write about complex and contested ideas in relatively simple language. This, inevitably, means that in places the result is an oversimplification – and that readers will disagree with some elements of the argument, though I make no apology for being, at times, controversial. I have included a glossary on page 203 to explain some of the more technical language.

Geertz (1993) argues that to describe culture with any degree of accuracy requires 'thick descriptions', which look at the local and specific details, rather than 'thin descriptions' which tend to generalize and to be vague and insufficiently specific. Therefore, I have included examples to illustrate points being made, while trying not to privilege my own views. While drawing on theoretical writing, I suggest some practical implications for how young children should be nurtured and those who care for and educate them.

It may be helpful to set out here some assumptions which I shall try to justify in subsequent chapters, namely that

- human beings, especially as children, are constantly trying to make sense of their experiences;
- while some aspects of any individual's identity depend on his or her genetic make-up and temperament, identities are constructed, and constantly changing, contrary to an essentialist view, which regards identity as fixed;
- culture is not static and more like a space (or spaces) for exploration than a thing or a collection of things;
- different levels of culture influence individuals within them in ways which are subtle and often unconscious and so hard to see or articulate;
- the groups to which an individual belongs exert a profound influence on how his or her identities are shaped;
- any stage-related theory of how identities are shaped should be treated with caution, when applied to a particular individual or group, even though it may provide a broadly accurate overall pattern;
- the years before adolescence are more influential in how identities are shaped than is usually recognized; and
- education is a process with the potential to improve both individuals and society.

Part I explores the complexities of what is meant by identity and culture, and how these intersect, and the current social, cultural and educational context, to indicate some of the challenges faced by young children and adults who care for, and educate, them. I highlight some groups for whom creating a coherent and robust, but flexible, sense of identity is particularly difficult and suggest the qualities and dispositions required to deal with a world of change and uncertainty.

Part II considers how young children learn, particularly how they construct their identities, and the role of culture, in its broadest sense, in this process, touching on the age-old question of the relative importance of 'nature' and 'nurture', discussing why culture matters, how culture influences children and the environments – the micro-cultures – within which children thrive. I argue that children need to exercise agency, imagination and creativity, within structures which enable and encourage them to do so. I explore different ways of representing experience and the role of language, notably the child's own talk and ability to listen to, and question, adults respectfully but not uncritically. I suggest that young children benefit from a broad, balanced and rich range of experiences, outside and in school, involving play, stories, the arts and the humanities. The importance of these, and the role of example and guided participation in how identities are constructed, lead to my advocacy of an approach based on the education of the whole child, involving inclusive environments and trusting relationships.

Part III explores the implications for adults, taking account of issues of power and authority, for instance in the extent to which adults should seek to control or influence children's identities and beliefs. The general implications are considered in Chapter 7, suggesting an approach based on the idea of apprenticeship. Chapter 8 explores the implications for parents/carers and those in roles of responsibility outside schools; and Chapter 9 for those who work in schools. The final chapter draws together the whole argument, highlighting that adults must recognize the complexities involved but not be paralysed by them.

In brief, I shall argue that

- culture operates in often subtle and contradictory ways to shape, but not determine, who we become;
- identity is like a tower constructed from many different identities, which requires secure foundations, established in early childhood, to be sufficiently robust to weather the storms of life;

- the construction of such an identity is like a journey, in which children require guidance and support to navigate the route through uncertain terrain and stormy waters;
- identities are constantly reshaped and re-negotiated, as a changing narrative, involving many varied, but interlinked, aspects of the whole person;
- more emphasis is required on children having a sense of agency and belonging and intrinsic motivation than at present; and
- adults should be wary of believing that their own assumptions and ways of thinking about nurturing and educating children are correct.

Underlying this is a belief that helping children to construct their identities is a task for a wide range of adults who

- are sensitive to children's cultures and backgrounds, without accepting what is damaging or unacceptable, or using these as an excuse for low levels of children's achievements or adult expectations;
- help children to recognize, understand and question often deeply ingrained assumptions, associated with their, and their family's and community's, identities; and
- challenge many of the messages about success and materialism with which children are currently presented.

Writing this book has led me into areas about which I had previously as a white, middle-class English man and as a teacher and head teacher, not thought very much. The journey has been circuitous, but fascinating and at times unsettling, raising profound questions about identity, the nature of success and what we want our children, and the society and culture we live in, to become. But these are questions of which parents/carers, teachers and others must take account if children are to be, and become, confident, resilient and compassionate citizens in a world of constant, often unforeseeable, change.

Part I

# Identity and Culture in a World of Uncertainty

# 1

# Exploring identity and culture

*People tell others who they are, but even more important they tell themselves and then try to act as though they are who they say they are. These self-understandings, especially those with strong emotional resonance for the teller, are what we refer to as identities.*

Holland et al., 2003: 3

## Unpicking the puzzle of identity and multiple identities

This chapter explores two complex concepts, identity and culture, which have no single, agreed meaning, and how they relate to a sense of belonging.

Identity is a construct which encapsulates all elements of who a person is, and feels that she or he is, in relation to aspects such as spiritual, moral, social, emotional, cultural, aesthetic, mental and physical development and factors such as gender, ethnicity, class, (dis)ability, religion and nationality. However, since identity deals with the whole person, separating these interlinked aspects is only a convenience, and they should be distinguished but not separated. As the quotation at the start of this chapter suggests, identities are self-understandings shaped by individuals, and are related to perceptions and feelings; but how these are constructed depends on other people and on the groups and cultures to which individuals belong.

Identity is loosely associated with concepts like personality, character and self. While personality and identity are similar, the former suggests something individual. In 'Western' countries, especially anglophone ones such as the United Kingdom and the United States, identity is usually understood mostly in individual terms and as a matter of choice. Other cultures and societies tend to see identity more collectively, emphasizing membership of, and conformity to, the norms of the nation, an ethnic group and/or a faith community.

As discussed in Eaude (2016: 109–11), I have reservations about the idea of character, if this is seen as just about grit and resilience in the face of adversity or involving the denial of one's emotions. However, character is a useful term if this refers to

- the sort of person one is, and how one acts, when one's inhibitions are down; and
- the behaviours and qualities one manifests when not observed by others or motivated mainly by tangible rewards and punishments

since, as Nagel (1986: 191) observes, 'if we are required to do certain things, then we are required to be the kinds of people who will do these things.' Such a view is the basis of virtue ethics, discussed in Chapter 3 and subsequently.

A person's character is made evident in to what extent, and how, she or he manifests qualities and dispositions such as courage, generosity or independence. In other words, how brave or timid, how willing to share or keep things to herself or himself, how independent or conformist she or he is. But, although an individual may manifest such qualities in general, this changes according to the context, especially for young children. For instance, a toddler who is usually adventurous may be scared by the presence of a dog; and a five-year-old who is normally willing to share his toys may refuse to be separated from a particular item, if worried.

Bruner (1996: 35–6) argues that perhaps the single most universal thing about human experience is the phenomenon of 'self' and that two aspects of selfhood are regarded as universal. The first is agency, the sense that one can initiate and carry out activities oneself, though even the most cursory view of young children – and we all – indicates that agency does not mean acting entirely on one's own. The second is that of evaluation, in that individuals evaluate their efficacy in what they hoped, or were asked, to do. Bruner calls the mix of these two 'self-esteem', combining a sense of what one believes, or hopes, oneself to be capable of and what one fears may be unachievable. But how self-esteem is experienced, and expressed, varies between cultures; and children's self-esteem is strongly affected by other people's perceptions, especially adults and, increasingly, members of the peer group. As we shall see, self-esteem can be too high and is fragile when based on external features such as possessions or looks, rather than intrinsic qualities.

Identity is closely related to questions such as Who am I? Where do I fit in? and Why am I here? which writers such as Eaude (2008) and Hyde (2008) associate with spirituality. While spirituality has a strong historic link with religion, such a search can be, to adopt McLaughlin's term, 'tethered' to religion or otherwise (see Best, 2014: 12). In other words, such existential questions are universal but can be explored within a religious framework or outside one.

Identities are retrospective and prospective. They are like the story which someone tells (in words and other ways) to herself or himself and to others of who she or he has been, is and may become (see McAdams and McLean, 2013). In Taylor's (1989: 47) words, 'In order to have a sense of who we are, we have to have a notion of how we have become and of where we are going.' And as Russell (2007: 54) indicates, 'Our concept of selfhood is derived from the unity of a narrative which links us to those around us from birth.' Narratives help to arrange and categorize disparate and often-confusing experiences, with identity best seen as a narrative created, and constantly shifting, over time, shaped and manifested within the context of culture.

In Jacober's words (2014: 97), 'Identity is what each of us discovers and creates in telling our story, both to ourselves and to others.' Identity is linked to memory in that who we are and who we become depend on what we have experienced and how such experiences have been understood, represented and internalized, individually and as a group. In Macintyre's (1999: 221) words,

> The story of my life is always embedded in the story of those communities from which I derive my identity. I am born with a past; and to try to cut myself off from that past, in the individualistic mode, is to deform my present relationships. The possession of an historical identity and the possession of a social identity coincide.

We are not just individual persons, but interdependent ones.

Some people are described by, and describe themselves as, 'hyphenated' or 'hybridized' identities such as an African American or a British Sikh, but identity is multiple in more profound ways. We all have multiple identities in that our sense of self alters according to the context. A four-year-old who is a confident speaker or artist at home may be more shy or reserved if expected to perform in an unfamiliar situation; and a seven-year-old who is self-assured when reading a familiar book to her mother may be more tentative when asked to do so in a group.

Jenkins (2014: 51–2) makes the distinction between 'self' as how each person feels and understands him or herself privately and 'person' as how she or he is seen by others. How individuals are perceived and perceive themselves may not coincide; and the aspect which an individual regards as predominant may not be that which other people see as most significant. For instance, a seven-year-old boy may be proud of his prowess at sport or cooking, whereas other people may categorize him more on his behaviour or skin colour. Individual identities are created and negotiated taking account of expectations which vary between different cultures and parts of children's lives, trying to create some coherence between those aspects of identity which one feels and those ascribed by others, with the latter influencing young children particularly strongly. Problems may arise if a child sees his or her identity in simple and unchanging terms, for instance mainly as a girl-who-can't-walk or as a naughty boy, since such identities easily become self-fulfilling.

A useful distinction is that between substantive and situational identities (see Woods and Jeffery, 2002). The former are more enduring, not immutable but less open to change, and the latter more context-related, fluid and transient. Situational identities often strongly affect individuals' sense of identity and actions, unless their substantial identity is firmly rooted. Each person is an individual, but his or her identities are influenced, though not determined, by a wide range of factors and, while identities are constantly changing, there is an underlying continuity, though one aspect of identity – as a girl, a Hindu, or a sports player – may be predominant in a particular context or time in a child's life; and which aspects predominate may shift, sometimes rapidly, between contexts.

For a very young child, his or her name, gender and the language she or he speaks and where she or he lives are important markers of identity. For slightly older children, being able to ride one's bike on one's own, no-longer-a-bed-wetter or one-who-can-swim may signify overcoming difficult challenges, while for most children approaching adolescence, appearance and popularity become increasingly significant.

Before children go to school they develop, as a sibling or friend, aspects of their identities such as being, and being seen as, friendly, naughty or serious – and a combination of such qualities. As well as being based on temperament, these are influenced by the environment in which children grow up and the expectations related to factors such as gender and class, whether explicitly or not. Complications often arise when children move into group settings. Children acquire new categories of identity, as a reader or an artist, a mathematician or an athlete, a nerd or teacher's pet, and some which may have mattered less previously, such as being sociable or quiet, eccentric or reclusive, come to matter more. How such identities are described changes over time and between cultures, but the underlying idea is similar. Such identities become, inevitably, more public, with some valued more than others. Recalling the situational aspect of identity, how a child is perceived and how she or he comes to see herself or himself matter more and frequently exacerbate low self-esteem. For instance, a six-year-old who wets the bed may feel ashamed about this, but much worse if this is known to his or her friends.

There is a hierarchy of identities, often implicit, where some aspects are seen, whether by oneself or by other people, to matter more than others. For instance, a child's home language is one important element in how his or her identity is defined, by the child and by other people. However, some languages are valued more than others. For example, English tends to be valued worldwide, and European languages more than South Asian or African ones. This relates both to language as such, which may indicate ethnicity, and to how it is spoken in terms of accent and dialect, both strongly associated with class and status and, by extension, to whether the speaker is seen to belong. Young bilingual children may feel proud of the language they speak at home but find that this are not held in high regard outside the home and immediate community; and as a result may have conflicting views about their home language and how and when to speak it.

This discussion inevitably reflects, to some extent, my own 'Western' assumptions about identity. Those from different cultural backgrounds may present a more collective, less individualistic view. But every child has to try to create a coherent sense of herself or himself from many often-conflicting identities, in relation to other people and the world around and how she or he fits in. By coherent, I mean making sense of a range of different experiences to try and answer questions such as Who am I? and Where do I fit in? This involves understanding oneself increasingly as part of larger narratives than that of one's immediate family and culture. Towards the end of Chapter 2, we return to what a coherent and robust identity entails, having discussed the factors which militate against that.

## Probing into what culture means

This section explores another complex and slippery construct – culture – which refers to several different, overlapping concepts and reflects various historical and cultural assumptions. Its meaning is not fixed – and changes over time and between different societies.

Williams (1959) argued that the original meaning of culture moved from a process of tending natural growth and, by analogy, human training, to one of becoming more like a thing in itself, a way of life, particularly one implying familiarity with the arts and what came to be called high culture. This idea is implicit in Arnold's view of culture as 'the best that has been thought' (1869), though, as Galton et al. (1999: 196) indicate, Arnold continues that culture is the medium through which to make sense of what it is to be human. Moreover, Arnold's emphasis was on knowing rather than doing. The unspoken question is who should decide what is 'the best that has been thought' and on what criteria – a matter for debate rather than being decided by only a few people, usually white, older men regarded as being highly educated.

Williams linked this change of meaning to industrialization to argue that working-class culture represented a collective idea and the institutions, manners, habits of thought and intentions which proceed from this, and that middle-class culture was, and is, based on a more individualistic view. As a result of social movements like the end of (formal) colonialism, feminism and globalization, the view of culture as largely associated with a particular, rational and cerebral view of knowledge and white, male, 'Western' superiority derived from Arnold has increasingly been questioned.

One persistent theme, historically, is that of a cultured person, in the sense of someone who is knowledgeable about, and takes part in, activities such as reading or writing literature and the arts and going to the theatre, opera and ballet. These activities are frequently seen as 'high', as opposed to as 'low', or 'popular', culture – such as reading romances and magazines and watching soap operas, which, however enjoyable, are often considered as 'just entertainment'. The boundaries and distinctions between high and low culture – for instance, in types of music, film or literature – have become more blurred as class has become less significant as an organizing feature of society. However, many people, including me, retain a strong sense that culture should improve people; and distinguish between what is highbrow, and seen as improving, and lowbrow, which is at best entertaining and possibly a waste of time – even though many teachers, parents and children – we all – quite reasonably spend a long time involved in lowbrow activities. Culture has a complex relationship with entertainment, explored further in the next section.

Young (1994: 12) cites Hatch's view that 'culture is the way of life of a people. It consists of conventional patterns of thought and behaviour, including values, beliefs, rules of conduct, political organization, economic activity, and the like, which are passed on from one generation to the next by learning – and not by biological inheritance.' In Eagleton's (2000: 131) words, 'Culture is not only what we live by. It is, also, in great measure, what we live for – affection, relationship, memory, kinship, place, community, emotional fulfilment, intellectual enjoyment, a sense of ultimate meaning.' Such broad views suggest that culture refers to much of what is significant in life, but underplay unpleasant aspects of culture and see culture mainly as what binds groups rather than what excludes outsiders.

Geertz (1993: 44) suggests that 'culture is best seen not as complexes of concrete behaviour patterns – customs, usages, traditions, habit clusters – as has, by and large, been the case up to now, but as a set of control mechanisms – plans, recipes, rules, instructions … – for the governing of behaviour'. These two do not seem contradictory, but the recognition that culture acts in a regulatory way helps in considering how individual identities are shaped; and the idea that culture can be understood by examining behaviour patterns and attitudes, many of them implicit and not easily observed, is useful in thinking how environments can be created and sustained.

The *Oxford English Dictionary* highlights several different meanings of culture, which can be summarized in three main groups

- related to cultivation and husbandry, as in agriculture;
- development or refinement of mind and manners, as in 'a cultured person'; and
- distinctive customs, achievements, products and ways of life of a society or a group, as in Scandinavian, or Jewish, or military, culture.

Alexander (2000: 163), recognizing Williams's point that culture is 'one of the two or three most complicated words in the English language', distinguishes two main usages

- a broader anthropological one, referring to aspects such as values, beliefs, ideas, institutions, networks of relationships, patterns of behaviour and artefacts; and
- a more restricted aesthetic one, based on artistic-cum-literary experiences – the arts and the humanities – but with powerful connotations of relative worth, shading into assumptions about class and status.

Alexander adds that 'we then find that we are left with a residual baggage that stubbornly refuses to be tidied into one or other of these definitions' and highlights the frequency with which the word culture carries various appendages, notably

- adjectives which demarcate, claim, reject, compare and tacitly evaluate kinds of culture such as 'high', 'popular', 'mass', 'youth' and 'ethnic';
- nouns which indicate what people and groups do with culture and what culture does to people, such as cultural 'capital', 'transmission' and 'relativism'; and
- prefixes such as 'postmodernist culture', 'subculture' and 'microculture'.

Alexander indicates that more recently its usage has expanded so that it can be, and is, appended to virtually any sphere of activity, as in 'business' or 'professional' culture. The word is frequently used as a shorthand for ethnicity, as in the term multicultural. Inglis points out 'how unusually all-inclusive the concept is (but it has swollen to embrace any manifestation of a society as well as becoming as synonym for society itself)' (2000: 113).

Alexander's analysis, while insightful, seems to underplay the extent to which the roots of the word lie in the language of husbandry, with culture like a garden which needs tending rather than being completely natural. This sense, where culture is seen as the environment(s) or space(s) in which people live and grow, is helpful particularly in thinking how children are brought up, nurtured and initiated into social groups.

Since culture frequently refers a loose consensus of norms, values and beliefs, it may be unwise to try to define what exactly it means, but more fruitful to consider how the word is used and to think of culture, not as a thing but more as the spaces where humans as groups live and have lived and within which experiences occur and identities are shaped – and like the soil within which we, all, are nurtured and grow up.

While terms such as European or Islamic culture are frequently used, the idea of any group having a common culture is problematic in that it suggests a homogeneity within the group that rarely exists. Those who are seen to belong to any culture may vary considerably in their beliefs and attitudes. In Krause's (2012: 12) words, 'Not all individuals who consider themselves to belong to the same culture share all meanings, and individuals also participate in cultural meanings of which they are not aware. … Thus meaning is not co-terminous with language and, indeed, might not be expressed adequately in words.' While an individual's identity is made evident to some extent by cultural signifiers such as clothing and accent, such signifiers may mislead an observer. Seeing any culture as homogeneous tends to lead to over-generalization and stereotyping. Especially with young children, generalizing can easily lead to stereotyping, as actions and attitudes which some members of a group manifest are conflated with other, irrelevant aspects.

Culture is to some extent made evident through language, though the assumptions behind language may differ. An example which amused me, obsessed with the weather like many English people, occurred in India, when after a long spell of dry weather, a heavy rainstorm was greeted by people running into the streets, saying to each other 'good rains'. Such differences can lead to misunderstanding. Some are well known such as when English and American people talk about 'pants' or a 'rubber' meaning different things. More subtly, and problematically, language which appears to be the same may have varying meanings, or connotations, in different cultures. The assumption in much of the United States that 'instruction' is largely equivalent to 'teaching' is different from mine that instruction tends to refer to a didactic approach. And, while most people are in favour of fairness (at least in theory), ideas of what this entails may vary significantly depending on deep-rooted beliefs. As Haidt (2012) argues, someone who is, broadly, on the right politically may see fairness in terms of what one deserves – and so be less worried about inequality; whereas someone broadly on the left is likely to see fairness more in terms of equal distribution. Likewise, while most readers probably regard democracy as desirable, they may vary considerably about what they understand democracy to entail and which models of democracy they prefer.

Language provides only one, somewhat smudged, window through which to view culture, which can be understood more clearly by observing commonly held practices and assumptions. A simple example occurred when I visited Finland and was driven along wide open, empty roads. I asked why my host did not drive faster. Puzzled, she explained that Finns almost always keep within the speed limit, not for fear of being caught but because doing so was expected and so became second nature.

Similarly, assumptions about what is desirable or otherwise may vary considerably between cultures. For instance, as a head teacher, I was sufficiently worried about the weight of a seven-year-old boy of Pakistani heritage to ask his mother to discuss what could be done to address what we, and medical staff, saw as his obesity. When I mentioned that I wanted to discuss his size, she broke into a broad smile, as to have such a well-nourished boy was to her a source of great pride.

Since assumptions linked to culture underpin how we all think and act, the next section explores how culture exerts influence and affects, and helps to shape, children's identities.

## Examining how culture operates and exerts influence

Geertz, an anthropologist, writes (1993: 5) of culture as 'webs of significance (man) himself has spun', emphasizing the role of human relationships. Cultures, and cultural signifiers, help to indicate who we are and to shape who we become, as individuals and as groups. The influence of culture operates at a micro-level of the family, local communities and groups to which people belong and within which young children learn what is expected of and can test the boundaries of acceptability; and the macro-level of society, nationally and internationally, which frequently offers contrasting messages.

Membership of any group tends to be made manifest by cultural markers or signifiers. Some are permanent, such as skin colour or circumcision, or only changeable with great difficulty, as with attitudes, assumptions and beliefs, while others like clothing or a haircut can be altered more easily. Some, for instance, a cross or a turban, are easily visible and usually intended to be so while others like speech patterns and ways of interacting are less obvious. Some, such as accent and attitudes towards those who are different, may be subtle with their significance evident only to some people or at certain times.

Some signifiers are seen to matter more in particular groups or cultures. For instance, the colour of someone's hair is usually considered less significant than skin colour, and the pitch of voice less important than accent. Features such as right- or left-handedness, hair colour, size, wearing glasses, having up to date clothes or being seen as a bully or a mummy's boy are both signifiers and creators of identity, for better or worse. Such relatively small or apparently mundane features matter more to children, especially as they approach adolescence, than adults tend to recognize. Moreover, many ordinary aspects of life such as dress and food have symbolic meanings, even though the child herself or himself and other children may not understand clearly what these symbolize to other people. Therefore, a child who dresses or speaks in a particular way may not understand, cognitively, why this marks him or her as an outsider, though may feel that she or he is.

Culture is associated with what is valued by a group (and by implication what is not or regarded as of less value) and has an inherently normative function. The title of Arnold's book *Culture and Anarchy* suggests that culture helps to preserve and protect what is regarded as special or worthwhile and staving off what is destructive. High culture is related to status, as well as (perceived) intrinsic merit. From this flows ideas such as 'guardians of culture', however much such people can easily become, or be seen as, bastions of reaction and privilege. The idea of a 'city of culture', in contrast, tends to focus on the idea of culture as transformative. In this sense, culture is mostly related to spaces where activities such as theatre, sculpture and music are seen as beneficial to individuals and help to create, or strengthen, a sense of group identity.

Culture can, like tradition, act as a force for stability, especially when used by the powerful who wish to defend the status quo. For instance, an appeal to study the classics reflects a wish for children to engage with what is seen as more enduring rather than with newer, possibly more transient, material. However, culture can also help to promote change, as when music or art is used to support a political argument or disseminate a new idea more widely.

Bauman (2000) suggests that culture is not static, but in a state of continual transformation. It is constantly being reproduced and changed and in this process changes the people within it to some extent, but at different speeds and in different respects. Some aspects of culture may change slowly, so that what was unacceptable in a previous generation may take many years gradually to become even broadly acceptable. In contrast, 'youth culture', expressed through fashion, music and language, indicates what is up to date, often influenced by those who sell these, change very fast – and increasingly so.

Attitudes towards issues such as gender, race, sexuality and disability have changed relatively rapidly, particularly in recent years, in my view for the better. However, they still vary considerably in different societies and cultures, with attitudes and often legislation discriminating against some groups. For instance, how mental illness and disability are understood varies between cultures, where some people think of these in terms of possession by spirits or regard disability as a punishment – ideas which I believe to be wrong and potentially damaging to children. And the law in many societies allows, and may even encourage, discrimination against individuals and groups based on their gender, ethnicity, sexuality or religion.

Culture influences what individuals experience, and how they interpret this, and their interests and allegiances. For instance, the media provide sources of entertainment and act as a conduit through which group assumptions and identities are expressed and usually strengthened. And the sorts of TV programme people watch, and shared interests in sport, help to create group identities, even though individuals within these may have different preferences and allegiances, which can be a source of rivalry.

Some aspects of culture as expressed through the media are a matter of taste, such as which sorts of music, television programmes or humour one likes, or which football team one supports, and apparently harmless. Others are more corrosive and potentially harmful, such as violence and those aspects which, however deliberately, may encourage sexist, racist and homophobic attitudes. These statements, inevitably, reflect my own cultural assumptions and beliefs and other people may disagree with this emphasis. However, in Chapter 3, I shall suggest that many apparently harmless messages presented in the media are more subtly damaging to young children's identities than they seem.

Culture creates and sustains expectations to be adopted in any particular context. Moreover, culture – at different levels – helps to shape the nature of debate and discourse and the views of those within a group. This matters particularly with young children, as they are often impressionable so that unkind or racist remarks when allowed to pass unchallenged easily become the norm; and where people are treated with respect and compassion this tends to influence how most members of that group respond.

The historical link between culture, especially in terms of gender, race/ethnicity and socio-economic background, and underachievement at school and exclusion from positions of power and influence subsequently, is common to most societies. Discrimination against women remains common, more overtly in some societies than others. In the UK, especially England, discrimination and disadvantage on the basis of skin colour is associated with an imperial past, and in the United States with the legacy of slavery. In many countries, such as Australia, New Zealand, Canada and the United States, the previous, and ongoing, treatment of the indigenous populations is correlated with lower outcomes in terms of literacy, educational attainment, health, incarceration and life chances. These are exacerbated by disproportionate levels of poverty, as discussed further in Chapter 2. The ongoing marginalization as a result remains a source of considerable and understandable resentment.

While the targets of prejudice and discrimination may change, whether on grounds of ethnicity – such as people of colour or travellers – or religion – such as Catholics, Jews or Muslims – the pattern of 'othering' those who are different, and frequently seen as threats, remains. Explanations for such trends are usually associated with connotations of the supposed superiority of some cultures and beliefs. While some of the underlying assumptions may have changed to some extent in recent years, many lie deep in the psyche of all those involved, both those who are historically advantaged and those discriminated against.

The ways in which culture is tacitly passed on makes it hard to notice and easy to take for granted, especially by those in positions of (relative) power and privilege. White-skinned people should recognize that the world looks, and is understood, very differently from the perspective of people of colour. The same is true of men and women, those who are physically able and those with a disability, the rich and the poor, adults and children.

This discussion indicates that issues related to culture are often sensitive and controversial but are linked to power, such as

- which practices are approved of and which thought to be objectionable; and
- whose history and traditions are most valued.

For example, cultural markers such as women being required, or expected, or choosing to wear the *hijab* (headscarf) evoke strong responses. Doing so is required in Iran, banned in France in public places and mostly acceptable in England, but even so may not be approved of by some people. I shall suggest that individuals cannot understand their own history without some knowledge of their cultural heritage and how they, and their family, fit into larger historical narratives, but the extent to which this occurs depends on how such narratives are presented and what is emphasized.

Any group or culture contains barriers, especially attitudinal ones, to participation and belonging, based on power differentials, which are often invisible to the powerful but all too real and apparently insurmountable to those who face them. For example, invisible barriers may make involvement of those with a disability difficult, even when those in the group may consciously try to be inclusive; and ethnicity or socio-economic background often excludes those who are 'other', sometimes in subtle ways, related to being made to feel unwelcome or not understanding cultural references, sometimes in blunter and more overt ways. In Part III, I suggest that helping to dismantle such barriers is a difficult but vital aspect of how adults create and sustain inclusive environments.

The last two sections have indicated that cultures are the contexts in which identities are constructed and negotiated. This discussion has implications for issues such as gender roles and identities, responses to ethnic and social diversity and how stereotypes are formed and whether, and how, these can be changed. As such, we are entering fascinating but dangerous territory. However, first, we consider why belonging matters, particularly in relation to young children and their identities.

## Asking why belonging matters

The Early Years Learning Framework in Australia (see EYLF, 2019) is called 'Belonging, being and becoming', indicating the close link between these three. This section considers why belonging matters so much in defining, and shaping, young children's identities. It suggests that the groups to which people belong and feel a sense of belonging exert a powerful influence on how identities and character are shaped, particularly for young children.

In Maslow's hierarchy of needs (1998), physiological aspects and a feeling of safety are the most basic requirements, followed by the need to belong in social groups. A sense of belonging is crucial to psychological well-being. Feeling part of a group both helps one to feel safe and provides a source of friendship and support. All people belong to many groups, each with its own norms and assumptions. But many children – and adults – feel insecurity about whether, and where, they belong as a result of many factors, some structural, others more individual such as a lack of opportunities to make friends and put down roots, maybe resulting from displacement or migration.

Erikson (1995: 29-30) argues that the organization of experience takes place at three levels: the physiological, the individual and the social. Identities are created at the social, as well as individual, level since, as Erikson (1995: 30) writes, 'the human being, at all times, from the first kick *in utero* to the last breath is organized into groupings of geographical and historical coherence: family, class, community, nation'. Who people are, and feel themselves to be, is defined in large part by the groups to which they belong. This may be less so in fragmented, individualistic societies than in the past, but remains the case to a significant extent.

In Eaude (2008), I argued that cultural development is closely linked to a sense of belonging, where a child fits in and how she or he learns to do so, in different contexts. In De Souza's (2016: 128) words, 'A sense of belonging to a group provides a person with their sense of self and place which, in turn, inspires in them a sense of purpose as they see themselves as having some responsibility to and for their group.' The construction of identities is not just an individual enterprise, but a process of becoming, not just as a separate person but as an individual within groups and societies. We are social, and interdependent, creatures however much some people may see themselves as rugged individualists, as I used to.

Eaude (2016) emphasized the importance of belonging in relation to young children's moral education – and the influence of the groups to which they belong in helping to influence and regulate behaviour. Membership of groups and communities provides the basis for how people learn to conduct themselves. How we conduct ourselves and learn to conduct ourselves depends heavily on those around us since as Bourdieu (1986) indicates practices form, and are shaped by, habitus, or social contexts, including both micro- and macro-cultures. We learn how to conduct ourselves largely through experience of the environments in which we operate – though some young children may not know what is expected and may take a long time, with support and guidance, to internalize this.

As Richardson and Wood (2000: 18) indicate, 'Allegiances, belongings and loyalties are sources of a sense of identity,' though these inevitably have different weightings. Groups, whether formal or informal, tend to be defined and held together by shared interests and cultural references and often by a common background or heritage. For instance, membership of, or support for, a sports team, visible symbols such as a uniform or the types of discourse like shared references and jokes help to define a group. Types of music or sport, especially those associated with people of a particular ethnic group and/or class, act as a bonding mechanism for some groups. Such shared interests tend to reflect what members of the group feel comfortable with and to shape their responses. Knowing these, or not, often indicates to what extent one is a member of the group, or an outsider. As a simple example, one's gender may make presence and participation in some activities or discussions, such as those related to fashion or football, difficult both for the outsider and the members of the group.

Visible symbols may provide a sense of belonging and pride, though this may lead to excluding other people, since loyalty to one's immediate social group is a basic instinct. However, where members of communities and groups – at whatever level – identify themselves as who they are not, rather than who they are, this can lead to distrust, dislike and even hatred of those who are, or perceived as, 'other'. Othering runs deep, lying behind racism and homophobia, at one, more destructive, end of a spectrum and clear distinctions between boys' and girls' roles and activities at a less obviously harmful one.

A shared cultural heritage is one basis for how people belong to larger groups, such as a nation, but in a diverse society, individuals especially from disadvantaged groups may not recognize existing narratives of national identities as reflecting their own experience and those of people like them. Hales (2018: 676) suggests that 'those at the lower end of the cultural hierarchy, often disadvantaged groups ... can find themselves in a "cultural vacuum"; being marginalized and segregated because they are unable to develop their own identity and place themselves within the wider group.'

A sense of belonging matters to all of us because if one does not know the references and other practices which bind the group together one feels like an outsider, and may be excluded particularly if this becomes public. For example, conversations or jokes may depend on one's knowledge of TV programmes, fashions or celebrities; and understanding a work of literature on knowing about references, sometimes quite subtle, to other aspects of a cultural or religious heritage with which one may, or may not, be familiar.

If children do not have a sense of belonging, they are likely to be unhappy or isolated. This can cause considerable personal distress, but has more serious long-term consequences. As Bellous and Clinton (2016: 358) indicate, 'If people are isolated, their own story of how the world works is the only one they hear. They have a hard time believing there are other ways to experience life. They tend to think and act alone and aren't self-aware.'

Children have no choice about some of the groups to which they belong, but choice in respect of others. For instance, in India, the caste into which a child is born exerts a significant influence on how she or he is seen by other people and his or her life chances. And children everywhere have no choice in terms of family, gender or class, at least initially. Where children can choose, membership is often based, at least to some extent, on shared interests or on factors such as age, gender and class.

For young children, their place in the family and immediate community is particularly significant. Local identities, as part of a neighbourhood, a nursery and a school, are likely to be stronger than global ones, and young children may have only a limited sense of belonging to larger entities such as a nation. A friendship group or a class – and similar micro-cultures – tends to matter more for young children, given the immediacy and proximity of these. A faith community may be, for some children, a significant source of belonging, initially at a local level and increasingly as part of the wider community of believers.

The need to feel part of the peer group is intense for most children, especially as they approach adolescence. For those who find belonging difficult, or are not popular, their wish to keep up can easily lead them to join groups which may be superficially attractive but lead them into trouble. For instance, belonging to an informal group of friends with similar interests appeals to young children, but may result in inappropriate behaviour, especially when children challenge the authority of adults.

Friendship groups matter to young children, both their peer group and, in some cases, the children whom they look up to, particularly those who are more attractive because they are older and apparently more successful. As children get older, the regulatory element to discourage deviance from group norms becomes stronger. How children are seen by others exerts a strong influence on whether they feel proud or ashamed, and the extent to which they conform or rebel. Especially as they approach adolescence, children become acutely aware of feelings of embarrassment and shame because of worries about status and not fitting in. The fear of missing out, or being excluded, becomes a strong motivator as children become older and more aware of how they are positioned in the peer group.

Bourdieu's (1986) idea of cultural capital helps to explain how what one knows, or feels familiar with, in one context may be of little or no use elsewhere. For instance, when I go into an environment where I feel comfortable, my anxiety and uncertainty reduces. Likewise, when I go to a loud party (if I do) or to a place of worship where I am unsure of the conventions or how to behave, I feel out of place and anxious. The resources, social and emotional, which served me well in other situations no longer do so. These examples may provide some insight into how a young child, who is less experienced and may lack the necessary cultural capital, feels when arriving in a new, unfamiliar setting and is uncertain how to behave and respond. However, one must recognize that children, especially those from disadvantaged backgrounds, do not lack cultural capital as such but frequently do not have what is needed, or know how to use what they have, in unfamiliar situations.

I shall argue, in Part II, that children need to extend their 'bank' of cultural capital and learn which aspects to use in which contexts; and in Part III that adults working with young children must draw on children's existing 'funds of knowledge' and cultural capital, especially when children are in unfamiliar territory. Having started to explore the complexity of identity and culture, Chapter 2 considers how these intersect, frequently in subtle ways, especially in relation to gender, race, class and religion.

# 2

# Thinking through the intersections of identity and culture

*Children – and all human beings ... – exist in multiple and often competing communities, exercising formative, shaping influences on the child's identity.*

Mercer, 2005: 174

## Seeing how gender affects identity

We have seen that culture, in various ways, affects how children's identities are shaped; and that many of the issues involved take us into contested territory. Recognizing Mercer's point, at the start of this chapter, that influences are multiple and often competing, this chapter starts to explore factors such as gender, race/ethnicity, class and religion, touching on age, health and (dis)ability. All of these, and many others, such as one's place in the family, affect how any child is socialized and how she or he sees herself or himself. These factors all intersect in that each affects how the others are understood and manifested, as addressed in more detail in subsequent chapters. So, for instance, a five-year-old boy's or a ten-year-old girl's identity will be affected by their own, and other people's (often unconscious), constructions of gender. These may vary depending on the child's ethnicity, social background and possibly religious faith; and be influenced by messages from the media and, increasingly, the peer group.

The ideas discussed in this chapter are inevitably filtered through my position and assumptions as a white, middle-class English man and therefore a member of several advantaged groups – and similar considerations will affect how readers respond. However, it is important to remember that variations within any group are significantly greater than those between groups (see Gaine and George, 1993: 6–9); and that these factors, and the expectations which accompany them, influence, rather than determine, individuals' identities. Therefore, many of the generalizations must be treated with caution and one should avoid labelling individual children on the basis of these factors, but should not ignore their influence.

This section suggests that there are strong pressures for boys or girls to conform to patterns associated with gender, remembering that culture regulates how members of any group are expected to act. However, there is a wide variation within both groups, though the statistical data on gender attitudes and behaviours indicate that most females cluster nearer the average, with males more widely spread and so tending to manifest more extreme attitudes and behaviours.

A person's sex is based on biology, but how children learn to act, or perform, in ways deemed socially appropriate to their gender depends on culture and upbringing at home and wider cultural influences, and changes over time. While children are (almost always) born biologically as a boy or a girl, Yelland and Grieshaber (1998: 2) indicate that 'non-Western' societies tend to have more fluid categories of gender than just male and female. But in 'Western' societies gender is one of the earliest and clearest categorizations which young children make, for instance, in choosing friendship groups; and how they are socialized affects what they tend to be interested in and how they tend to respond.

How boys and girls are regarded and adults' assumptions about, and expectations of, boys and girls vary in different societies and cultures. At the most serious level, male children are prized more highly, with strong evidence of female foetuses being aborted in some cultures, for instance in India. At a less extreme level, men and boys and their achievements are generally given greater priority and have historically been regarded (particularly by other males) as more capable than women and girls. While such attitudes have changed to some extent in recent years, they remain deeply embedded in most cultures.

Women have a lower status than men and are discriminated against in most societies. However, men

- commit far more crime and acts of violence;
- constitute the vast majority of the prison population;
- act more often in anti-social ways;
- are more likely to commit suicide; and
- have more mental health difficulties, though the types vary between men and women.

Cross-cultural research (see Blackmore et al., 2008: 8–9) indicates that women participate much more than men in childcare and that girls are more likely to be socialized to be nurturant, obedient and responsible, boys to be self-reliant and achieving. Girls are usually expected to care for others and to be less competitive or forceful and tend to be more protected than boys are. Boys are expected to be independent, take risks and be tough, and not to express emotion, except at sporting and similar events. This is captured in the idea that 'big boys do not cry', leading, when they are older, into the belief that a 'hard man' fights rather than discusses.

Men, and boys, tend to be interested in things, competition and winning; and women, and girls, more in people, relationships and emotions. Most males seem more at ease when talking about sport or motor cars than emotions and relationships; and the reverse is true for females. In part, this is because of shared interests but also assumptions about what is appropriate for boys or girls to discuss.

Boys tend to dominate equipment and discussions and be less able than girls to take account of other people's responses and to take turns. Many boys have a restricted emotional repertoire and find it hard to regulate their behaviour and to display emotions other than anger, often through violence. Girls tend to internalize their emotions and may be more reluctant to interrupt in group discussions. Many girls become more anxious, especially about their physical appearance, as they approach adolescence, exacerbated by the media's tendency to present femininity in terms of sexualization, though social media has increasingly affected boys in this respect.

Difficulties may manifest themselves in different ways for boys and girls. For instance, where boys have fragile identities, this may result more from emotional inadequacies, whereas girls' identities may be fragile more because of societal pressures which undermine their confidence and increase their anxiety.

The reasons for such outcomes are enormously complicated. The simplistic view 'boys will be boys' (and likewise for girls) is still sometimes considered as a valid explanation not just for interests and behaviours being differentiated by gender but for seeing behaviours and attitudes as inherent and not open to change. However, Engel (2005: 23–4) argues that 'to understand the development of gender differences we have to think of the phenomenon as interpersonal rather than intrapersonal'. How gender is learned and masculinities and femininities internalized is a societal and cultural issue. In Yelland and Grieshaber's (1998: 1) words, 'At a very young age … we learn what girls and boys *should* be and what they *should* do' (emphasis in original). Such behaviours and attitudes are learned, based on expectations embedded in culture, and hard to unlearn.

To explore how such outcomes are influenced by early experience, it may help to distinguish

- activities and interests;
- behaviours;
- attitudes; and
- expectations,

although these are linked in that genderized activities and expectations affect behaviours and attitudes.

Gender identities are strongly influenced by example and expectations, both from adults and from the peer group. Socialization as a boy or a girl starts from a very early age. For instance, the most common question about a newborn child is about its sex and name, and babies are usually dressed in pink or blue and encouraged to play with different types of toy, depending on their sex.

Different behaviours for boys and girls are frequently expected and encouraged (or discouraged). Girls tend to be allocated care-giving roles more than boys, who assume that they will be catered for. Boys are expected and encouraged to be more active and challenging, and girls to be quieter and more conforming in most cultures, especially many South Asian ones, with a view to preparing them for marriage and motherhood. Cross-culturally, boys tend to engage in more 'rough and tumble' play than girls and young boys and girls to participate in, and, play predominantly with children of their own gender, with each gender preferring different types of activity. As a result, boys tend to be seen as boisterous and to like rough games and more interested in science and maths; and girls expected to concentrate more on pleasing adults and be interested in quieter activities such as reading and in clothes.

'Laddish' behaviour – involving bravado and opposition to authority – is associated more with working-class than middle-class boys (see Connolly 2002). Such bravado frequently hides emotional fragility. Boys, especially those from working-class backgrounds, are frequently told to 'hit back'. To look weak or show fear or weakness is often, for a boy, to risk ridicule or exclusion, which discourages the expression of emotional difficulties and intimacy and encourages boys to concentrate more on activities and things than on emotions and relationships.

Adler, Kless and Adler (1992) describe how, among the mainly affluent pre-adolescent children they studied, boys and girls constructed, within their gendered peer subcultures, idealized images of masculinity and femininity on which they modelled their behaviour. These images were reflected in the factors affecting children's popularity among their peers. Boys achieved high status through their athletic ability, coolness, toughness, social skills and success in cross-gender relationships. In contrast, girls gained popularity because of their parents' socio-economic status and their own physical appearance, social skills and academic success, though the social skills which they manifested were more based on sensitive interactions than the boys'.

Adler and Adler (1998: 209) argue that

> from their parents and the mass media, (girls) learn that the woman's role is to attract a man who will bestow on her his status'; and that passivity is also inherent in the 'ideology of domesticity' ... that characterizes girls' play and interaction. Unlike the boys, who search for the physical limits of their bodies and the social limits of their school, group and society through their effort to challenge these limits, the girls ... live indoor lives, draw indoor scenes, and concern themselves with nurturing, smoothing over problems or inequalities, and gathering others around them. They focus on the emotional dimension of expression and become more adept at intimate contact than at openly competing against others.

Expectations easily become self-fulfilling. For example, boys tend to have poorer fine motor skills and find it harder to sit still and to concentrate in school. Boys are more likely than girls to be diagnosed as being on the autistic spectrum, as having attention deficit hyperactivity disorder (ADHD), a behavioural condition that includes symptoms such as inattentiveness, hyperactivity and impulsiveness and to be excluded from school. Increasing numbers of children, disproportionately boys, especially those from disadvantaged backgrounds, are medicated as a result of diagnoses of ADHD. However, Timimi (2005) highlights that how boys' behaviour is understood and encouraged varies significantly between cultures and that expecting young boys to sit still for long periods contributes to them finding it hard to regulate their behaviour. Moreover, he points to the dearth of medical evidence supporting ADHD as a medical condition, arguing that it would be better approached not as a disorder but as a cultural construct in a society that seeks to relocate problems from the social to the individual. This reflects a trend to see problems in individual terms, often on a medical model, and label children as problematic (see McCann, 2016 for a wider discussion of how mental illness is socially constructed).

This section has suggested that masculinities and femininities are largely learned, depending on assumptions embedded in cultures. However, one must take care that the trends outlined do not become stereotypes. Many boys and girls do not manifest such behaviours and attitudes. But I suggest that many children, especially boys, need to be helped to change their behaviours and attitudes, rather than their interests, by seeing models of masculinity, in particular, and femininity which differ from those encountered at home, in the community and in the media.

## Understanding the effects of ethnicity and race on identity

Ethnicity and race, as important elements of, and factors affecting, children's identities, are complex, linked and multifaceted concepts. Since the two concepts are hard to separate and sometimes used interchangeably, it is necessary to explain how they are used in this book. Moreover, as Hirsch (2018: 161) points out, 'discussions about race, and especially mixed-race, are difficult to get right'. In addition, the appropriate terminology is frequently a matter of dispute and, as indicated in the Introduction, it is easy to use words in ways which reflect careless assumptions and may unwittingly cause offence.

Race has historically been seen in biological terms, and ethnicity as a combination of biology and culture. However, both are socially constructed and associated with power relationships. There is no valid biological basis of dividing humanity into separate 'races'. Such crude categorization, usually with implications of superior (and inferior) intelligence, based on small biological differences, notably skin colour, is unhelpful and inaccurate.

While ethnicity is to some extent based in biology, such as skin colour, it is also related to aspects such as nationality, language and religion; and, sometimes, to distinctive types of clothing and food. As Modood (1997: 297–9) indicates, to base ethnicity mainly on skin colour tends to be a 'Western' response, whereas, for Asians, culture and religion tend to be more important signifiers of identity.

Hirsch (2018: 61) writes that 'genetic difference between racial groups is negligible and is far overshadowed by the range of ethnic difference within groups'. However, having a black or brown skin, and associated physical features, has historically been linked with being dirty and bad, with a darker skin seen in negative terms. Dark-skinned children have frequently tried to lighten their skin colour by scrubbing or by bleaching; and many black girls, especially, to straighten their hair.

'Race' continues to be a way of categorizing people which exerts a strong influence on how all people are seen and treated and how they see themselves. Those with black, brown or yellow skins are frequently stereotyped, especially those who are more powerful, on the basis of characteristics such as intelligence or trustworthiness. Enduring attitudes include a sense of superiority and inferiority, of entitlement or of exclusion (and resentment), as a legacy of colonialism and slavery, despite challenges and changes to these attitudes in recent years.

Societies treat race in different ways. For instance, Hirsch (2018: 10) highlights how in Britain white people are taught not to 'see' race and to believe that race does not matter, whereas such issues are discussed more openly in the United States. However, racism remains an important factor in how different groups are treated and in outcomes.

'Race' and ethnicity are strongly correlated with outcomes, especially when linked with levels of wealth. People of colour, especially black men and those living in poverty, tend to have higher levels of illness, disability and mental health difficulties, be more involved in crime both as victims and as perpetrators and have low levels of literacy and educational attainment. The overrepresentation of black children in special schools in England was noted by Coard in the 1970s (see Wright, 2013 on issues related to black children's attainment subsequently), and concerns about low levels of attainment for some minority ethnic groups remain. Similar patterns of attainment and disproportionate numbers of children diagnosed as having special educational needs (or learning disabilities), especially those related to behaviour, are evident, and a source of concern, especially among people of colour and indigenous groups, in all societies.

Gillborn and Mirza (2000) highlight differences of educational attainment based on race, class and gender, though the pattern of attainment varies between groups, and there is much more variation within groups than between groups. For instance, children of Chinese and Indian heritage tend to score more highly in terms of academic attainment than indigenous children in England, whereas those Pakistani and Bangladeshi heritage tend to score lower, with traveller/Roma children usually the lowest attaining ethnic group. Girls on average score more highly than boys in most ethnic groups and children from poor backgrounds lower than those from more affluent ones.

Many reasons are given for these trends. For instance, Chinese and Indian families tend to be seen as ambitious and hardworking, but the parents tend to be better educated and wealthier. Some adults still associate children learning English as an additional language with low attainment, although the evidence suggests that such children initially score lower in language tests (understandably) but then catch up with and, frequently, overtake those for whom English is a first language. But, as Gillborn and Mirza highlight (2000: 7), 'emphasising *difference* in attainment between groups can be part of a necessary analysis of inequalities in educational outcomes. However, care should be taken that such an approach does not lead to a hierarchy of ethnic minorities based on assumptions of inherent ability' (emphasis in original).

Ogbu (1974), studying an urban neighbourhood in California many years ago, highlighted three main arguments given for why black children fail academically

- inferior intelligence;
- cultural deprivation; and
- the culture of schools.

Drawing on Durkheim's insight that when a whole group does not conform to expectations, the cause is usually related to the group, Ogbu argued that black children are encouraged to fail and are taught that their effort does not bring the same rewards as for more advantaged children. There is a well-established association with poverty, since many families and children from black and minority ethnic backgrounds live in poverty; and those minority ethnic groups where children attain highly tend to be more affluent. However, as Ogbu writes (1974: 253), 'not all of those from a background of poverty fail in school; nor do all who fail come from such a background'; but disproportionate numbers of those in his study who failed at school were both poor and black. He highlights that since people tend to measure themselves against those whom they know and who are closest, low expectations, especially in terms of effort, easily became self-fulfilling in a culture where success and effort are not seen to go hand in hand.

Different groups and individuals fail or succeed for differing reasons, but mainly for systemic ones. For example, many successful children from migrant communities come from a background of prior success and aspiration, whereas those from less highly educated groups have a more difficult task, especially those living in poverty. For many children from minority ethnic backgrounds with a history of migration, a further complication is added by whether they are migrants themselves or the children or grandchildren of migrants. Those of the second and third generation, especially where parents retain a traditional, conservative view of how children should be brought up, often find themselves torn between the expectations of their parents, families and communities.

Such children are torn between conflicting loyalties as they explore how their culture and religion contribute to, and fit into, the emerging narrative of their identities.

Whether manifested in skin colour, religion, language or other ways, race/ethnicity frequently is a source of discrimination, as some groups and individuals are positioned as 'outsiders' and denied access to as wide a range of opportunities as those available to other ethnicities. As a 'white' person, I may feel uncomfortable in a context where visible differences mean that I am in a small minority, but this operates much more strongly for people of colour, because of considerations of power. However, being of a different skin colour to the majority of the group can lead to paradoxical results. People of colour may stand out because of their visible difference, but are often ignored in public space, apparently invisible despite their visibility, or demonized as unwelcome outsiders because of their visibility, particularly in the case of young men.

The conclusion that a major cause of black children's underachievement is racism, built into the educational system, is supported by the evidence of young children of Afro-Caribbean heritage starting school in England as relatively high attainers and then gradually (as a group) attaining less well compared to other groups as they progress through school (see Wright, 2013). And Connolly (2002) highlights how teachers disproportionately focus on the disruptive behaviour of groups of black boys, especially, from a young age, and thereby tend to reinforce this as part of such children's racialized, and gendered, identities.

Racism has serious consequences psychologically. Results from many studies have linked experiences of discrimination and racism to a range of psychosocial difficulties in African American youth, including low self-esteem and depressive symptoms (see Harris-Britt et al., 2007). Sanders-Phillips et al. (2009: 180) argue that 'exposure to racial discrimination in children of color is ... consistently related to internalizing (anxiety, depression, and withdrawal) and externalizing (anger and aggression) behaviour and these associations increase during adolescence'. While most of these studies have focused on adolescents, the foundations are established beforehand.

Studies of the effects of racism on those doing the discriminating are strikingly absent. However, as Troyna and Hatcher (1992: 196) suggest, 'the intricate web of social relations in which children live their lives and the particular set of material and cultural circumstances in which this is embedded have the potential to heighten the salience of racism as an appealing and plausible explanation for the "way things are"'. In other words, ideas of racial superiority can easily become normalized and apparently unchangeable.

The effects of racism are even more complex than those of sexism because there are so many different ethnic and linguistic groups; and this complexity becomes even greater when one takes account of social class.

## Working out how social class affects identity

Social class is another complex and contested factor which affects how children's identities are constructed. Reay (2017) highlights two main meanings related to

- socio-economic background and level of family income; and
- values, norms, beliefs and practices, which demonstrate status and what is deemed to matter.

Drawing on this, class is conceptualized in this book mainly in relation to poverty and status.

While most sociologists (e.g. Savage, 2015) agree that terms such as 'working' and 'middle class' are hard to define exactly, and boundaries have become more fluid with greater social and ethnic diversity and the expansion of higher education, these concepts remain useful. Both are linked to occupation, education and wealth but sometimes in contradictory ways. For instance, someone who is not well off financially but exhibits values, beliefs and practices associated with middle-class life may continue to see themselves, and be seen, as middle class. And a person brought up as working class is likely to retain some affiliation to such an identity and beliefs even if she or he acquires a high level of qualification and income.

Although Todd (2015), rightly, sees class as a relationship defined by unequal power rather than a way of life or an unchanging culture, class identities are created and maintained by particular activities and expectations. In England, class is strongly associated with status and how one should behave – and by implication how one should not, sometimes in apparently trivial and implicit ways. For example, I was brought up that one should always put milk on the table in a jug, rather than a bottle, and certainly not to play with working-class children, though it was not deemed necessary to explain why. Assumptions related to how one should behave based on one's own and other people's social background are often implicit until they are broached.

Class in terms of status may be an English pre-occupation, though the associated expectations and allegiances have become more fluid. In other societies, such as the United States and Australia, distinctions based on status are less pronounced. However, poverty is a reality for many children and their families and has a profound effect on children's opportunities, achievements and identities in all societies.

Many accounts of working-class communities in the past suggest that, even though people were poor, the communal spirit and willingness to help each other compensated, at least to some extent, though this may downplay the difficulties associated with poverty. Those living in poverty tend to suffer from worse physical and mental health and low levels of literacy and attainment. Poverty is associated with problems such as low birth weight and a reduced ability to deal with infections; and inadequate nutrition leads not only to hunger but also to illness and obesity. Poor people are more likely to be unemployed and insecure as a result of having to move house frequently or parents having no job or juggling the demands of more than one job to make ends meet.

Chapter 3 highlights growing concerns with children's mental health as a result of stress. However, children are affected in different ways, depending to some extent on social class. For instance, there is increasing evidence of affluent, middle-class children, especially girls, being anxious, manifested in adolescence in rising rates of self-harm and anorexia. And children who are poor, especially boys, tend to manifest more conduct-related difficulties, with various groups, notably black and working-class boys, disproportionately excluded. This results in such children often being seen by teachers as problematic notably in terms of behaviour.

Brooker (2002) highlights three main reasons given for the low level of school attainment of disadvantaged groups

- language and literacy practices at home;
- cultural and child-rearing practices; and
- parents' lack of interest in their children's education.

Whether, and how much, poverty is related to status varies between societies, but it is a mistake to conflate economic with cultural deprivation. Many working-class children do not have the broad and rich experience of language and reciprocal conversation which helps them to succeed at school. However, Brooker cites a wealth of research (e.g. Tizard and Hughes, 1984) which attests to the richness of working-class children's language experience at home, though often not evident in schools. Heath's (1983) comparison of two contrasting, though geographically close, communities in the United States indicates vividly how, in the disadvantaged community, children's existing skills in storytelling were not transferred to the classroom because they were not able to draw on familiar language and cultural practices.

Rogoff (2003: 291) highlights that an emphasis on verbal instructions and adults' explicit structuring of contributions to conversations, and giving clues where necessary, tends to be a feature of middle-class parenting. Similarly, Lareau (2011), in her study of middle- and working-class families, argues that middle-class parents, regardless of ethnicity, tend to act in ways which she describes as 'concerted cultivation'. This is characterized by regular discussion between parents and children, where the former reason and negotiate and tend to control leisure activities; and this approach often leads to middle-class children having a sense of entitlement to challenge adults and the ability to do so.

Lareau argues that, in contrast, many working-class parents do not consider the features of concerted cultivation, particularly organizing children's leisure activities, as necessary to good parenting. They tend to adopt an approach she calls the 'accomplishment of natural growth' which involves being directive towards children but allowing them more freedom. This does not mean that such parents do not work hard at being good parents, but their children experience long stretches of leisure time and child-initiated play, clear boundaries between adults and children and regular interactions with other family members. However, this often leads to a sense of constraint in children's, and adults, interactions with institutional settings where middle-class expectations are the norm.

Middle-class children are more likely to

- have a wider experience, and range, of language;
- visit the theatre or museums or go to drama, or music, or swimming lessons out of school; and
- receive help with homework and/or additional tuition,

all of which help in formal educational settings. So the transition into, and between, formal settings tends to be easier for middle-class children because the settings and associated expectations are more familiar. However, Lareau emphasizes that many middle-class children squabbled, whined and talked back to adults in ways that would not be tolerated in working-class homes. Moreover, she indicates that many aspects of children's lives, such as favourite TV shows, meals and playthings, were not strongly differentiated by class.

Social class tends to replicate itself between generations. Children's academic success is strongly correlated with family income and parental, especially the mother's, level of education. Middle-class parents have access to a wider range of social capital – networks of influence – and are more likely to have 'sharp elbows', where they play the system to gain advantage for their children, since they know how to exert influence. Brantlinger (2003) indicates how educated middle-class parents do so by knowing how to exercise choice, and being better at doing so than less educated parents. As a result, poor children frequently have less choice of school and attend schools where academic standards are lower.

The school system mirrors and reproduces the hierarchical relationships in wider society – and always has done. Moreover, the structure of schools is not neutral in terms of motivation. In Brantlinger's (2003: 13) words, 'Because (working class and lower income families) rarely benefit from it, the competitive school structure does not play the same motivating role for them as for middle class students. Class advantage may be invisible to those who benefit, but subordinates are acutely aware of barriers to opportunity.' An overemphasis on performance excludes many working-class children, however unwittingly.

Class distinctions run very deep. Middle-class professions, like being a doctor, a lawyer or a teacher, tend to be valued more than becoming a plumber, a cook or a train driver. And activities such as going to the theatre or museums are usually held in higher regard and confer more status, whereas those associated with working-class activities such as fishing or darts are not.

Lower attainment at school for children growing up in poverty – and the lack of opportunities which flow from that – is associated with a more restricted vocabulary. However, one should not assume that poverty necessarily leads to educational difficulties, though these are correlated. The findings of the EPPE project (Sylva et al., 2010) emphasize the importance of the home learning environment in children's success at school, but see this as depending more on relationships, expectations and facility with language than poverty as such. Constant stress and chaotic lives are damaging to children of whatever social class and many children, including those from middle-class families, experience a poverty of relationships.

Families where parents have a low level of qualifications, often living in poverty, are frequently described in derogatory terms as having a culture of low aspirations. While this is true of some individuals and families, uncertainty about how to support their children's education, or inability to do so, is far more salient, for many working-class parents, than lack of interest.

Benjamin and Wrigley's (2013: 144) suggestion that the two main emotional effects of poverty are shame and futility helps to explain why acquiring a high sense of self-esteem is harder for children from poor backgrounds than for those from more privileged ones. Children from poor backgrounds are frequently looked down on by children and adults from more affluent ones, implicitly or overtly. This may be because of visible signifiers such as names, clothing or possessions, but is often more subtle. Reay (2017) writes of how she, as an academically successful working-class girl, always felt out of place in schools where most children were middle class; and of the petty humiliations and insults which were all too evident to her and other working-class girls. Some were the result of deliberate actions and comments, some less intentional. Members of dominant groups may exclude deliberately at times, but not even notice the petty humiliations. Like adults, children can be kind and caring, but can also be cruel and exclusive, especially to those whom they see as 'other' – and perhaps a threat.

Reay points out (2017: 153) that white working-class communities may have different collective memories of formal education, mostly related to exclusion and failure, from those in minority ethnic groups, especially if the latter are migrants from societies where education offered more hope of escaping from poverty and educational failure. Reay (2017) argues that seeing these issues in individual rather than structural terms tends to place responsibility for success or failure on individuals and their families, leading to feelings of guilt and a sense of hopelessness for those who do not succeed. And while working-class families tend to be more attached to particular localities and communities, this becomes impossible when poverty means that they have to move frequently.

Structural reasons provide more convincing explanations of low attainment, and possible solutions, than deficit models where poor children are blamed for their failure. We shall return to ideas such as cultural capital and 'funds of knowledge' but one should remember that working-class children do not lack cultural capital but that what they bring is often not valued in schools and settings which tend to manifest and encourage middle-class values and ways of working. This highlights the need to review the aims and processes associated with schooling, as discussed in Chapter 9, and to create more inclusive settings which dismantle or minimize the barriers to high achievement and self-esteem.

## Exploring the relationship between religion and identity

As discussed in Chapter 1, religion has a strong association with associated questions with spirituality – those related to identity, meaning and purpose. However, many religions have had an ambivalent attitude towards young children, where they are frequently presented as examples for adults to emulate, but excluded and even mistreated in practice. Attitudes towards children, expectations in terms of behaviour and approaches to punishment may vary in faith communities from what children experience elsewhere, especially at school.

The part which religion plays in identity and how identities are shaped, especially for young children, is controversial, not least because religion has always roused strong feelings and continues to do so, for instance in terms of many parents' wishes to bring their children up as members of a faith community and concerns about indoctrination. Religious affiliation is one protective factor in relation to mental health, but can also be narrowing and restrictive; and I shall suggest in Part III that indoctrination tends to make children's religious identities brittle.

Current portrayals in the media frequently highlight the role religion plays in conflict and extremism, rather than how it is a normal and essential part of life for many families in most societies. Historically, religion has influenced societies in both positive and negative respects. Religion has made major contributions to culture in the sense of music, art and literature, such that all children need to know about religion, for instance the stories and practices of faith, if they understand how other people think and avoid religion becoming a source of conflict and discrimination. Religion has been influential in encouraging both altruistic and conforming behaviour and remains for many children a source of motivation and identity, but has also had a history of intolerance and oppression. Discrimination on the basis of religion has been persistent throughout history, for instance, in how overt anti-Semitism keeps reappearing and how anti-Muslim sentiment has been widespread in recent years.

In many 'Western' countries, religion tends to be associated primarily with beliefs and individual choice. This is mostly a Christian – especially a Protestant – view and, as Brown (2013: 17) points out, 'the conceit of religion as a matter of individual choice … is already a distinct (and distinctly Protestant) way of conceiving religion, one that is woefully inapt for Islam and … Judaism'. Many other religious traditions place greater emphasis on ways of acting and being, a framework for living in and understanding the world, than on beliefs and individual choice.

While the roots of the word 'religion' lie in what binds a group, membership of any group is, necessarily exclusive of those not accepted as, or deemed to be, part of that group. Religion provides structures and routines designed to enable individuals to belong, for instance, through clothing and practices such as prayer, fasting and observance of holy days and festivals. Religious affiliation is frequently evident through such visible symbols or markers of identity, but it can be hard to distinguish cultural practices and beliefs from religious ones. Many practices regarded as essential by some adherents may be seen by others (and outsiders) as not essential, such as particular forms of worship or prohibited activities or, more controversially, attitudes towards groups such as women or gay people.

Religious traditions are often seen as inflexible, with particular beliefs and practices expected in order to belong. Although some religious traditions are like this, Macintyre (1999: 222) writes that 'traditions, when vital, embody continuities of conflict', with Winston indicating that 'Macintyre understands a tradition as a living argument, not a set of precepts to enforce conformity' (1998: 21). But the wish to protect the beliefs and practices associated with a religious tradition is frequently used as an argument against change.

One should be careful about generalizing about religion. For instance, some faith communities keep men and women, or adults and children, separate during worship, whereas others encourage worship together. Images are widely used in some religions, seen as idolatry in others. Moreover, one should be wary of seeing any religion as homogeneous, in the sense that statements such as 'Christians believe that ...' or 'All Muslims act ...' are accurate, except at a very general level, and even then being cautious. There is considerable diversity within most religions. While all Muslims are careful to avoid what is *haram*, forbidden, and regard the Q'uran as a holy text, different groups express their faith and worship in distinctive ways. Likewise, while images of Yahweh are forbidden in Judaism, not all Jews practice their faith in the same way. And within Christianity faith is expressed through liturgy and rituals which reflect a diverse range of traditions and theologies.

However, while religions are characterized by diversity when considered overall, local congregations frequently reflect greater homogeneity, often associated with ethnicity and class. For instance, many congregations of charismatic Protestant Christians consist mostly of black people; and the Anglican Church (at least in England, though not worldwide) consists mainly of white, middle-class people.

In many industrialized societies, notably in Europe, there has been a rapid decline in religious affiliation in the last fifty years (see Woodhead et al., 2016). As Davie (2012) observes, 'At precisely the moment that we need them most, we are losing the vocabulary, concepts and narratives that are necessary to talk intelligently about religion.' While the idea that organized religion is in decline as a result of secularization is largely a Western view, religion, worldwide, is flourishing and remains an essential part of many adults' and children's identities in Western societies, especially among minority ethnic groups. In many other, especially Muslim, countries, religious affiliation remains the norm, even though with varying levels of active participation. In some societies, notably the United States, religion is seen as a largely private matter with teaching religion in publicly funded schools forbidden by the constitution.

As a result, religion is for many children a central source of identity; and for others something of which they have little or no experience or understanding. And those for whom religious affiliation is an essential part of their, and their family's, identity may see this something to be kept mostly to themselves, especially at school. The rise of secularism, and wariness about religion and indoctrination, has led many people to talk, instead, of values, a term considered further in Chapter 3. However, religious faith remains a significant factor in how many people understand themselves and the world and how young children's identities are shaped.

The influence of religion on individual identities is perhaps the area hardest to understand for those who have grown up in a secular environment without religious affiliation. Haidt (2012: 116–20) highlights three different foundations for ethics – those of autonomy, community and divinity. The first sees people mainly as individuals with wants, needs and preferences, the second as primarily members of larger entities from families up to nations. The ethic of divinity is based on the idea that people are children of God and should act accordingly. As a result, religion provides a foundation for how individuals see themselves and understand the world, and how to act and interact, rather than this being a matter of personal choice. Seen like this, religion becomes more like a way of life than a set of beliefs. Moreover, in many religions, individuals either cannot choose to relinquish a religious identity or must face serious consequences if they try to do so.

Religious identity is strongly based on the beliefs and practices of a faith community, about which outsiders may know very little; and even when they know a certain amount they may find their knowledge and sensitivity lacking in important respects. For instance, I was shocked as a young teacher when a mother asked me, on religious grounds, to avoid giving her daughter reading books which portrayed witches, a point I had not even considered. When I became a head teacher two eight-year-old Muslim boys who were friends had an argument when one said that the other drank beer. I suggested that one was provoking the other and that it didn't really matter. They agreed that I was right on the first point but not on the second. What may appear to an unthinking outsider not to matter may be far from trivial to a child.

This chapter has highlighted several intersecting factors which affect how identities are constructed, suggesting that everyone's sense of belonging – as insiders or outsiders, as 'one of us' or otherwise – is affected by considerations of gender, race, class and religion, though I have done no more than mention (dis) ability and age.

The issues raised are far from straightforward, with complex, and sometimes serious, social and psychological implications, addressed in more detail in Parts II and III. Although children from different backgrounds are in many ways similar, they frequently occupy somewhat separate worlds. Boys and girls inhabit different micro-cultures in various respects, as do children from particular ethnic groups and social backgrounds, since considerations of ethnicity and class frequently affect who children are allowed to play with, other than at school.

Exclusion and discrimination are frequently the result of one or more of these factors, but these should not be seen as completely separate. For instance, while wealth tends to 'trump' gender and race or at least ameliorate levels of disadvantage, this is not always so. Middle-class black children may be discriminated against in the public sphere because of skin colour, despite their family being relatively wealthy.

The difficulties with establishing a robust identity as a boy or a girl or a member of a particular ethnic, linguistic or religious group are exacerbated by poverty, and, in different ways, by coming from an affluent background with the expectations and pressures that may accompany this. The struggle for coherence may be harder for those who move – physically or psychologically – from the culture in which they grow up, especially in terms of ethnicity or class. Such a move tends to pull children, often painfully, in different directions, choosing between conflicting loyalties and identities. While the effect of this is most evident in adolescence, such pressures also affect younger children.

I shall argue that behaviours, and the attitudes and values associated with these, are internalized from an early age and that, since the factors discussed above, and different elements of identity, affect each other, children should be viewed and treated holistically. However, the next chapter considers the changing context in which young children grow up and the challenges and opportunities this presents.

# 3

# Understanding the changing social, cultural and educational landscape

*This is the era of globalisation, and perhaps of unprecedented opportunity. But there are darker visions. The gap between the world's rich and poor continues to grow. There is political and religious polarisation. Many people are daily denied their basic human rights and suffer violence and oppression. As if that were not enough, escalating climate change may well make this the make-or-break century for humanity as a whole.*

Alexander, 2010: 15

## Looking at how childhood is understood in different times and cultures

This chapter considers how childhood has been, and is, perceived in different times and cultures and the changing social, cultural and educational context to argue for more emphasis on the sort of person a child is and the qualities and dispositions associated with global citizenship.

There are few certainties about childhood, except that all adults have been children. For instance, there is no common definition of the age at which childhood ends, with UNCRC (1989) defining it as continuing to age eighteen and in some cases beyond that. Lancy (2015) highlights how conceptions of childhood differ both historically and across societies and cultures, and the extent to which psychological research and the explanations offered are affected by culture. Lansdown (1994: 33–4) argues that 'for many adults, childhood is imbued with a rather romanticized notion of innocence – a period free from responsibility or conflict and dominated by fantasy, play and opportunity. Yet for many children of all cultures and classes the dominating feature of childhood is powerlessness and lack of control over what happens to them.'

Historically, children have not been the centre of attention as they are frequently in 'Western', middle-class societies. In the nineteenth century, children in poor families were usually sent out to work or worked at home from a young age. In more affluent families, children were expected to be seen and not heard. In most societies in Asia and Africa, children learn from an early age that they have a duty towards their family, associated with a sense of shame when such an obligation is subsequently not adhered to. Childhood is still seen in many societies primarily as a preparation for adult life and employment and, for girls especially, marriage, rather than a time when children are allowed to grow up without much concern about the future.

Children inhabit a world of which adults have at most a partial knowledge, in terms of games, humour and interests. This has been exacerbated by the influence of technology, as discussed in the next section. Play has, historically, been one defining feature of childhood in all cultures and societies, though its prevalence and types vary, as discussed further in Chapter 5. However, while it is usually recognized that very young children need to play, many cultures manifest a strong suspicion of play in favour of more formal instruction, particularly as children move out of early childhood. For instance, Brooker (2002: 161) indicates how the Bangladeshi parents she interviewed viewed play as something to be indulged rather than encouraged and did not wish to encourage young children's independence and autonomy.

Most adults have strong beliefs about how children should behave and be taught, usually based on factors such as gender, race, class and religion, and the expectations which accompany these, as discussed in Chapter 2. In 'Western' societies, young children are often treated as incapable. For instance, most three-year-olds in Vietnam can handle chopsticks, and are expected to fend for themselves, whereas in most 'Western' societies such a skill would usually be seen as too complex for such young children. Parents in the United States and England, particularly middle-class ones, tend to focus more on children being stimulated and protected than those in most other societies, including many industrialized countries such as the Scandinavian ones and France. As Marano (2008: 83) suggests, 'Parents … infantilize their children by overprotecting them and assuming them incapable of handling any challenge', with children frequently not expected to do chores or look after their own space and possessions. However, adults have a somewhat ambivalent attitude towards protecting children, with Cross (2004: 185), for instance, writing that 'Americans (are) eager to protect children from dirty words and pornography but not to shelter them from consumer desire'.

Adults in most societies historically have tried to control children's behaviour primarily by punishment. Corporal punishment, whether as a smack or a more formal beating, was widespread until the 1980s and still is in many cultures. It is still allowed and used in many African and Asian societies and in the United States – in nineteen states in school and all states at home – whereas it is forbidden in many other Western countries. However, increasingly, there has been more emphasis on rewarding good, rather than punishing bad, behaviour, through tangible rewards such as stickers or money or by approval and affirmation. And other sanctions such as 'time-out' are commonly used to indicate disapproval and encourage children to change how they behave. Which of these are used, and how, varies significantly across and within different groups defined by ethnicity, socio-economic background and religion. Such beliefs and approaches may vary within a family, especially between generations, but they affect how children are expected to conduct themselves and therefore how their identities are shaped. So, children have to negotiate their identities in the face of often-conflicting messages within and beyond their immediate family and may therefore be confused if they are unsure what is expected.

While the age of starting school varies, there is increasing pressure in most societies to start activities associated with school learning, and formal instruction, with very young children. Mayall (2002) argues that children's lives are increasingly 'scholarised', with less freedom to, and time for, play, especially unsupervised by adults, and families expected to take more responsibility for children's academic attainment. Moreover, in Heath's words, 'childhood is becoming one prolonged stretch of spectatorship. Passively waiting to be entertained by others, children miss out on the kind of learning that comes through direct experience, participation, and collaboration' (Demos, 2010: 115).

Erikson (1995: 13–14) suggests that a long childhood tends to make for technical and mental virtuosos but leaves a lifelong residue of emotional immaturity. This is not necessarily to argue for or against a long childhood, where children can explore their own identities free from the pressures of adult life, but to indicate that different ways of bringing up children may have benefits and disadvantages in terms of independence and emotional resilience.

Lancy (2015: 360–4) points out the resistance in WEIRD societies to schooling from a significant minority of children and what parents expect in terms of effort, in contrast to many cultures where education is highly valued and conformity expected. 'Concerted cultivation' – and middle-class parenting styles – tends to lead to better outcomes at school as measured by tests, but whether this is so in other respects is far from obvious. If many children in 'developed' societies are growing up unhappy, anxious and often brittle, it is at least worth asking whether the ways of bringing up and educating children currently assumed to be correct are appropriate. I shall suggest, drawing on the work of Rogoff (2003), Lancy (2015) and others, that less sophisticated cultures may have a view of child-rearing from which more sophisticated ones have much to learn.

One significant issue is the extent to which children are seen as individuals or part of a group. Individualistic cultures emphasize self-sufficiency and collectivist ones the dependence of individuals on the groups of which they are a part. This is manifested in the extent to which children are considered to have rights and responsibilities, as individuals and towards other people. The United Nations Convention on the Rights of the Child (UNCRC), adopted in 1989, reflects a growing emphasis during the twentieth century on children's rights, with the United States the only industrialized country not to have signed. The UNCRC emphasizes universal rights for all children, such as those to

- life, survival and development;
- not be discriminated against;
- their views being respected; and
- their best interests to be considered in all matters affecting them.

While some rights are unconditional, such as those to life, others seem to be conditional in that they imply responsibilities or children will require (at least some) adult help to exercise them. For example, Article 15 states that 'children have the right to meet together and to join groups and organizations, as long as it does not stop other people from enjoying their rights. In exercising their rights, children have the responsibility to respect the rights, freedoms and reputations of others.' And, while Article 12 states that 'every child has the right to have a say in all matters affecting them, and to have their views taken seriously', young children's views may need to be mediated by adults, since they may not yet be capable of making decisions likely to benefit themselves – or others – in the long term.

Wall (2010) sees the discourse of human rights as systematically excluding children, while recognizing (2010: 123) that adding participation rights to those related to provision and protection is a step forward. He argues that children rarely receive a proper hearing, in a world dominated by consumer or parental choice, where those who shout loudest are heard most clearly. Wall writes, 'In a world structured around agency, individuality and autonomy, those who are relatively less independent in life will tend to be assumed, however benignly, to be second-class moral citizens' (2010: 89). Moreover, the UNCRC focuses on individual rights, whereas many cultures see rights more collectively and emphasize responsibilities as well as rights. While I shall argue that children require a sense of agency, Lancy (2015: 393–6) indicates that many cultures see children's agency as something to be restricted if they are to learn not to focus unduly on themselves.

This section has indicated that beliefs about childhood and expectations of children vary substantially between cultures and societies. Adults are often ambivalent and uncertain about issues such as how, and how much, to protect children and to encourage their individual rights. The importance of these points will become evident in Chapter 6 and Part III, when considering whether, and in what sense, children require a sense of agency in constructing and negotiating their identities and can be supported in doing so.

## Surveying the changing social and cultural context

As Alexander's words at the start of this chapter state, globalization presents many challenges such as climate change and environmental degradation, inequality, polarization and oppression, as well as opportunities. Among the significant social and cultural changes in recent years which the Cambridge Primary Review (Alexander, 2010: 53–5) highlights are

- changing patterns in the immediate and extended family and communities;
- a much improved level of physical health, though greater concern about mental health;
- a higher level of disposable income and possessions for most but not all;
- a rapid change in types, and availability, of technology; and
- a less deferential approach towards authority.

Social and cultural change has led to more diverse types of family, both the immediate and the extended family. For example, many children do not live with both birth parents, or in a traditional nuclear family, as I did. This results from the increased frequency of events such as the breakdown of relationships, adoption and different ways in which people become parents. As a consequence of migration, far more children are of mixed heritage and most children live in communities with greater linguistic, cultural and religious diversity. As discussed, many children have no affiliation to a faith community, whereas for others religion forms an important source of identity and belonging. The fragmentation of communities and weakening of support structures, such as faith-based and community groups (see Putnam, 2000) which have traditionally offered a basis for shared identities and a protective function, has led to what Giddens (1991) calls 'disembeddedness' and people relying more on themselves as individuals. With globalization and secularization, cultural affinities and identities have become more fluid.

There is growing concern about obesity and its likely long-term consequences; and physical and mental health difficulties affect disadvantaged groups disproportionately, especially those living in poverty. Advances in medical practice have led to an increasing number of children surviving whose brains were damaged before birth and who may have significant disabilities because of very premature birth or conditions such as foetal alcohol syndrome. But the physical health of most children is much improved in recent years, in terms of nutrition and susceptibility to illness.

However, there is increasing evidence of precursors of mental health difficulties such as unhappiness, loneliness, anxiety and low self-esteem becoming more common in young children (e.g. Palmer, 2006; UNICEF, 2007; UNICEF, 2013). While young children are rarely diagnosed medically as having mental health difficulties, the early signs of anxiety-related and behaviour- (or conduct-) disorders are widespread. As we have seen, diagnoses, especially for conduct-related disorders, are being made earlier and the use of medication to control children's behaviour has risen considerably in recent years.

While most societies have become more affluent in recent years, with far greater availability of material possessions, inequalities of wealth in most industrialized societies have become significantly greater (see Wilkinson and Pickett, 2009; Dorling, 2015; Wilkinson and Pickett, 2018). Wilkinson and Pickett (2009, 2018) argue that inequality is detrimental to the bonds which hold societies together and that more people feel insecure as manifested in the rise of populism and xenophobia; and that behaviours such as bullying are more common in unequal societies.

Technology has a prominence in children's lives unthinkable in my childhood. From a young age, they look at computer and television screens, often for considerable periods of time, and are influenced by advertising and subtle messages. The long-term consequences generally and in terms of identities are uncertain. Technology may bring significant benefits in broadening cultural horizons and understanding of other cultures, but the ready availability of information may result in children being uncritical of what they see and hear, without explicit guidance. There is growing evidence that the anonymity provided by the internet and social media leads to less considered and more hurtful comments than people would make face to face. However, studies such as O'Keeffe et al. (2011) identify several benefits as well as risks in children using social media, and highlight that such means of communication are widespread, especially for adolescents, though less so for younger children.

Young children are often absorbed when watching screens, even though they may be more volatile in other situations. They expect to be entertained more than previously. Moreover, technology and the media help to create a world characterized by immediacy and gratification which tends to favour simple solutions and to discourage sustained and critical thought. Greenfield suggests that 'children come to school with shorter attention spans and often with less developed speech and imaginations. They are used to receiving information mainly iconically and visually in short, sharp bursts rather than socially including talking through or reading in any sustained way that helps to develop concentration and the building of conceptual frameworks' (Baldwin, 2012: 31, summarizing Greenfield's work).

Automatic respect for adults has diminished with the decline of deference in many cultures, especially in Western societies. While such a trend may be welcome in some respects such as encouraging independent and critical thinking, it has resulted in children being less respectful towards their parents; and many parents, and children, showing less respect for teachers, in ways that seem strange in societies where children are expected to listen to, and obey, the teacher.

The current macro-culture seems to offer the chance to pick from a smorgasbord, a pick'n'mix, of apparently attractive options of who one will choose to be. Hargreaves (2003: xi) argues that these changes mean that 'the demands *on* young people and challenges facing them are vastly different from what they were', continuing that this is also true of the demands which they make. In particular, these changes have opened children to being, and being seen as, commodities and consumers and many of the worries traditionally associated with adolescence are increasingly seen among younger children.

Westerlund (2016: 224) argues that the consumer culture, together with the chance and encouragement to create one's own lifestyle, has led what she calls a performance culture, where one has to perform to maintain one's identity but is constantly measured and compared with others. The influence of advertising, television, computer games and, increasingly, social media, and the messages about happiness and success presented, encourages children to focus on themselves and how they look. The emphasis on body image results in many young girls, especially, dressing in what most adults probably regard as inappropriately sexualized ways. These messages are often targeted at young children and operate in subtle ways, presenting a view where success is usually based on possessions and good looks, often in the context of sport, fashion and celebrity. Paradoxically, the appearance of choice frequently leads children to conform with the peer group, for instance on shared markers of identity such as having the 'right' clothes or mobile phone. Such influences, especially the focus on individuals and how they feel, tend to lead to children becoming passive, individualistic and narcissistic (see Ecclestone and Hayes, 2009). This does not mean that all children are like this, but the emphasis on looks and body image seems likely to affect particularly strongly those who are less resilient, by preying on their insecurities.

A consumerist culture emphasizes material pursuit and trivializing which Hyde (2008: 141–59) identifies as key factors undermining children's spirituality. Williams (2000) argues that a consumerist culture provides seductive and alluring choices to children (and others) who may be unable to recognize the possible consequences of such choices. Moreover, he suggests that 'the reluctance to think about nurture and the learning of choice is fundamentally ... a reluctance to think about the role of time in the formation of identities' (2000: 49).

One should be careful about such interpretations. Older people, like me, frequently lament change and overstate its adverse effects. Engagement with technology may tend to be addictive, but as a little boy I was fairly obsessive, though not about technology. And while I and many others worry about the casual violence in computer games and films, it is worth recalling many fairy stories are very violent. However, the world in twenty, let alone fifty, years is likely to change even more than between my childhood and now, with the wider application of technology and artificial intelligence as well as the challenges highlighted earlier. Further erosion of separate cultural and class-based identities, with more mixing of ethnicities and cultures, is likely. Children now grow up in a world with fewer certainties than in my childhood and stronger, often conflicting, influences on their attitudes and identities, and mixed messages about how they should act.

One significant change for the better, in my view, has been the greater visibility of women, people of colour and those with disabilities, in the media, both in general and when they are shown succeeding in a wide diversity of roles. While such groups remain underrepresented and are more evident in areas such as sport and the arts than in business or in science, such a change provides a far more diverse range of role models. This reflects a greater awareness of the discrimination which such groups face and a wish to publicize the success of individuals and to change the outcomes for disadvantaged groups, with the last of these, unsurprisingly, proving much more difficult.

Despite these changes, children grow up in a society where discrimination on the grounds of gender, race and class is still prevalent. In all societies, most positions of power are held by men, with roles in the home and at work strongly influenced by gender. Women are still far more likely to be in caring roles, and men less likely to be a regular presence, either physically or emotionally, in young children's lives, though the extent of this varies between cultures and has changed to some extent in recent years. Sexism, racism and homophobia remain widespread in both affluent and poor communities, though these tend to be more overt in the latter. Such attitudes may not be manifested much in a child's class or school, but she or he will certainly encounter these in wider society.

All children face challenges in constructing and sustaining robust but flexible identities as a result of the changes outlined previously. However, many face particular difficulties, especially those who

- have had disrupted lives;
- live in an environment with unpredictable relationships;
- have experienced traumatic incidents or long-term abuse or neglect; and
- have a parent, usually the father, who is absent, actually (such as those living far away or in prison) or emotionally.

The difficulties which some children face may be fairly obvious, as with refugees, asylum seekers and those displaced by family circumstances and the lack of a secure geographical base, or children being hungry, cold or scared because of poverty, crime or the easy availability of drugs. For others, these difficulties may be more hidden, such as children who are carers or the victims of, or witnesses to, child abuse, domestic violence or substance abuse or where adults are in debt or addicted to gambling. Many of these disproportionately affect poor, and often diverse, communities and the children who live in them.

Many, though not all, children in such groups are what a teacher whom I interviewed called 'unanchored ships', struggling for a coherent narrative of identity, so that they may require particular types of support and sensitivity. However, the next section describes how young children are educated in most school systems, as the basis of the subsequent argument that a broader, more holistic approach is required if children are to construct coherent, robust identities.

## Assessing the current educational context

This section provides an overview of recent trends in primary (or elementary) education internationally, recognizing that priorities and practices in different systems vary (see Alexander, 2000) and that what is espoused in policy may not be reflected in practice. These trends are considered in terms of the curriculum, pedagogy, assessment and accountability, though these all affect each other. Although most examples are drawn from an English context, similar trends apply elsewhere. A more detailed discussion is available in Alexander (2010, Part 3) and Eaude (2016, Chapter 4).

Curriculum organization varies between systems, with some using broader 'areas of learning' and others maintaining separate boundaries between subjects (Pepper, 2008). Despite this, there has been a remorseless emphasis in recent years, in most systems, on what Alexander calls Curriculum 1 – the 'basics' or the core curriculum – the content of which varies slightly but always includes those elements of English and mathematics which are most easily tested. The written curriculum frequently sets out the content to be learned in the core subjects in great detail. Often much of the school day is spent on skills related to Curriculum 1, with Curriculum 2 – the rest including the humanities and the arts – marginalized as desirable but not essential. Moreover, the curriculum is usually based on a Western-centric view of the world, with too little recognition of the contribution of other cultures and of women, people of colour and those living in poverty.

Recognizing that knowledge, skills and understanding are all interlinked and necessary to make sense of oneself, the world and the interaction between the two, it helps to distinguish between three main types of knowledge

- propositional, or factual, knowledge – 'know what';
- procedural knowledge – 'know how'; and
- personal/interpersonal – 'knowledge of oneself and other people',

with the latter two particularly important in how young children's identities are constructed.

The emphasis on Curriculum 1 reflects a view of education in which, as Trevarthen (1992) points out, cognition has, since the Enlightenment, been emphasized above conation or emotion, that is will or feeling; and propositional knowledge has been privileged over procedural, practical knowledge, reflecting Arnold's view of culture, discussed in Chapter 1. Such a view reflects the sharp division between academic and vocational education, and the prioritization of the former, though such a divide is greater in England than in many countries in mainland Europe. Moreover, it is associated with a neoliberal approach which emphasizes what is deemed necessary for economic productivity, with less concern for other views of the purposes of education and approaches which might result from these.

The marginalization of Curriculum 2 reflects how what Bruner (1996: 39–40) calls logical-scientific thinking and the analytical, cognitive type of intelligence is seen to matter most and other types, such as those posited by Gardner (1993), devalued. Bruner argues that logical-scientific thinking is helpful for understanding physical phenomena, while narrative thinking is a more appropriate way for human beings to organize and manage their knowledge of the world and structure their experience, and to understand people and their plights.

Much of the recent emphasis of policy is based on the thinking of E.D. Hirsch (1987), who, in arguing for what he calls cultural literacy and core knowledge, emphasizes that if they are to succeed children must be taught knowledge of literature, history and scientific principles associated with the culture in which they live. Hirsch argues that, without this, allusions and connections cannot be understood, especially by those from disadvantaged backgrounds. However fairly, this view has been associated with an emphasis on propositional knowledge and rote learning (see Gardner, 1991: 188–9). Chapter 4 considers why such an emphasis is unhelpful in enabling young children to construct robust identities.

The rationale given for the increased emphasis on Curriculum 1 is to ensure greater consistency and an entitlement for all children – a way of raising standards of attainment, notably those of children from socially disadvantaged backgrounds and some minority ethnic groups. However, the result has often been a narrow and fragmented curriculum, especially for those who find school learning hard, with much time and effort spent on trying to ensure that children attain high scores in tests. Concern about emotional and behavioural difficulties and low-level disruption and disaffection, especially among boys from low-attaining groups, has grown. This has led to methods of managing behaviour being recommended where children are expected to conform, with rewards for compliant behaviour and sanctions otherwise, and to exercise choice, by recognizing the consequences of their actions.

As a result of concerns about the loss of enjoyment and creativity and about children's behaviour and mental health, many governments worldwide have introduced policy initiatives designed to address children's needs more holistically and programmes to improve children's social and emotional development. However, the main thrust of educational policy has remained constant. Despite the rhetoric emphasizing aspects such as creativity, social and emotional development and, more recently, character education, these have in practice been sidelined in the context of what Ball (2003) calls performativity – that success is mainly about measurable outcomes in decontextualized high-stakes tests based largely on attainment in skills associated with literacy and numeracy – often called the 'standards agenda'. Where the results form the basis of inspection judgements, teachers' priorities are understandably skewed to achieve high scores, at the expense of breadth.

Children with disabilities and special educational needs have been integrated much more in mainstream classes. However, the standards agenda takes little account of differences related to gender, race and class, except in relation to attainment, in part because of an understandable wish for such factors not to be used as an excuse for low attainment or aspiration. While frequent worries are expressed about the low levels of attainment of some groups, such as white working-class boys and some ethnic minority groups, the proposed solution is almost always 'more of the same', so that additional support or extra classes are provided to try and raise test scores, rather than offering a broader and more engaging curriculum.

Pedagogy – the how rather than the what of teaching – has traditionally been the preserve of teachers. In recent years, teachers of young children have increasingly been expected to

- teach and manage classes in prescribed ways, reducing the extent to which teachers exercise professional judgement;
- focus mainly on narrow elements of children's identities, as readers (or rather decoders of text) or mathematicians (or correct completers of sums); and
- cover a very wide range of content, usually in discrete subject-based lessons, and often requiring an approach based more on direct instruction than on facilitation.

As a result, young children are expected to listen and practice skills for much of the week, with limited time for play or activities associated with the arts and humanities or physical education. However, more recognition in policy of the importance of children talking and articulating their ideas has led many teachers to encourage this, though the pressure to cover the curriculum frequently reinforces teachers' tendency to speak too much.

Accompanying these changes has been, especially in the 'core subjects', more emphasis on differentiation with children grouped based on perceived ability, or prior attainment. While this may make it easier to pitch lessons at a level which provides suitable cognitive challenge, Chapter 9 argues that such an approach often disadvantages children in the early stages of learning English, children of colour and those from working-class backgrounds.

Teachers in many systems have been under pressure to introduce formal instruction at an ever-younger age, on the assumption, put crudely, of 'the sooner, the better', with less emphasis on play-based learning, even for children as young as three or four. However, some systems, notably in mainland Europe, delay formal instruction until the age of six or seven, with teachers of younger children concentrating more on social and emotional development and learning through play.

While these trends are stronger in some countries than others, most systems and schools are very data driven, with strong pressures related to performativity and accountability. Each system's position in the league tables resulting from the Programme for International Student Assessment (PISA) dominates the thinking of politicians and policy-makers. Despite a widespread recognition among teachers of the benefits of formative assessment which enables children to know what to do to improve and informs teachers' pedagogy, outcomes as measured through summative assessment are usually deemed to matter most. Tests of what can easily be measured have come to define the success of children, teachers and schools, with regular and publicly available inspection reports. A huge industry based on devising and marking such tests, and saying how they should be interpreted and influence pedagogy, has resulted.

What Alexander calls a 'culture of compliance' (2004) among teachers results from this greater emphasis on high-stakes assessment and accountability mechanisms. Fear permeates the system, leading to the marginalization of the arts and the humanities and less trust in teacher judgement and professionalism. Inevitably, such changes have affected how teachers learn, and are encouraged, to teach and see their role.

Significant discussion of the aims of education, and what it is to be an educated person, has been stifled by the assumption that educational success can, or should, be measured largely in terms of test scores in those areas of the curriculum which are most easily measured. Such an approach sidelines one key aim of education, which in English legislation and policy is children's spiritual, moral, social and cultural (SMSC) development. Eaude (2008) suggests that, while what SMSC development entails is not easy to articulate, provision should enable children to explore, within or outside a framework of religious belief, questions about meaning, identity and purpose, some of which may be difficult and distressing. As such, SMSC development makes an essential contribution to the development of the whole child. RSA (2014) presents a brief but cogent discussion of SMSC development, arguing that it is in danger of being marginalized in all but the most confident schools, partly because of a lack of time for reflection about the purpose of education.

To summarize, most young children, in schools worldwide, experience a curriculum focused on decontextualized skills in literacy and numeracy, which marginalizes the humanities and the arts and activities and experiences, such as play and story, which I shall argue are vital in the shaping of children's identities. As a result, the experience of school is not very engaging for many young children, especially those from historically disadvantaged groups, particularly as they approach adolescence.

Among the underlying assumptions of the current approach are that

- the most important knowledge is that which can be tested;
- young children learn mainly through instruction;
- regular testing is necessary to ensure that children learn; and
- when children are not learning well, they need more of the same,

all of which I shall challenge. Part III, particularly Chapter 9, argues for a significant change of priorities, within and beyond schools, to address the needs of the whole child, holistically, if children are to be equipped for a world of change.

## Identifying the qualities and dispositions required for an uncertain world

The current context is one of social and cultural change. Three main types of response to change and the uncertainty which accompanies this are to

- fall back on to what is familiar and retreat into defensiveness;
- become highly individualistic and competitive; and
- welcome and celebrate the possibilities that this presents.

I shall argue that the first two of these do not form the basis of a robust identity. This section suggests that, to flourish in an uncertain world, more emphasis is required on the qualities and dispositions associated with global citizenship, and indicates what some of these are. By qualities, I mean characteristics which are manifested by, and influence, observable behaviours. Dispositions are orientations towards certain types of behaviour and response and refer to the motivation to manifest qualities even when unobserved or not acting to be rewarded or avoid punishment. As Claxton and Carr (2004: 91) write, an emphasis on learning dispositions considers long-term learning trajectories rather than the accumulation of particular bodies of 'knowledge, skill and understanding'.

Such a view is the foundation of my argument for adults to adopt an approach based on virtue ethics and an apprenticeship approach. Virtue ethics – usually associated with moral education – concentrates on the sort of person who will act appropriately when expected to make specific decisions, and therefore seeks to strengthen the qualities and dispositions – or virtues, though the word may seem old-fashioned – associated with character (see Eaude, 2016: 33–36). An apprenticeship approach is discussed in more depth in Chapters 7 and 8, but in brief involves children working alongside someone with more experience and learning mostly by example and practice, over time.

While there is no agreed definition of global citizenship, UNESCO (2014) describes Global Citizenship Education (GCED) as aiming to empower learners of all ages to assume active roles, both locally and globally, in building more peaceful, tolerant, inclusive and secure societies. GCED is based on three interlinked domains of learning

- cognitive: knowledge and thinking skills necessary to better understand the world and its complexities;
- socio-emotional: values, attitudes and social skills that enable learners to develop affectively, psychosocially, and physically and to enable them to live together with others respectfully and peacefully; and
- behavioural: conduct, performance, practical application and engagement.

Bourn et al. (2016: 12–13) argue that this view of global citizenship is integral to education for sustainable development, with the two concepts representing different sides of the same coin and focusing on similar capabilities

- cognitive skills: learners acquire knowledge, understanding and critical thinking about global issues and the interconnectedness/interdependency of countries and different populations;

- socio-emotional skills: learners have a sense of belonging to a common humanity, sharing values and responsibilities and holding rights; learners show empathy, solidarity and respect for differences and diversity; and
- behavioural skills: as a result of which learners act effectively and responsibly in local, national and global contexts for a more peaceful and sustainable world.

Bourn et al. continue that UNESCO – and to some extent the UN Sustainable Development Goals – advocate that global citizenship in education should promote universal human values, including human rights, gender equality, cultural diversity, tolerance and environmental sustainability (UNESCO, 2014). I doubt whether the capabilities outlined should be seen as skills, as this may imply that they are techniques rather than deep-seated beliefs and dispositions, and shall challenge the idea of universal human values. However, global citizenship implies looking beyond a locality or a nation and a recognition of interdependence not just with other people but with the natural world of which we are all part – and acting accordingly.

In many societies, historically and still, religion has been seen to provide the basis for identifying and developing the qualities associated with character and morality. As indicated in Chapter 2, secularization and the decline of religious affiliation in many 'Western' countries has led to more use of the term values. Halstead (1996: 5) defines values as 'principles, fundamental convictions, ideals, standards or life stances which act as general guides to behaviour or as points of reference in decision-making or the evaluation of beliefs or action and which are closely connected to personal integrity and personal identity'. How values and motivations are internalized is considered in Chapter 6, but, as discussed in Eaude (2016, Chapter 7)

- the term values is often used to suggest that these are universal;
- values is used in two senses, descriptively and aspirationally; and
- values are demonstrated in a person's actions more than what she or he says.

Although the idea of universal values has considerable appeal, let us consider some difficulties which this presents. Some values, such as honesty, courage and generosity, would seem to be so widely approved of as to seem universal, Yet, in Alexander's (1995: 24–5) words, 'values are not absolutes. They are by their nature contestable and contested'; and, as Katayama (2004: 70) writes, 'in a plural society like ours people agree in valuing virtues like justice and honesty but do not share the same interpretation of these terms. ... The more detailed interpretation such words are given, the more difficult it is to achieve a broad consensus.' Moreover, values inevitably clash in real situations so that the question is usually not whether to be honest, courageous or generous but how honest, courageous or generous to be, and how to ensure that aspirational values are manifested in practice.

Haydon (2004) argues that the idea of universal values carries the (usually implicit) assumption which privileges the liberal values of relatively rich and 'developed' countries and so fails to recognize that what is valued changes over time and differs between – and within – cultures and societies. Moreover, there is a hierarchy of values, where some are seen as more important than others, however much values are interconnected. So, I believe justice to be ultimately more important than courage or patriotism while other people and cultures may prioritize different values or considerations such as religious faith or personal aggrandizement.

In Eaude (2016: 115–17), I explored five potentially controversial values, or attributes – patriotism, ambition, humility, modesty and deference – and three more likely to be seen as universal – fairness, respect and honesty – to demonstrate that the importance and the meaning ascribed to them varies between cultures. However much one may wish to argue for universal values, what these entail in practice will always be a matter of debate, given that values are only general guides to behaviour. Moreover, many people understand their lives more in terms of a narrative based on how people act and are treated, rather than on abstract concepts such as values. It may be more beneficial and practical, especially with young children, to focus on qualities and behaviours since these are more easily observed and understood.

Which qualities adults wish to strengthen will depend to some extent on their aims – and the sorts of identities they hope and expect children to manifest. For instance, if children are to become robust and resilient, they must learn to cope with a variety of unexpected or unfamiliar situations. If adults wish children to be kind and compassionate, opportunities to develop empathy will come to the fore. And if adults want children to succeed, whatever the cost, they may encourage ambition and ruthlessness.

Let us consider which qualities children require to cope with change, as global citizens, recognizing that no list will ever be complete or agreed. Claxton (2002, 2007) sees what he calls the 4Rs – resilience, reciprocity, resourcefulness and reflectiveness – as the basis of 'learning power' and that these can be learned, though may be, to some extent, a matter of temperament. Hargreaves (2003: xviii) argues that in a 'knowledge society' young people need capacities such as deep cognitive learning, creativity, ingenuity, problem-solving, risk-taking, trust in the collaborative process and the ability to cope with change. 'First Steps', a report by the Confederation of British Industry, an employers' organization, highlights similar characteristics such as

- tenacity, self-control and curiosity;
- enthusiasm and zest, gratitude, confidence, ambition and creativity; and
- humility, respect and good manners and sensitivity to global concerns,

as essential for the twenty-first century (CBI, 2012: 33), not only for employment but also for life more generally. The International Baccalaureate curriculum emphasizes similar qualities and dispositions, in contrast to the curricular focus in most systems on (largely propositional) knowledge.

Critical thinking is necessary to assess the veracity of information when this cannot be assumed and to decide whether this, and the people providing it, should be trusted. In Bailin et al.'s words (1999: 281), critical thinking involves 'the kinds of habits of mind, commitments or sensitivities (which) include such things as open-mindedness, fair-mindedness, the desire for truth, an inquiring attitude and a respect for high-quality products and performances'.

The qualities which seem particularly important for children in constructing a robust identity as global citizens are set out in Table 1, recognizing that their relative importance will always be a matter of debate and vary to some extent across cultures and contexts. For instance, while Bloom (2018) argues that empathy – at least when it gets in the way of rationality – is less important than compassion, I shall suggest, especially in Chapter 6, following Nussbaum, that empathy is essential in understanding other people and treating them compassionately. However, it is worth noting that

- while most may be seen as intrapersonal, several are interpersonal;
- many are qualities which young children manifest, but which are not encouraged, or strengthened, by the macro-culture and the current educational system; and
- one box is blank for you to add your own.

**Table 1** Qualities contributing to a robust but flexible identity

| Courage | Curiosity | Generosity | Agency | Creativity |
|---|---|---|---|---|
| Resilience | Imagination | Open-mindedness | Resourcefulness | Reciprocity |
| Playfulness | Reflectiveness | Fair-mindedness | Flexibility | Empathy |
| Compassion | Confidence | Respect | Optimism | |

Parts II and III consider how such qualities and dispositions are best strengthened, with Part II discussing the processes involved from the perspective of how children learn, and Part III the role of adults.

The first three chapters have explored what is meant by terms such as identity and culture, arguing that culture, especially micro-cultures, can, and should, help to

- provide a sense of place and belonging;
- set and regulate the parameters of acceptability; and
- create, and potentially expand, individuals' expectations of what they can achieve.

In relation to young children, the first of these matters especially in the child's search for where she or he belongs though this is hard in a fragmented and confusing world. The second helps to civilize, or at least socialize, children by encouraging them to act and interact in ways which are acceptable in particular contexts. The third enables each child to imagine new possibilities and, to some extent, make these more attainable. Together, these help to shape robust but flexible identities.

Part II

# How Young Children's Identities Are Shaped

Part I explored the social and cultural context in which young children grow up and their identities are constructed. It introduced the idea of identity as a constantly changing narrative integrating multiple, often-conflicting identities, arguing that a robust but flexible identity involves internalizing a wide range of qualities and dispositions.

As well as being constructed and shaped, identities can be seen as

- woven, suggesting that different strands are intertwined;
- forged, like metal in a fire, implying that the qualities involved are strengthened by a manageable level of challenge and adversity; or
- grafted, or overlaid, on to existing ones, though identities can be left behind, or wither, when new ones emerge, such as when a child may see herself or himself as 'no longer a baby' in adopting a more grown-up identity.

The process can also seem as like trying to complete a jigsaw without knowing exactly which pieces one has to work with. However, I mainly use the metaphor of identities being constructed and shaped, indicating that the process is incremental and reciprocal.

Part II considers how young children learn and particularly how their identities are constructed, and constantly reshaped, so that they can make sense of many different, possibly contradictory, feelings and experience and the role of culture, broadly interpreted, in this process. As they do so, children are engaged on a life-long and life-wide journey, navigating a route through uncertain terrain and stormy waters, where

- the route is not necessarily, and often not, linear;
- what is involved is determined to some extent by the context;

- the child herself or himself has to undertake much of the work; and
- there is no obvious end-point or destination.

I shall gradually build up the argument that

- insecurity provides a weak foundation for constructing a robust but flexible identity;
- such an identity cannot be imposed, but must be constructed by each child, albeit with support and guidance, especially when she or he feels anxious, confused or vulnerable;
- identities are constructed, and reconstructed, gradually and mostly through small, ordinary actions and interactions; and
- since this process occurs through every aspect of life, not just at home, or in a faith-based group or in school, let alone only in some aspects of the school curriculum, a holistic approach is required.

One distinction explored is between those aspects which are learned directly or indirectly – or more accurately with or without conscious awareness and effort. We shall see that norms and qualities are learned mostly by example, practice and habituation. Identities are constructed more as a by-product of relationships and experiences throughout life than by explicit instruction. Constructing a coherent identity involves exploring, imagining and creating new possibilities, within supportive cultural spaces and environments. Since this is a reciprocal and multifaceted process, children have to gain, and retain, a sense of agency, and engagement, but other people, especially trusted adults, have crucial roles, though how these are carried out is fraught with dilemmas, puzzles and paradoxes, to be discussed in Part III.

A second area considered is how beliefs and assumptions embedded in the family and other cultural traditions and activities associated with culture in the sense of the arts and the humanities influence children's identities. Young children's identities are strongly influenced, and regulated, by relationships with adults and each other and by expectations set by, and feedback from, the home, family, faith communities (for some children), the peer group and the wider social and cultural context. Therefore, how identities are constructed and re-negotiated is not just a matter of individual effort and choice and the process happens slowly, and unevenly, over time.

Part II is structured broadly in terms of the learning processes (Chapter 4), activities and experiences (Chapter 5) and environments (Chapter 6) which help create a robust sense of identity and belonging, although such distinctions are somewhat artificial. For instance, imagining and exploring new identities involves processes which occur in specific activities or experiences, but the result depends heavily on the context and environment. Similarly, how values, beliefs and motivation are internalized depends on the environment and how rewards and sanctions, routines and rules are applied by adults and understood by children. Throughout Part II, I try to highlight where factors such as gender, race, religion, class and disability are influential and where the needs of children in early childhood and pre-adolescence differ.

4

# Constructing identities

*Identity ... is forged out of interaction with others. Who we are is inextricably bound up with who we are known to be.*

Salmon, 1995: 63

## Exploring how young children learn

This section provides an overview of how young children learn, as a basis for the more specific discussion, which follows, of how their identities are constructed. Learning involves extending the boundaries of, and building on, existing knowledge, skills and understanding. We have seen the importance of procedural and personal/interpersonal knowledge. Gonzales, Moll and Amanti (2005) use the term 'funds of knowledge' to describe the types of knowledge which many children from disadvantaged backgrounds have but which tend not to be highly valued in school. These usually relate to activities associated with working-class cultures, but the idea can be extended to a wide range of activities and interests of which the schooling system takes little or no account, but which are important aspects of children's identities, now and in the future. These are as diverse as chess, cooking or computer games; electronics, farming or geology; and knowledge of dinosaurs, martial arts or sacred texts – and many more. What counts as success at school may not be what is seen to matter outside. For instance, Jason as a ten-year-old with low self-esteem could not read fluently or write comprehensibly and hated dance, but was brilliant at building or fixing anything electrical and mechanical. In Part III, I suggest that, especially with young children, adults must value, and build on, such funds of knowledge.

Let us consider briefly the long-standing debate of the relative influences of 'nature' and 'nurture'. There is no doubt that genetics is a major factor in how people develop and, as Kagan (1994) argues, temperament plays a crucial part in how children act, interact and respond. However, early experience and socialization affect profoundly how a child makes sense of the world. Nature, whether one's genes or temperament, and nurture, or experience, interact. Therefore, this debate is not very fruitful, in this context, except insofar as one must recognize that some aspects of how children act are 'in-built' and not open to change and that experience triggers, and so enhances or limits, how children develop.

Piaget, and many other psychologists, argued that development occurs through a series of discrete, consecutive stages, such that children must have reached a particular point of readiness before moving on to the next. However, in Engel's words, 'young children's behaviour is dynamic and often inconsistent, shifting rapidly from one orientation to another. Because they are in such a rapid period of change, their abilities, feelings, motivations and behaviours are often in transition and hard to characterize in a neat way' (2005: 11–12). And as Donaldson's research (1982) demonstrates

- young children's emotional state affects their cognitive abilities to a considerable extent;
- a child must see activities as purposeful and meaningful if she or he is to be engaged; and
- the context and relationships with the person setting a task is very influential in how young children understand a task and respond.

James (1998: 47) writes that 'once it had been realised that expectations about the abilities and competences of the child had been shown to vary cross-culturally and over time, it was suggested that biological development must be seen as contextualizing, rather than unequivocally determining, children's experience'. So, as David and Powell (1999) argue, views of developmentalism are more culturally determined than usually recognized. Seeing children's development in terms of discrete, linear stages is too limiting particularly in relation to complex, fluctuating aspects such as how identities are constructed.

As discussed in Chapter 1, identities are actively created and constantly re-created, as opposed to an essentialist view – that how a child at any point is how she or he will always remain. Jenkins (2014: 81–2) sets out, with some reservations, Poole's summary of a general sequence for the 'emergence of identity in childhood', drawn from ethnographic studies across many cultures. Jenkins's reservations, and mine, relate mostly to Poole's rather exact timing of many of the processes outlined saying that they only 'begin' then, whereas signs of these are frequently evident at an earlier age. This said, one may adapt Poole's summary as follows

- an individualized attachment to mothers and caretakers being created within the first few months of life;
- from twelve months on, naming and categorization emerging and being directed to an understanding of the human world;
- by the age of two basic conversational capacity being established and, thereafter, the child's ability to represent and act out individual other people and their practices – 'in pretend' – growing in complexity;
- between two and four years of age, the child's narratives and understandings of self and others indicating the appearance of a more elaborated map of persons in an expanding sense of community, entailing self-identification and identification of other persons through observation, differentiation, imitation and affiliation; with gender, during the same period, becoming an increasingly significant dimension of selfhood;
- from five to six years of age, the child assuming more responsibility for his or her actions, gaining a greater understanding of the statuses she or he occupies, with their related roles, acquiring a public face to control how she is perceived by others and doing more as she or he would be done by; and
- during middle childhood, the peer group, often segregated by gender, replacing the family as the primary context within which identification occurs and develops.

These points are elaborated in this and subsequent chapters, taking account of Jenkins's (2014: 82) reminder that

- children are understood and childhood experienced differently depending on many factors; and
- children are active contributors to, and makers of, the human worlds of which they are members.

Let us first consider some insights from neuroscience and psychology about learning, in relation to young children. As indicated by Howard-Jones (2010), Tommerdahl (2010) and others, one should be cautious about thinking that lessons from neuroscience lead to clear and definite recommendations for parents or teachers. In part, this is because the brain is not the same as the mind, which is shaped and reshaped by culture and experience. However, the evidence from neuroscience (see for instance Blakemore and Frith, 2005; Goswami, 2011) and psychology indicates that

- the brain, and the mind, are more plastic and changeable than previously thought, with early experience very significant in how these develop, though major changes occur subsequently, especially in adolescence;
- anxiety and excessive stress affect adversely people's ability to concentrate and behave appropriately;
- young children only gradually learn 'theory of mind', which enables them to understand what another person thinks, knows or believes, and to use this to predict that person's behaviour;
- emotion and cognition are closely linked and inhibitory processes – the ability to self-regulate – crucial, with pre-adolescence usually when these processes become gradually stronger and more reliable;
- much learning occurs tacitly and indirectly through illustrations, analogies, metaphors and stories;
- habituation, example and practice are essential, especially in internalizing deep and lasting patterns of learning; and
- engagement and motivation may be greater when rewards are not wholly predictable (see Deci et al., 2001).

Blakemore and Frith (2005: 167–75) emphasize that normal brain function depends on regular routines of sleeping, exercise, eating and drinking. Sleep enhances processes such as the consolidation of long-term memory, with too little sleep reducing children's ability to concentrate. Exercise and a healthy diet contribute to good health, both physical and mental; and a lack of these is likely to affect health adversely.

While being challenged and feeling unsettled is an integral part of learning, and some stress is necessary, too much makes it hard to concentrate and repeated stress affects the chemical responses in the brain, making people more fearful, wary and often aggressive or withdrawn. Emotional intensity tends to add to feelings of stress, helping to explain why children who are suffering deprivation and abuse face an uphill struggle in relating appropriately to other people. While short-term stress may downgrade or upgrade the immune system activity, chronic or intense stress impairs the immune system and its functioning, causing long- and short-term health problems, with prolonged stress causing long-term biological changes. These affect self-esteem and self-concept adversely and may be even more debilitating and undermining of self-esteem than one-off traumatic events (see Cornwall, 1999 for a more detailed discussion of how behaviour is affected by stress).

Bruner (1996) highlights the centrality of children making meaning and what he and Trevarthen (1992) call 'intersubjectivity' and is often called theory of mind – how humans come to know each others' minds. Over time, young children come to recognize that other people have beliefs and desires which vary from their own, and so make inferences about other people's behaviour and motivation. How, and at what age, children understand their own and other people's emotions and behaviour is complex and not well understood. But Engel cites (2005: 87) Nelson's research which suggests that children start to develop theory of mind earlier than previously thought, and that they do so not by applying logical rules but by drawing on recollections and narratives of previous interactions with people.

Thompson (2009: 163–4) indicates that, by the end of their first year, infants demonstrate an awareness of other people's attention, behaving and feeling and, in their second year, they start to develop self-referential emotions such as pride, guilt, shame and embarrassment. By the age of three, children recognize the importance of other people's beliefs, and by five or six they begin to perceive people in terms of their individual characteristics and motives. For instance, Dunn and Brown (2001: 91) highlight that teasing and jokes involve, respectively, knowing what others will find annoying and anticipating what others will find funny because it is unexpected. Similarly, comforting someone else requires the recognition that she or he is distressed and what will decrease this, and Bloom (2013: 31) argues that babies have the capacity to make judgements between kindness and cruelty and to show compassion for other people. Harris (1989: 94) writes that experiencing emotions such as pride and guilt precedes understanding them more abstractly so that at about six or seven years old children can attribute such emotions to their parents and by eight give examples of themselves feeling such emotions without reference to someone else.

Children from a very young age categorize even when they may not be able to name the categories and may not select the same criteria of importance as adults do. Since young children tend to think in binary, black-and-white, terms, they frequently 'other' those who are different. Nussbaum (2010: 33–4) suggests that being afraid of 'the other', what is alien or threatening to us, is part of our basic instincts and that all human societies have created 'out-groups' who are stigmatized as shameful or disgusting or both. While young children can be welcoming and inclusive, they often exclude other children, particularly those they dislike or who are different for whatever reason.

Young children tend to be impulsive and excitable especially as a group, because of what Engel (2015: 50) calls the 'more undiluted emotions of early childhood' and their tendency to be easily influenced by other people. Their working memory and inhibitory mechanisms which enable to regulate their emotions and their behaviour are usually not well developed. As Cowan (2012) indicates, working memory is vital if one is to attend to a range of different ideas but has a limited capacity, with excessive information leading to overload, impaired processing and reduced memorization. Reasoning, in particular, makes considerable demands on working memory and attention, helping to explain why young children find this difficult. As a result, young children may find it hard to concentrate on what adults want them to do, but, when engaged, even very young children can do so for long periods.

## Becoming attached and socialized

Pollard (1985: x) writes that 'individuals are thought to develop a concept of "self" as they interpret the responses of other people to their own actions. Although the sense of self is first developed in childhood, … it is continually refined in later life and … provides the basis for thought and behaviour.' Holland et al. (2003: 5) argue that identities are lived in and through activity and are therefore social products; and, in Salmon's words at the start of this chapter, identity is forged out of interaction with other people. Champagne (2009: 2) writes that 'identity cannot be "taught". It is rather experienced, supported and developed, like a language, within a community.' Identities are shaped by relationships and experiences where the child is trying to make sense of a range of often-confusing emotions and experiences and are, in a sense, by-products of activities, experiences and, particularly, relationships. This section discusses how the foundations of identity are established, right from the start.

The process starts very early. Tiny babies are literally working out what is part of themselves and what is not, as they suck and grab and feel. As Bruner indicates, babies are more active learners than used to be assumed, writing that they 'were much smarter, more cognitively proactive rather than reactive, more attentive to the immediate social world around them, than had been previously suspected ... they seemed to be in search of predictive stability from the start' (1996: 71–2).

Dunn (1988: 1) argues that

> babies are born pre-disposed to learn about sounds and sights that are characteristic features of *people*. They are particularly attentive to shapes and patterns that are like faces and to sounds that fall in the frequency range of the female human voice. As babies, they learn especially fast about stimuli that change in a way that is contingent upon their own behaviour.

Every baby's physical and mental development is affected by how she or he is treated – and loved and cared for (see Gerhardt 2004, especially chapter 1). The prime carer, usually the mother, is vital in ensuring that those needs which the baby cannot meet unassisted – such as for nourishment, warmth and reassurance – are met. For instance, when the baby is hungry, or cries, most mothers are attuned to recognize what they want and respond appropriately. This, in turn, acts as a cue for the baby, where the baby recognizes that his or her own actions affect this. How, and especially how predictably, such relationships are established, based on the mother's attunement to the baby's needs and responses, affects how babies learn to respond and to regulate their behaviour.

Such ideas provide the rationale for attachment theory (stemming from Bowlby's work, for example 1965 and see also Goldberg, 2000) which, put simply, states that babies develop internal working models which

- are constructed as a response to anxiety during early infancy through the baby's relationship with the prime carer;
- influence how the baby regulates emotion; and
- strongly affect how she or he acts and interacts with other people.

Models of attachment may be secure or insecure, with the latter usually divided into avoidant, anxious (or resistant) and disorganized. Children with secure models of attachment can cope better with adversity because they can access a 'secure base' which provides emotional support and enables the child to be more adventurous and to take more risks. Infants with avoidant models explore but take little notice of their mother and are not worried either at her departure or at her return, sometimes being more sociable with a stranger. Having learned not to rely on their mother in seeking comfort, such children are less prone to express their emotions. Those with anxious models of attachment are reluctant to explore in their mother's presence and distressed when she leaves, reacting to moves to provide comfort either angrily or passively.

A small number of children with insecure attachments fit neither of these categories, showing both avoidant and anxious responses. Described as disorganized attachment, this leads to paradoxical behaviour, for example crying loudly but avoiding the mother's comfort or approaching her without seeking comfort and support. Such children are thought to have strategies to access the security they crave but be unable to implement them, having learned that these do not work predictably.

As children grow older, their need for the mother to be present diminishes, but anxiety still has to be contained. Loving relationships and predictable responses matter most for those who have least experience of them. Children leading very fragmented lives tend not to have experienced such relationships, for a variety of reasons, such as those mentioned in Chapter 3. What a child used to predictable relationships and responses may find relatively easily may be beyond what those with disorganized models of attachment can manage. Without caring and supportive relationships, children are really deprived.

Primary socialization, to use Berger and Luckmann's (1967) term, occurs during very early childhood, especially within the family, when a child starts to internalize the attitudes and values appropriate to members of a particular culture. Subsequently, broader social interaction leads to secondary socialization, but 'the world internalized in primary socialization is ... much more firmly entrenched in consciousness than worlds internalized in secondary socializations' (1967: 154). Early experience imprints itself very deep, as we saw in relation to attachment. For instance, even at my age, when with my mother, I tend to respond differently, more anxiously and sometimes defensively, than I would otherwise in similar situations, despite conscious attempts to do otherwise.

Discussing primary socialization, Berger and Luckmann (1967: 151) emphasize how the significant others who mediate the world to the child modify it in the course of doing so, selecting aspects depending on their own place in the social structures and their own individual experiences. As a result, 'the child takes on the significant others' roles and attitudes, that is internalizes and makes them his own. And by this identification with significant others the child becomes capable of identifying himself, of acquiring a subjectively coherent and plausible identity' (1967: 151-2). This process inevitably means that often-implicit assumptions and expectations about gender, race and class are internalized very early. This is most obvious in relation to gender, as we have seen, but how a child is nurtured and expected to respond in relation to other factors contributes to how she or he learns to act and interact and comes to see herself or himself.

Jenkins (2014: 72) suggests that selfhood is the earliest and most enduring primary identification, the stem stock on to which other subsequent identities are grafted, though identities may subsequently be discarded, to some extent, and overlaid on existing ones. Primary identifications are very hard to change, though not completely set in stone. So, identity is individually and socially constructed; that is, we make choices about who we are and who we want to be but within constraints which strongly influence conscious choices. Secondary socialization, where one learns how to act and interact in groups outside the home, whether the extended family, faith-based or other groups or formal settings such as nurseries and schools, can only alter one's actions, assumptions and attitudes to some extent.

Children search for predictable patterns from a very early age. Engel (2005: 68–71) summarizes Nelson's argument that children in the first five years of life

> easily detect the underlying scripts that shape and guide daily life, by experiencing a series of routines (such as breakfast, going to day care or visiting the park) that offer them a set of maps, that tell them what to expect. Children's understanding of how the world works, therefore, emerges from everyday encounters with a world full of people and events. (2005: 68)

Engel (2005: 164) writes that such early scripts act as organizing frameworks which enable children constantly to compare their expectations with what seems really to be happening. This helps to explain why routines and structures matter, but Chapter 6 returns to what I call the puzzle of predictability – the extent to which children benefit from adults who are predictable and consistent.

Vygotsky (1978) argues that what is internalized depends on the interaction between the child's internal world and external events. Put simply, what goes on outside the mind helps to structure what happens within, with knowledge created reciprocally rather than deposited from outside. One cannot make sense of new experiences outside cultural assumptions. However, many of these assumptions are tacit. Young children learn many things of which they are not conscious, helping to fill the well of memory on which they can draw in later life. For instance, they learn to speak by listening to, and using, language, without much direct instruction, and responding to cues and to feedback, that is reciprocally. Young children use, and learn to use, language (and the messages which surround spoken language) to get what they want, by requesting, signalling intentions and negotiating references (see Dunn and Brown, 2001: 88) – all of which involve using, and assimilating, cultural assumptions automatically.

Learning is a reciprocal process, involving watching, imitating, receiving feedback and trying again, so that learning becomes embedded, through practice and habituation. Rogoff (2003: 282–326) indicates how young children in many cultures are expected to behave and to learn to do so primarily by watching and listening and then by copying. Children watch for cues and respond to feedback, often subtle and silent affirmations that they are acting appropriately or corrections so that they adopt a different approach. They are not, and do not expect to be, the centre of attention. While such an approach fits well with how tacit knowledge is learned, it accords less well how in modern 'Western' cultures, especially middle-class ones, children from an early age are expected and encouraged to perform, coming to depend on adult encouragement and praise to complete even simple tasks.

As Goswami and Bryant (2010: 143) state, social interaction plays a critical role in learning, continuing that for children verbal mediation is not enough and that 'shared activity is required to mediate the child's acquisition, mastery and internalization of new content'. Tasks must be within the child's Zone of Proximal Development (ZPD) – just beyond what they can do on their own, but which they can with sensitive guidance and support; and children must retain their sense of agency – the idea that how they act makes a difference. If children feel helpless, out of control or believe that how they act does not matter, their identities are likely to become fragile.

## Learning through example, habit, practice and feedback

Building on the discussion of the reciprocal way in which identities are constructed, this section considers why example, habit, practice and feedback are so influential, especially for young children. In considering this, we should remember Salmon's (1995: 20) insight that 'our personal construct systems define the understanding we each live by. This means that learning is never the acquisition of a single, isolated piece of knowledge. Our ways of seeing things are inextricably intertwined. To alter one assumption means that others, too, are brought into question.'

Engel (2005: 117) highlights primary and secondary processes of making sense of experience: the former mostly unconscious, the latter more logical, rule-governed and conventionally organized. Constructing identities does not just involve accumulating factual knowledge or learning a collection of discrete skills. Much of the knowledge required is procedural and personal and interpersonal, and tacit so that it is learned more through example and imitation, as if by osmosis. Since young children rely less on cognition than adults, much of their learning takes place through processes and activities such as play, songs, stories, art and music, not just spoken language, and is reinforced through habit, practice and routine, unconsciously as well as consciously.

How imitative processes work is a matter of debate. Research, such as that summarized in Baldwin (2012: 33–5), suggests that mirror neurons play a major role in how humans learn, as they do in monkeys, with these triggered when an action is performed and when it is observed in another person. So, in Blakemore and Frith's (2005: 161) words, 'by observing an action, your brain has already prepared to copy it'. And, as Bellous and Sheffield (2017: 168) suggest, 'we anticipate what we expect'. However, how mirror neurons operate, and even whether the human brain has such neurons, remains contentious. And, as Engel (2015: 69) argues, children do not just copy adults, but pattern their intentions on the intentions of those whom they observe – and so are selective about what they imitate, not, for instance, copying what they perceive as mistakes.

Lacan provides another explanation, from psychoanalysis, describing the mirror stage as vital in how identity is created (see Woodward, 2002: 18–20). This is based on the belief that infants from the age of about six months recognize themselves in a mirror (or something similar), encouraging the child to see herself or himself as an object which the child can view 'from outside'. However, children do not recognize that the images are reflections of their own bodies until the age of about fifteen to eighteen months. When the child becomes fascinated with his or her own reflection, she or he sees a coherent self, a self that is somehow integrated as one. But it is a sense of self at odds with his or her own internal incoherence and uncoordinated bodily functions. The search for coherence involves working out how the split between different images of oneself can be repaired. This discrepancy, or splitting, between the image and the subject is often resolved in favour of the image, which becomes a controlling source of how we think about who we are. Lacan came to consider this process not as a stage in the infant's life but as representing a permanent structure in how we come to see ourselves. In Erikson's (2000: 128) words, 'Psychosocial identity develops out a gradual integration of all identifications.' However successful or quick this integration may be, the process is usually uneven and non-linear.

Children see, identify with and emulate many different role models, some positive, others less so, including adults in their own families and communities; teachers and other adults in schools and other settings; other children, including older ones; and celebrities through mass communication and advertising.

Children recall, and are influenced by, how other people make them feel more than what such people say. The importance of reciprocal relationships over time in how young children learn leads me to believe that face to face, sustained, relationships with trusted adults are more significant in the long run than images of famous and successful people, however attractive the latter may be. More immediate role models help children to see, understand and internalize how to conduct themselves, for instance in how curious, confident or creative to be in particular contexts. In contrast, the influence of more distant role models tends to relate what is visible rather than what is felt or experienced. However, seeing examples of successful people who are 'someone like me' seems to matter particularly for those from groups which have been historically disadvantaged and are underrepresented in the images which children encounter.

Young children find it hard to understand abstract ideas, especially out of context, and need to experience, see and feel what these entail. Since stories, examples and embodied experience help bring abstract ideas to life, these are important in constructing identities, especially those based on concepts such as a nation or a religion. Such identities tend to be superficial and fragile if based on ideas which children have not understood and internalized through living them. A sense of national identity, or patriotism, may be created by singing the national anthem or saluting the flag, but is unlikely to become embedded without exploring what being a member of the nation entails, through stories and examples. Similarly, a robust religious identity is created more through hearing stories and engaging in worship than by listening to, or reciting, statements of belief or creeds.

While knowing what action is appropriate depends on an interplay of emotion and deliberation, qualities and dispositions become embedded mainly by practice and habituation. For instance, we learn courage by being brave and to be generous by practising generosity. Similarly, children – we all – learn to trust, and to be trustworthy, by being trusted and to be respectful by respecting, and being respected by, others. Children's minds are malleable, so that the qualities they manifest and the values they espouse can be changed, but doing so becomes more difficult later on. Any characteristics, if constantly reinforced, become harder to change through conscious processes, for better or worse.

Habit becomes self-fulfilling in that one becomes more skilled at doing what one practices repeatedly. But this can embed undesirable, as well as desirable, habits, and it is essential to practice in the correct way. Bateson (see Bateson and Bateson, 1988: 42–6 and Eaude 2018a: 75) writes of his unsuccessful efforts as a nine-year-old to play the violin, earnestly practising separate skills rather than learning to act fluidly, and so practising the wrong things. He contrasts how two different types of action are learned, shooting at a fixed target and a moving one such as a bird. When shooting at a fixed target, one can adjust one's aim deliberately on the basis of feedback about the accuracy of a previous shot, having time to adjust one's aim. This does not work with a moving target, where the movement of aiming and firing must be a whole, single action, based on intuition, experience and practice to form good habits.

When aiming at a fixed target, one can use information, as feedback, to correct one's aim after the event. But, with a moving target, concentrating on every small action tends to stop one from acting fluently. One has no time to correct one's aim consciously and so must rely on habit and internal response mechanisms. Bateson calls this calibration, learning through doing and habituation, rather than relying on cognitive processes. If skills, procedural knowledge and qualities are to become embedded they must be learned and applied fluently in context. Calibration is particularly important for young children, since their cognitive processes are usually less well developed or efficient than adults', though they benefit from reflecting consciously on what they have done and how they can improve.

Bellous and Clinton (2016: 240–69) discuss the idea of memes as chunks of culturally transmitted information and practices, types of procedural knowledge like baking a cake or looking after a baby. Although these practices consist of separate skills, they – and the identities associated with them – are best learned as a whole, because they fit well into existing patterns of thought and schemata, explanatory structures which codify disparate bits of information and through which we make sense of experience, and because learning through activity helps such procedural knowledge to become internalized.

We have touched on the importance of feedback and will discuss adult feedback in more depth in Part III. In general, we all, especially children, respond more positively to reinforcement of what we have done well, rather than telling off or criticism. Criticism tends to affect children strongly, especially those who are unsure or have low self-esteem and when criticism is related to a child's substantive identity rather than his or her actions. Feedback comes from many different sources, with that from trusted adults especially significant, but other people who seem attractive, for whatever reason, such as older children or members of the peer group, exert influence on young children. While young children are often over-trusting of what adults say, Harris (2012) indicates that even very young children are more discriminating about whom they believe than adults tend to assume. He writes (2012: 41) that they manifest 'sensitivity to anomaly rather than passive acceptance', giving increasing weight, as they get older, to the (previous) reliability and accuracy of the informant. Feedback from other people can be verbal or non-verbal, with Jackson et al. (1993) suggesting that non-verbal feedback, such as a smile and nod of approval, is particularly significant. However, feedback can also be to oneself. For children to recognize their own strengths and abilities and what they must work at contributes to their sense of agency and ultimately to a more robust identity.

My emphasis on habituation and practice might be seen as an argument for rote learning. As indicated in Chapter 3, followers of E.D. Hirsch advocate a didactic approach to teaching children, especially from disadvantaged backgrounds, the types of knowledge required to succeed. However, this tends to overlook the importance of procedural and personal and interpersonal knowledge and children retaining a sense of agency if they are to remain in control of their learning and create robust, coherent but flexible identities. Moreover, it ignores the huge levels of advantage and disadvantage which result from children's backgrounds and the contexts in which they live – quite apart from the social capital on which parents of advantaged children can draw.

This section has suggested that much of the learning associated with identity and character takes place unconsciously or only partly consciously and deliberately. The next considers more conscious processes.

## Representing experience

While much knowledge is learned tacitly, representing experience helps to embed learning in long-term memory and make what has been learned available for conscious processing. How this happens affects how deeply and efficiently learning occurs. Bruner (2006: 23) argues that representation takes place in three main modes

- first, kinaesthetic, by doing and enacting;
- then iconic, by observing and drawing; and
- increasingly symbolic, especially through language.

The kinaesthetic, or enactive, mode embeds learning most deeply and the iconic more so than the symbolic. Throughout life, in Wall's (2010: 75) words, 'embodiment is more primordial even than language'. And, as Bruner (1996: 79) observes, 'we seem to be more prone to acting our way into thinking than we are able to think our way explicitly into acting'. Adults can use all of these modes, though they rely heavily on language, but young children only gradually come to learn efficiently through language, especially listening to, and processing, other people's words and ideas. While young children must learn to use and understand language clearly, they learn more deeply through their actions and visual representations than through using language. Young children benefit from being active, not just for health reasons but because they learn most profoundly in the kinaesthetic mode, so that learning becomes embodied, or 'second nature'.

Language is a tool which is both receptive and expressive – for hearing and for articulating, and so clarifying, ideas. Vygotsky saw language as a psychological tool which helps one in organizing one's thoughts and wishes and a communicative and cultural one to express these. Children benefit from expressing in words how they think and feel, so that they can process their feelings consciously and extend their emotional repertoire; but into middle childhood, and beyond, language is a necessary but a limited tool for learning. Talking about different ways in which people do, and might, respond can enable even very young children to think about how they should conduct themselves, though they may have only a limited idea of what the words mean. Most children find doing so easier in spoken than written language, because the former is quicker and less permanent. However, the public nature of spoken language may be more threatening, unless children feel that those listening will treat their ideas with respect.

Issues of identity raise many puzzling and sometimes painful questions, for young children as for older people. Young children may find it easier to address such issues through other modes of representation than language, such as play and painting, not least because these enable emotion to be expressed and processed more easily and with less threat. It is no coincidence that play, drama, art and music are all associated with therapy, enabling troubled children to deal with difficult issues. This is partly because they do not rely on language and cognitive processing and so allow the unconscious to work, notably in processing emotion. Such activities can be therapeutic in that they can help children to come to terms with what is puzzling and potentially distressing, though in more severe cases children may require skilled therapy.

Salmon (1995: 56) argues that 'our most important constructions are often unavailable to consciousness, and therefore to explicit verbalization'. She continues, 'Trying too soon to find words for something felt but not yet known can often drive it into inaccessibility. Only after it has been anchored within a visual form can efforts to give it clear verbal formulation be valuable' (57–8). As advertisers know and use very cleverly, young children are strongly influenced by percept as well as concept, and are open to emotional responses rather than rational, logical thinking, emphasizing the importance of images. Using images is a key way in which young children categorize experiences, mainly because the parts of the brain essential to rationality and the conscious processing of emotion are not yet well developed. However, as Bruner (1996: 159) observes, 'images are not only prototypes of categories, but also stopped action frames in narratives'.

As mentioned, Bruner (1996: 39–40) distinguishes between logical-scientific and narrative modes of thinking, arguing that

> we frame the accounts of our cultural origins and our most cherished beliefs in story form, and it is not just the 'content' of these stories that grip us, but their narrative artifice. Our immediate experience, what happened yesterday or the day before, is framed in the same storied way. Even more striking, we represent our lives (to ourselves as well as to others) in the form of narrative. (1996: 40)

Bruner points out that, while these two ways of structuring experience are universal, narrative has varied modes of expression in different cultures which may privilege different forms of doing so, such as song, poetry, drama or spoken stories.

One function of narrative is to mesh cognition, emotion and action together and thereby to give meaning to human experience. Narrative provides coherence to otherwise disparate events, since stories are (usually) about human agents with desires, beliefs, knowledge, intentions and commitments (see Bruner, 1996, chapter 1). As Bruner (1996: 21) indicates, 'Telling stories, about ourselves and about others, to ourselves and to others, is the most natural and the earliest way in which we organize our experience and our knowledge' (see Bruner, 1996: 121-3). Narrative comes more easily to young children than logical-scientific ways of thinking – even if such narratives may, to adult eyes, seem confused or fanciful. Through narrative, we recognize ourselves in other people and other people in ourselves. Narratives do not necessarily unfold logically. They ramble and go backwards or sideways as well as forwards, reflecting the non-linear nature of how identities are constructed.

Engel (2005: 114) argues that 'children use stories (their own and other people's) to differentiate between what they consider to be fact and what they believe to be fiction'. She highlights (2005: 109) how toddlers use stories to sort out the usual from the unusual, and argues that 'when children are between two-and-a-half and five, they energetically and enthusiastically, if unconsciously, exploit the potential for using narrative as a way to construe and reconstrue their world. That is, they simultaneously explore their world through narratives and explore narratives themselves' (2005: 111). However, she points out (2005: 111) that as children get older (than about five or six) their stories become more conventional and therefore less crafted by and reflective of the author's inner life.

Part of what is involved in constructing one's identity is finding new ways of telling one's story, when the old one no longer fits or describes accurately enough new realities. Narratives of identity are not created solely, or primarily, through language, but language plays a significant role in embedding a sense of who one is in consciousness. In part, this is because representing experience through language helps to structure children's thinking as they learn to categorize and make sense of experience. As Mercer (2000: 15) suggests, 'Language is not simply a system for transmitting, it is a system for thinking collectively,' jointly creating knowledge and understanding and linking 'individual thought with collective resources and procedures'. Language helps to relate local, personal experience to abstract ideas – and vice versa. Words enable half-formed thoughts to be articulated and understanding to be enriched, with more experienced users of language helping to reframe these and add new layers of complexity or nuance. However, young children, especially those from disadvantaged backgrounds, tend to use what Bernstein called restricted, rather than elaborated, language codes (see Abbott, 1988). Restricted codes are appropriate in some contexts, but elaborated codes are necessary to operate successfully in a wider range of contexts, especially in schools.

Learning to use language as a tool to construct meaning, and with it identity, is an active, reciprocal process where children talk, listen and think, rather than just listen passively. In Mercer's words (2000: 9), 'Dialogue stimulates thought in ways that non-interactive experience cannot.' What young children say and the conversation which ensues tends to matter more than what they hear. They benefit from being encouraged, and able, to take the lead and express in words how they feel and think. While adults may have to make explicit some points, a child may be more likely to internalize messages when she or he has articulated these – or another child has done so. However, adults can help to reshape children's understanding by reframing what they say in more precise or complex ways.

Discussion and conversation help to articulate, and shape, children's thinking and encourage reflection both on what has happened and on what they might have done, or might do, differently. Such a process is much easier in discussion with one trusted adult or in small groups where children can respond immediately. While group discussion is commonly used in formal settings, young children, especially those who are not used to expressing themselves in words or listening to other people and wait their turn and find such dialogue hard, particularly in large groups. Many boys in particular find listening carefully to other children difficult. And those children who are not used to reciprocal conversation and what was described in Chapter 2 as 'concerted cultivation' are likely to find it difficult and frustrating to articulate their ideas, to listen to others and to remember what they wish to say. Children in the early stages of learning a second or subsequent language may find it hard to express their thoughts in words, though ironically their experience may make them more attentive listeners.

This chapter has outlined some fundamental points about how young children learn, emphasizing relationships, activity and interaction and example, habituation, practice and representing experience, particularly through enactive and visual modes. Young children must have opportunities to express themselves through play and using a range of materials and media – such as drama, dance, paint, clay and music – as well as language, both spoken and heard. Constructing a robust identity is a slow process, through small steps such as the example which children encounter, the questions they ask and the feedback they receive. This requires both time and space, which the insistent demand for instant gratification and success preclude. The next chapter looks at agency, creativity and imagination and the types of activity which are most influential in enabling children to make sense of their experiences and construct a robust and coherent sense of identity.

5

# Exercising agency, creativity and imagination

*Young people are living in times of rapid cultural change and of increasing cultural diversity ... The engine of cultural change is the human capacity for creative thought and action.*

NACCCE, 1999: 7

## Reaching beyond what is familiar

Bruner (1996: 41) writes that 'finding a place in the world, for all that it implicates the immediacy of home, mate, job and friends, is ultimately an act of imagination'. This chapter argues that constructing a robust identity requires children to exercise a sense of agency, creativity and imagination, and considers what this entails, though one must bear in mind how adults can constrain or enable this, as discussed in Part III.

Let me start with a story which illustrates various themes in this chapter. Leigh was a rather troubled and disorganized six-year-old, often late for school and with little self-belief, though plenty of enthusiasm. In a project on electricity, we made working models. He designed and successfully built a lighthouse, with a switch, overcoming the challenges he encountered mostly on his own though with some discussion with his friends and advice from me. For several weeks afterwards, first thing, Leigh would dash into the classroom. Before anything else he would reconnect the wires to see that his lighthouse still worked. I believe that he had not just constructed a model lighthouse, but in doing so he had strengthened his own identity and enhanced his own self-esteem and resilience, using his imagination and creativity and persisting in the face of difficulties.

All Our Futures (NACCCE, 1999), a report commissioned by the Government in England, but one which did not alter the emphasis on performativity, sees creativity and culture as closely linked and describes four central roles for education in cultural development as to

- enable young people to recognize, explore and understand their own cultural assumptions and values;
- enable young people to embrace and understand cultural diversity by bringing them into contact with attitudes, values and traditions of other cultures;
- encourage an historical perspective by relating contemporary values to the processes and events that have shaped them; and
- enable young people to understand the evolutionary nature of culture and the processes and potential for change. (1999: 48)

This summary presents a view of cultural development somewhat focused on cognitive processes and by implication older students, but let us consider some implications for young children. First, the emphasis on 'cultural assumptions and values' and on diversity recognizes the need for learning much more than just propositional knowledge. Second, the recognition that culture is not static provides a source of optimism that change, both personal and societal, is possible. Third, NACCCE suggests, albeit implicitly, that education in cultural development requires children to be active, creative and imaginative to reach beyond what is familiar.

NACCCE (1999: 29) defines creativity 'as imaginative activity fashioned so as to produce outcomes that are both original and of value'. Moving from a plan, or a hypothesis, to an original outcome is an act of imagination which requires creativity. Creativity entails children being able to create their own questions, to find their own answers and to enjoy solving real problems. It is an active process, leading towards an original outcome, not mere imitation. Creativity entails children having a sense of agency but also requires structure if a worthwhile outcome is to ensue. Structure is ideally self-created but for young children usually has to be provided by, or negotiated with, someone more experienced. However, structure must be enabling rather than restrictive, as discussed later.

This raises the question of whether, and in what ways, young children can be creative or original. NACCCE (1999: 30) answers this by presenting three categories of originality

- historic or uniquely original;
- relative, compared to other people who are broadly similar; and
- individual, compared to one's own previous work.

While it is highly unlikely that a child will manage the first, except in so far as anything is original simply by being different, they can achieve the second or third. Craft et al. (2001) captures this succinctly with the distinction between 'big C' and 'little c' creativity, where the former is reserved for just a few people and the latter embedded in everyday activities and achievable by everyone, including young children like Leigh.

Creative thought and action requires a context, enabling some divergence from what other people, and perhaps the person doing the creating, expects. For Leigh, this context was building the lighthouse, but creativity can flourish in many other activities. Creativity, as described by Craft et al. (2009), is situated in a context where creative learning involves authentic tasks and genuine risk-taking, with children gradually taking more control in a relationship based on that of an apprentice and a novice. While children require a sense of agency to ask questions, whether in language or other ways, they often benefit from being guided by someone more experienced as to which questions to explore. Much of the research (e.g. Craft et al., 2013) emphasizes that creativity should be seen as a collective, rather than just an individual, process, re-affirming that we are interdependent rather than independent, autonomous beings. Similarly, agency is usually strongest when it is exercised collectively, working with other people.

Creativity relies on children being and remaining curious, with curiosity being in Engel's words, 'the human impulse to resolve uncertainty' (2015: 10). As such, creativity is linked to curiosity and questioning, especially when children generate their own questions. Most young children are naturally curious but their curiosity tends to diminish between the ages of five and twelve (see Engel, 2015: 6). Young children inhabit a world of imagination and playfulness unless and until adults restrict this. Some may find it hard to act in creative, divergent ways, maybe as a result of fear or a background where adults have discouraged this. The latter may be because of parents'/carers' beliefs, possibly based on religious or cultural grounds, but often because adults do not see why acting in this way is valuable or lack the physical or psychological resources to provide suitable opportunities. But, as we shall see, in Chapter 9, schools and teachers frequently discourage curiosity.

Identities are frequently reshaped in response to uncertainty. Finding about oneself and the world involves reaching beyond what is familiar and comfortable and involves exploration of areas which may be confusing and painful. The types of question which enable children to explore such issues are usually open, encouraging divergence, within an environment which feels safe, so that children can go beyond the information available to them and ask further questions; or not if they do not wish to do so. Since many of these questions do not have easy answers, children need the chance to ask and explore and revisit these, when necessary, possibly several times.

If defensive or scared, children are unlikely to be creative. As Donaldson (1992: 254) writes, 'When you are deeply and persistently worried about the "sort of person" you are, concern about this will soon intrude; and instead of wanting to solve a problem you will be wanting to prove that you are the sort of person who can solve the problem. This is generally at the root of the fear of failure.' This affects all children, but especially those whose identities are fragile, whether because of family history or personal experience, or both.

Cultural development and creativity is associated with emotional and aesthetic development, in part because culture deals with people and their feelings. While children's aesthetic development is an under-researched area, it seems to require a wide range of experiences, including those of the arts, both as watcher (or hearer) and as participant, and detailed observation and appreciation. Doing so needs time and space, rather than superficial contact before passing quickly on to some new experience. Since a sense of beauty is subjective, and varies between cultures, children will decide what they deem to be beautiful, though frequently guided by adults. Rather than being confined to any one discipline, opportunities occur in mathematics and science, in literature and poetry, in design and construction, indeed in almost any activity. As in other respects, young children benefit from a wide range of experiences, and dwelling on and representing these in an appropriate mode, rather than responding superficially or just trying to memorize information.

The rest of this chapter discusses activities which are particularly influential in enabling young children to construct robust identities and strengthen the qualities and dispositions associated with these. This inevitably happens within a context and in activities as varied as play, stories, games, music or discussion, especially when interacting with other people, and in many types of activity. For instance, singing songs or hearing stories as a group helps to encourage a sense of belonging and working together can take place at the playground, in a science experiment or in dance or drama. As we shall see, how children learn to collaborate and the environment and the relationships in which they do so influences how robustly identities are constructed more than the activity as such.

## Discovering oneself through play and drama

In Winnicott's words, 'It is in playing and only in playing that the individual child or adult is able to be creative and to use the whole personality. It is only in being creative that the individual discovers the self' (1980/2002: 63). While this is, in my view, an exaggeration, it emphasizes the importance of play, and creativity more generally, in how children explore, construct and strengthen their identities.

The official commentary on the United Nations Convention of the Rights of the Child sees 'play as an essential component of physical, social, cognitive, emotional and spiritual development' (CRC, 2013: para 14c). And, in Engel's words, 'play is a central and vital process during childhood. It is not merely that children need time to unwind or have fun. Rather, without play, they will be much less likely to develop just the kinds of thinking we feel are so vital to a productive and intelligent adult life' (2005: 184–5). However, as discussed in Chapter 3, different cultures hold varying views on whether play is worthwhile, and its value, especially beyond early childhood. Many highly competitive individuals and cultures regard play as a diversion from 'real learning' even for very young children, and certainly once they start school; and childhood has become 'scholarised' at an increasingly young age.

Finding a satisfactory, agreed definition of play is difficult because the term covers several types of activity and process. However, McMahon (1992: 1) describes play as 'a spontaneous and active process in which thinking, feeling and doing can flourish since they are separated from the fear of failure or disastrous consequences'. One key feature is that people and things can assume, or be given, different identities. So, a stick can become a magic wand, a conductor's baton or a gun. A timid girl can become a princess or a dragon and a macho boy dress up as his grandma or a wolf. In imaginative play, object-substitution reduces children's dependence on external stimuli, and children can explore different selves, with the meaning of something detached from what it appears to be, or is, in reality.

Even very young children are acutely aware of the difference between real and imaginary worlds and usually able to flip between these without difficulty. For example, while a five-year-old may seem totally immersed in an imaginary situation, she can, where necessary, recognize, and tell others, that it is 'only pretending' and then move back into her imaginary world. This fluidity helps children to explore their own and other people's feelings and responses in safe space and to strengthen their sense of agency. Through play, as Wood (2014: 14) suggests, 'children are not simply influenced by their environments but act in ways that change them'.

Play – and her sister drama – offers the chance to perform different identities without having to live with the difficulties that doing so in the real world entail, notably the emotional pain associated with failure and disappointment. Meek (1991: 88) writes that 'in play, children ... experience a release from the inexorability of the here-and-now. They enter alternative worlds ... where they try out what they are to learn and experiment with the rules. Then, in play, children "walk tall"; their limitations are not confining, their imagination lets them invent new possibilities.' Meek's words refer to how children become literate, but play more generally is a process which strengthens many different aspects of children's identities.

Nussbaum (2010: 101) points out that 'play teaches people to be capable of living with others without control; it connects experiences of vulnerability and surprise to curiosity and wonder, rather than to crippling anxiety'. A child who finds it hard to communicate or express his or her feelings in words can practice doing so in play. For some children, especially those who are most insecure or anxious, play may be the only way of enabling this. I recall how a six-year-old who had experienced a very traumatic event could not talk about it, but was able to start reliving it through play, and so begin to come to terms with his worries. Where children have experienced severe trauma, they usually require specialized, long-term support but opportunities to play on their own can help children to start processing such feelings.

Children may find it hard to talk about their own feelings and difficult issues either because they do not have the vocabulary or confidence or it is worrying or painful to do so. It may be easier for them to address difficult issues by engaging with animations, puppets and other non-human characters which seem to understand the child. Such figures can help to reduce the emotional intensity of real-life relationships, are less threatening than real people and encourage metacognition – the ability to think about one's own thinking. In this way, a child may be enabled, over time, to recognize how the issues raised may relate to his or her own situation and self.

Tassoni and Hucker (2005: 9) characterize five stages of play – solitary, spectator, parallel, associative and cooperative – whereby individuals learn about, and practice, relationships with increasing levels of interaction and cooperation. Jarvis et al. (2014: 56) argue that 'peer collaboration in play-based activity is crucially important in the intricate interconnectedness of children's social, emotional, intellectual and linguistic development. In such activity, children develop an ability to contribute which in turn produces an emergent sense of competence and, within members of a highly social species, feelings of "belonging", "usefulness" and subsequent well-being.' This helps to explain why cooperative play matters so much in the construction of identities, but one should not overlook more individual forms of play, either solitary or as a spectator.

As Wood (2014: 16) indicates, recognizing that, and how, power relationships operate in free, unsupervised play can be uncomfortable for adults. For instance, she suggests (2014: 14) that 'motivation and agency appear to be linked through expression of the children's identities, such as being seen as a competent player and play leader, being a member of a skilled peer group or having the confidence to subvert adults' rules'. And, more fundamentally, 'the freedom to choose may advantage some (children), but disadvantage others' (2014: 16).

As discussed previously, technology has altered how young children spend their time and considerations of ethnicity and class frequently affect with whom children are allowed to play. Moreover, which types of play children engage in differs according not only to age and gender but also to ethnicity and class (see Wood, 2014). Girls tend to choose more pretending, and boys more exploratory, types of play. Boys are often socialized into playing with construction toys and competitive games and girls more towards dolls and quieter, more interactive games such as skipping.

Engel (2005: 27) cites the research of Gaskins and her colleagues over twenty-five years showing how Mexican children play in different ways from middle-class American children, though there are some commonalities. For instance, the Mexican children do less imaginative scene enactment, though both groups engage in role-playing in familiar domestic settings. And Lancy (2015: 222) indicates that Japanese pre-schools are raucous and loud where children run, wrestle, hit, rough-house and climb on and over everything, although older Japanese children are expected to conform.

While very young children enjoy play, they may not be able to articulate why. However, Baldwin describes (2012: 50) how children between eight and eleven said what they liked about dramatic play, categorizing their responses as

- feeling in control;
- reducing stress;
- raising levels of stimulation; and
- socially including or excluding others.

Play has an inherent potential for inclusiveness, because it relies more on unspoken and negotiable assumptions than on language and unchanging rules. However, research such as Thorne (1993) and Renold (2006) indicates that identities based on gender, and particular ways of being a girl or a boy, usually based on 'normal' heterosexual behaviours, are reinforced through the groups in which children play. Similarly, playing is frequently based, especially as children approach adolescence, on groups mostly of one ethnicity and class, where others are excluded unless there is a strong reason to include them such as shortage of numbers or a particular aptitude.

Play is both an activity and a process. As an activity, it is what all very young children do and is associated with activities such as drama and games. Playing as an activity remains important in many adults' lives, as in sport, or music, or acting. However, such activities are more structured and rule-bound than children's play, and (usually) are linked to leisure, something peripheral to, or in contrast to, the world of work, with 'real learning' supposedly taking place only when one 'works at it.' Seeing play as a process, a way of thinking and working, helps to indicate how it is linked to playfulness, which is applicable in most types of activity. Similarly, Engel (2005: 95) sees playfulness as an orientation towards reality, encouraging imagination, divergence and new strategies, an approach which can be adopted in most situations.

Play must be enjoyable or it ceases to be play. However, play is also the 'work' that young children do to make sense of themselves, each other and the world. In Engel's (2005: 185) words, 'When children are given plenty of time and encouragement for their play, they initiate and sustain complex scenarios, experiments, and inquiries in pursuit of skills, without any direct instruction.' Play does not require adult involvement (see Lancy, 2015: 252), and adults can easily undermine or inhibit children's play. Hyde (2009) highlights what he calls pseudoplay where adults take too much control so that the activity ceases to be play. Pseudoplay is dangerous since it disguises itself as play, with participation

- required rather than inherently pleasurable;
- based on predetermined learning outcomes rather than engaged in for its own sake;
- directed rather than spontaneous; and
- passive rather than requiring engagement.

Hyde identifies four dangers in pseudoplay

- compulsion, misusing power to take control of the activity and the outcome;
- entertainment, making children into passive consumers;

- manipulation, exerting undue influence; and
- competition, since making meaning is inherently non-competitive and for every winner there are losers.

This does not mean that entertainment and some level of competition are to be avoided, nor that adults should not exert influence, but that adults must be careful how they do so, and enable children to retain as much agency as possible, in ways explored in Part III.

Drama is historically associated with the persona, as a mask, and character, where someone pretends to be someone else. Drama provides a space for exploring different identities, usually requiring participants to communicate, cooperate and collaborate, and helping them to explore their feelings, whether in words or not. Both performers and watchers are participants in making meaning. Such a process can foster creativity and thinking skills, raising pupils' self-esteem and confidence through self-expression. But drama can also makes many people feel vulnerable, especially when performing in public, because it requires them to move out of their comfort zone. (see Winston, 1998 for a thoughtful discussion of the link between drama, narrative and moral education).

This section has highlighted how play and, by extension, drama help young children come to understand the world, themselves and the interaction between the two, and explore their own and other people's identities, linking this with imagination and creativity. However, Engel (2005: 109) argues that 'while play is the main activity of three- and four-year olds in our culture, it recedes during the first years of life, until its earliest form all but disappears. Storytelling, however, in all its manifestations not only appears early in life but also remains a central way that people make sense of their world and communicate with others.' The next section explores why stories are such a powerful means through which learning occurs, particularly in how young children construct a coherent sense of identity.

## Shaping identities through hearing and telling stories

Children under the age of four or five may not have developed the cognitive skills that facilitate learning from formal instruction. Moreover, they tend to find dealing with abstract ideas difficult for a considerable time after that age. But as Bruner (1991: 9) indicates, 'Narrative comprehension is among the earliest powers of mind to appear in the young child and among the most widely used forms of organizing human experience.'

Hearing and telling stories may just seem an enjoyable activity which encourages and enables children to listen carefully. When heard, stories are enjoyable and accessible and help listeners to understand experience, both their own and other people's, and to integrate the two, without much cognitive effort. However, as discussed in Eaude (2016, Chapter 9) and this section, there is far more to stories than this, especially in relation to how children construct their identities.

While we tend to associate stories with words, a story, especially when told, involves many other elements, such as inflection, gesture and body language, as part of the fabric of storytelling, not just an adornment, and so helps to model how to engage the storyteller and the listeners at an emotional as well as a cognitive level.

Identity has been presented as a constantly changing narrative, where a person's own story is reconstructed to indicate how she or he fits into larger narratives and tradition, such as the family and different types of community. Narrative or 'storied' identity is a term used by scholars such as McAdams and McLean (2013) to describe how life experiences are integrated into an internalized, evolving story of the self. This is especially important in how members of historically disadvantaged groups gain or recover a sense of identity and belonging.

We have seen that narrative is one of the earliest ways in which children structure their experiences. Cupitt (1995) suggests that we all, throughout life, constantly seek to create new narratives which describe our lives more appropriately than previous ones writing that '(stories) shape the process of life. It is through stories that our social selves, which are our real selves, are actually produced' (1995: ix). Understanding who one is, and where one fits in, depends on the stories that one tells about oneself in relation to other people and cultures – whether in words or through other means. In Macintyre's (1999: 216) words, 'Deprive children of their stories and you leave them unscripted, anxious stutterers in their actions as in their words.' Stories are essential elements in creating and sustaining identities. Let us think why.

Good stories are open-ended and can be revisited frequently, so that new layers of meaning emerge. They allow for alternative possibilities and courses of action, though most stories reach a conclusion, where the questions raised are resolved, at least provisionally. As Erricker (1998: 109) indicates, 'Real stories by virtue of being lived are necessarily unfinished and beg questions rather than provide answers. ... They involve a continual re-membering of the story itself.' In Engel's (2005: 112–13) words, 'Narratives are a potent tool for thinking because they are simultaneously bound by real-world rules and expectations, and can also violate those rules.' Their open-endedness and provisionality, and the questions raised about how one should act, help to introduce complex issues, suggesting rather than prescribing.

Most good stories provide an engaging and unthreatening route into reflection about choices and dilemmas. They enable listeners to cope with mystery and ambiguity, since in Arendt's (1970: 105) words 'storytelling reveals meaning without committing the error of defining it'. Good stories provide insights into how people feel, with characters feeling and thinking in authentic and, usually, complex, ways, raising questions rather than providing definite solutions. They suggest and resonate, rather than preach, and so bear repeated retelling by both teller and listener. As Winston (1998: 21) observes, 'Stories ... inform our choices in life, they do not dictate them', so helping to guide children in the struggle to understand, and shape, their own identities, their place in the wider scheme of things. Stories enable children to see events and themselves as part of bigger groups and longer traditions, maybe to do with a religion, nationality or ethnicity, and so to define themselves and reshape their narrative in relation to others, countering the tendency to see themselves only as individuals.

Stories, whether told or read or seen, help to explore human emotions and experience, actions and interactions; and how people respond, and have responded to, situations which may be similar to those which we encounter. In doing so, they can help to reveal perspectives and truths wider than one's own, necessarily limited, experience. Stories provide a bridge between the listener or reader and other cultures and generations and are fundamental to understanding history, religion and literature – and so ourselves and other people – providing a framework for linking otherwise disjointed factual knowledge.

As Wilson (2007: 110) writes, 'Stories ... create links to other possible stories, looping back and forth in memory and imagination. We retain stories from our families, from our teachers, from literature and popular media including film and theatre. They can carry enduring messages that are personal to us and harbour meaning that only we can know.' So, 'stories learned in childhood become powerful constituents of the world we inhabit as adults' (Nussbaum, 2010: 36).

Stories have always been used to pass on profound truths. Stories of faith are central to most religious traditions, from those told about Abraham and Mohammed to those used by Jesus and the Buddha. The myths of different cultures act in similar ways. Such stories matter not just for people of that faith tradition or culture but also as part of a wider cultural heritage. In an increasingly diverse world, all children benefit from hearing and knowing stories from a range of faith and other traditions and sources.

Stories are powerful tools for the exploration of beliefs and values, because, in Kimes Myers's (1997: 18) words, 'story connects us with that which lies beyond ourselves and this process makes us ask questions about the meanings of our lives'. They can help even very young children recognize and understand qualities such as courage and patience and to develop those such as curiosity and empathy. For instance, the stories of the Iliad and the Odyssey raise questions about love, selfishness, revenge and bravery without being too didactic. Greek, Norse or indigenous people's myths are not just about heroes and gods long ago, but help one to explore, and understand, universal themes such as love and jealousy, honour and deception, courage and betrayal. Through hearing or reading stories, a careful listener or reader comes to identify with other people, their emotions, their responses and their motivations – and so to understand, to some extent, how it is to be other than who one is. This may be easier when hearing or reading about those who are similar to oneself but, as they get older, children can be introduced to an increasingly diverse and complex range of characters.

Stories often help illustrate a point and hearing or reading them provides an easily accessible route into alternative realities. As Anning (1997: 9) suggests, 'For children the function of narrative can be to enable them to move from the here and now of their immediate experiences to the more distanced ideas about what happened then and what might happen next. In other words, the narrative form is a potent resource to help children move to abstractions.' Stories, therefore, help to link the child's own experience to more abstract, general ideas – and vice versa – reaching beyond their immediate reality. Although children do not necessarily need to retell such stories, doing so through actions, pictures or words can help them to internalize such messages and how these apply to their own situation.

Hearing and reading stories help children to retell and enrich their own stories of themselves by encountering those of people (or imaginary characters) who are similar or different. For instance, a story such as 'The Hungry Caterpillar', apart from being enjoyable, explores how appearance, and identities, change over time; 'Willy the Wimp' enables, in a humorous way, a young child to realize that her fears can be overcome and how she can participate in this process; and 'Voices in the Park' encourages children to consider diversity, as four different voices tell their own versions of the same experience. Thousands of other beautiful and well-written stories can be found to help children to explore what it is to be human, whether for themselves, other people or both.

To summarize, stories work in subtle, often unconscious, ways, including

- posing questions to encourage investigation of inference and motivation;
- connecting with other people and cultures;
- helping to provide a language and a space to explore feelings and beliefs where each listener can respond in their own way;
- nurturing the imagination; and
- prompting reflection.

Let me add a few words of warning. I have mentioned 'good' stories. There are many wonderful stories from both traditional and recently published sources – of heroes and villains, of different faiths, cultures and communities – along with others which preach at, or infantilize, children. So, which stories adult should use requires judgement and how they are read, or told, matters; but one should not be too precious about what constitutes a good story, or think that this is confined to books. Indeed, soap opera and comics frequently present profound ideas in narrative form and may be more accessible to young children.

Those who tell or read a story well rarely explain its message, but rather allow listeners to come to their own understanding of the questions raised. For example, in the Jewish and Christian scriptures, Cain who has killed his brother, Abel, is asked by God if he knows where Abel is. Cain asks, 'Am I my brother's keeper?' This question, left hanging, prompts hearers to reflect on our responsibility to other people. For a six-year-old, this might be to what extent she should be kind to those who are not her friends and for a ten-year-old how much responsibility we bear for those less well-off than ourselves, whether in our community or on the other side of the world.

As with play and pseudoplay, adults can easily over-control a story's message. Since the meaning of stories are multiple and have to be constructed by the listener, adults should be wary of too much explanation, but be prepared to listen to and discuss young children's responses and questions. Adults are often tempted to read stories with a definite 'moral' – and emphasize this – and so close off, rather extend, reflection (both out loud and in the child's head), and, with young children, to present stories with a binary view of good and bad and to avoid stories which raise difficult issues. However, fairy stories and the stories in the Torah (or Old Testament), for instance, do not shy away from such issues and gather much of their power from this. Similarly, the arts and the humanities enable children to address complex issues associated with their own and other people's identities.

## Creating new identities through the arts and the humanities

Chapter 1 highlighted that one enduring sense of the word culture refers to 'a cultured person' with a wide experience, and deep knowledge, of the arts and the humanities. These have long been seen as an essential aspect of being an educated person, though, as indicated in Chapter 3, are marginalized in primary schools in most systems. This section discusses why the arts and the humanities can contribute so much to how young children's identities are constructed.

The boundaries of what constitute the arts and humanities are fluid, with some disciplines, such as drama and geography, not easily categorized. I suggest that the arts should be understood with loose and permeable boundaries, including music, visual art, film, sculpture, design, architecture, drama and dance, all with scope for activity and creativity. Similarly, Eaude (2017) argues that the humanities are best seen as the study of one's own and other cultures, those areas of learning which help one to understand what it is to be human, and potentially to become more humane. Such a view includes not only history, geography and Religious Education (in schools where this is permitted) but also citizenship, literature, languages and philosophy, and many activities which reach far beyond the school curriculum.

NACCCE (1999: 69) sees the arts as 'concerned with understanding, and expressing, the qualities of human experience', enabling people to explore feelings and responses – and in doing so come to understand themselves more deeply. The arts involve creating and producing new artefacts and responding to, and judging, existing ones, individually or collectively; and encourage children to operate in flexible, imaginative ways, as both creators and observers, though not as passive ones. NACCCE (1999: 33) emphasizes how 'composing and playing music, writing poetry, making a dance … is not simply (a process) of discharging feelings – though it may involve that – but giving them form and meaning'. The arts operate through unconscious as well as conscious processes and allow the unconscious to work. So, experiences and activities such as watching films, creating visual art and listening to, and composing, music work at a level different from, and potentially more influential than, language. This matters for people of all ages but especially young children since they rely on unconscious and emotional processes more than conscious and cognitive ones.

The sorts of art which are approved of, or otherwise, vary according to culture, broadly understood. For example, many regional and national identities are expressed through particular types of dance, music or costume; and some cultures and religions may disapprove of, or even forbid, art or music, either in general or in particular forms. Various forms of artistic expression are associated with a particular gender or class, such as ballet and certain types of music being seen as mainly for middle-class girls and construction as more suitable for boys. While such attitudes are somewhat stereotypical, usually as a result of socialization, dealing with, and trying to counter, these, can require considerable sensitivity, as discussed in Part III.

To summarize Eisner's (2002) view, children can through the arts

- learn to make good judgements about qualitative relationships, with judgement rather than (rigid) rules prevailing;
- learn that problems can have more than one solution and questions can have more than one answer;
- celebrate multiple perspectives, since there are many ways to see and interpret the world;
- learn that in complex forms of problem-solving purposes are seldom fixed, but change with circumstance and opportunity, requiring them to be able and willing to surrender to unanticipated possibilities as the work unfolds;
- recognize that neither words nor numbers exhaust what we can know;
- come to know that small differences can have large effects;
- learn to express what cannot easily be said in words, so that when they are invited to disclose what a work of art helps them feel, they must reach into their poetic capacities to find the words to do so; and
- have experiences that they can have from no other source and through such experience to discover the range and variety of what they are capable of feeling.

The humanities provide many similar possibilities which can enrich and strengthen children's identities. Drawing on Nussbaum's (2010) view, Eaude et al. (2017: 390) wrote that

> the humanities ... provide a foundation for how children become active and engaged citizens in a democratic society. This leads us to suggest that there is a pressing need for humanities education in an increasingly complex world; and to argue the case for humanities on the grounds of the development of the 'whole child'. In particular, we would advocate for children:
> - understanding concepts related to human culture such as time, space and belief in how human beings can understand themselves and their relationship with the natural world, places and with each other;

- developing skills and habits associated with critical thinking such as assessing and interpreting information;
- exploring their own identities, values and beliefs and enabling them to be interested in those of other peoples; and
- learning to understand, and empathize, with people who are different, as well as those who are similar, challenging stereotypes and becoming more humane and compassionate individuals.

The ways of thinking and working, and the kinds of evidence and outcome, associated with the arts and the humanities such as observation and fieldwork, and representing experience kinaesthetically and visually, help to nurture creativity and a sense of agency and to engage many children not fully engaged with more 'academic' learning. The types of activity and experience involved do not just take place in formal settings and are particularly valuable for children whose backgrounds and prior experience mean that they find using agency, creativity and imagination difficult.

The emphasis on complexity and nuance which results from dealing with unpredictable situations means that children have to weigh up, and interpret, different types of evidence, encouraging curiosity and critical thinking, rather than conformity and deference. Such an approach involves learning more than factual knowledge and skills and helps to avoid brittle identities, as children learn to question and be critical, while remaining respectful, and to create understanding of, and empathy for, other people. For instance, as Morpurgo (2011) suggests, 'it is through literature, not simply literacy, that we learn to understand and empathise'.

There is not enough space to discuss how all the disciplines associated with the arts and the humanities can help to strengthen children's identities. However, let us consider briefly history, geography and the study of religion as ones with explicit links to time, space and religious beliefs and practices.

History is associated with cultural and national identities and heritage and helps to define these, as well as dealing with concepts such as time and causation. While history can help engage children's imagination, it may not do so, not least because children's sense of abstract ideas such as the passage of time and the order in which events occur is not yet well developed. For young children, particularly, history may be best understood – and taught – through visits, artefacts, stories and drama. A memorable incident occurred when I was teaching history to a class of ten- and eleven-year-olds, mostly from disadvantaged backgrounds, using drama in small groups. Two quiet girls were acting out being evicted from their houses, as a result of enclosure. They brought the class to a standstill when one banged the table and shouted that they would not be driven off the land their families had occupied for years – to my utter amazement and that of the rest of the class. This illustrates both how children can explore identities, and develop empathy, through learning history and the power of drama. Incidentally, the theme of enclosure and the associated injustices captured the imagination of that class in ways that the lives of the wealthy in the same era never did – indicating the extent to which content and context affect children's levels of engagement.

Geography has an obvious link to global citizenship in that it encourages children to explore how humans live in different types of place and space. Enquiry into, and investigation of, questions about the world and people's place in, and influence on, it lie at the heart of geographical thinking. Such questions include those of identity, such as 'Who am I?' and 'Where do I come from?' and place, such as 'Where do I live?', 'How is it changing?' and 'How can I influence this?' As well as questions about the physical world such as what the world is made of and how this alters, geography deals with human environments and cultures, such as who decides who gets what and why. Exploring these enables children to enrich their understanding of the physical world and human environments and their own lives and concepts such as

- interdependence linking the physical world and human environments to recognize the importance of sustainable development;
- place and space, recognizing similarities and differences; and
- scale and the significance of local, regional, national, international and global perspectives.

However, the places where young children live and where their families come from, and maybe still live, are likely to have particular significance and meaning because of their knowledge of, and emotional attachment to, such places and those who live there.

As discussed, religious affiliation is a central element of identity for some children, but hardly at all for others, though religion retains an important place in the social and cultural heritage of most societies, worldwide. Children, whatever their background, need to understand that religious affiliation is normal for most people in the world and to avoid crude characterizations of any religion as homogeneous rather than encompassing a range of different practices, viewpoints and beliefs. Such understanding, preferably through direct experience of people from different religious traditions and their practices and beliefs helps to create a greater awareness of what religion entails and its influence. This is necessary in a macro-culture where religion is frequently portrayed in negative terms and where many young children, whether from faith communities or not, have little understanding of different types of religious practice and beliefs, and sometimes a limited one of their own, even if they are members of a faith community.

This chapter has suggested that play, story, the arts and the humanities have a vital place in helping all children to sustain a sense of agency and develop qualities such as imagination and empathy, and so to create and sustain a robust but flexible sense of identity. Play and stories are natural parts of most children's lives, but activities associated with the arts and the humanities may have to be set up more deliberately. The types of activity and experiences discussed

- are usually enjoyable and engaging for children, though different children may enjoy different types of activity;
- enable children to interpret their own experience, in the light of other people's; and
- have the potential to change individuals, by enabling them to see and understand what may seem familiar, or be taken for granted, from a new perspective and how other people feel.

This said, relationships and environments have more influence than activities and experiences, as such, in how children's identities are constructed. The maxim 'act local, think global' helps to highlight that qualities and dispositions, such as those discussed in Chapter 3, are best learned in local, inclusive environments. While the ultimate aim of global citizenship is greater care for the planet, this starts with care for the immediate environment. The next chapter considers what inclusive environments are like and explores some of the cultural and religious sensitivities involved.

6

# Belonging and participating in inclusive environments

*Education has to be a mixture of haven and challenge. Reassurance of course. Stability. But also incentive. ... At the very least you offer the kids support. You care for them. You offer them security. You give them an environment where they feel they can grow. But you also make bloody sure that they realise that learning is hard. Because if you don't ... if you only make it a safe haven ... if it's all happy-clappy and 'everything the kids do is great' ... then what are you creating? Emotional toffees, who've actually learnt nothing, but who then have to go back and face the real world.*

Hare, 1995: 62–3

## Feeling nurtured and being challenged

As we saw in Chapter 1, the groups to which children belong matters because this influences how they act and interact, and learn to do so, at least in that particular context. And Chapter 3 highlighted how hard it is for many children to feel secure and a sense of belonging.

Children's identities are constructed and negotiated, influenced by expectations in many different types of environment, particularly the home, schools, faith communities (for some children) and the peer group, as well as the wider social and cultural context. But informal groups exert a strong influence, with the peer group becoming increasingly influential, given most children's wish for approval and a sense of belonging. These may exert a positive influence for some children, less so for others, especially those living in disadvantaged communities.

The more uncertain the situation, the more qualities and values, and the motivation and the disposition to base one's actions on them, matter. Since such groups usually operate in spaces to which adults have limited access, children must be equipped from an early age with the qualities and dispositions to deal with uncertainty, including resilience and confidence. For instance, children will have to deal with discrimination and cyberbullying largely on their own, albeit sometimes with adult help. This chapter argues that being nurtured in an inclusive and caring environment helps to strengthen such qualities and the disposition, or intrinsic motivation, to manifest them, though this cannot guarantee that children will always do so. It explores what such environments entail for young children and highlights several puzzles for adults, to be considered in Part III.

Any group, by definition, is exclusive of those who are not members, but groups must be inclusive of those who are, if they are to have a sense of belonging. In formal settings, inclusion is usually used to mean that most children, including those with disabilities, are educated together. However, as Graham and Slee (2008: 278) indicate, 'to include is not necessarily to be inclusive'. And, as discussed in Chapter 1, some children have always been valued less than others, based on factors such as gender, race and class and so de facto excluded, at least to some extent. This section argues that an inclusive environment entails every person in it being treated as a somebody rather than a nobody and feeling welcomed, and that, whatever a child's background, his or her worth is not conditional on being clever, attractive or wealthy – or anything else, other than a human being.

In inclusive environments, factors such as gender, skin colour, language, disability and class do not define how individuals are seen or treated by other children or adults. Young children make strong categorizations based on gender from an early age, especially once they interact in groups. Some adults think that very young children do not make distinctions based on race or class, but children's actions suggest that they do, though not necessarily in what they say. For instance, when we looked out for racist attitudes at a school where I taught, we were surprised how frequently these were evident, even with five- and six-year-olds. Connolly (2002) concluded that racism played a significant part in the lives of the young children whom he studied and that even five- and six-year-olds were able to reflect on how gender, race, class and sexuality affected their identities.

More obviously, and understandably, children may not want to play or interact with children who are different, especially those who are rough or dirty. While such behaviours may be manifested by children of all backgrounds, exclusion on such a basis is most keenly felt by those who are the least powerful and whose self-esteem is most fragile. An inclusive environment entails that barriers which are often invisible to those who do not face them, but all too real and apparently insurmountable to those excluded, are minimized. Chapter 7 considers the nature of these barriers and how adults can try to remove or minimize them.

All children must have their physical needs, such as for food, shelter and safety, and emotional ones, such as being loved, cared for and attended met, if they are to flourish and be creative, in line with Maslow's hierarchy of needs (1998). Children thrive in environments where they feel nurtured, at ease and have a sense of belonging and being in control, providing the social and emotional bedrock on which a robust identity is based. However, as Hare writes, at the start of this chapter, children require challenge, as well as haven, if they are to learn to cope with adversity. The nature and extent of haven and challenge varies depending on age and between individuals and for the same person at different times. As suggested in Chapter 3, many children are like unanchored ships and require more haven, especially in emotional terms, and benefit from anchors, albeit ones with a long chain (metaphorically), if they are to be creative and take risks; but they need also to be challenged, both intellectually and in terms of their behaviour and attitudes. And those who thrive on intellectual challenge benefit from being nurtured and reassured, particularly when they are feeling anxious, stressed or confused. Therefore adults have to exercise judgement and be attuned to individuals, in ways explored in Part III.

Young children must be cared for, and protected from harm, but also must be able increasingly to care for themselves and be equipped to cope with difficulties without becoming over-dependent on adults. What may be less obvious is their need to care for other people and things and how this helps to develop empathy, which, as Nussbaum (2010: 37) suggests, helps supply some of the crucial ingredients in acting ethically. Caring for others is based on emotion, rather than on rationality (Noddings, 2013: 61) and involves a recognition of, and response to, how others feel or might feel. This is one reason why young children benefit not only from caring for real people but also from dolls, pets or imaginary friends, even when how 'the other' responds is in the child's imagination. Indeed, caring for non-humans may be easier than caring for people because there is less risk of rejection. While caring for others is essential for all children, it is especially beneficial for those, many of them boys, who are troubled or focused on themselves but unused to caring for others.

Familiarity and predictability help to contain children's anxiety, but providing the appropriate level and variety of opportunities is far from simple. Engel (2005:

167) argues that familiarity with the context and the expertise which accompanies this enhances the quality of a child's understanding and response. Chronic, repeated or intense stress tends to make children wary and hypervigilant, and so less likely to trust other people, even familiar adults. For instance, a child who has an insecure model of attachment and regularly experienced adults responding unpredictably and perhaps violently is likely to become withdrawn or aggressive and to benefit from the security which accompanies familiarity. If an environment is too stressful, it will be damaging, but if too cosy and unchallenging may create dependency and undermine resilience. So, activities must be familiar and not too daunting, but also provide opportunities and encouragement to experiment and take risks.

In Eaude (2014), I discussed the idea, and the nature, of hospitable space, arguing that such space is welcoming and not too competitive, providing chances for children to explore, to play and to create both on their own and with others. As Claxton indicates (1997), deep learning requires what he calls 'the tortoise mind', which operates slowly, as well as what he calls 'the hare mind'. In constructing their identities, children benefit from space and time to relax and to be calm and quiet in a world full of pressure and noise and to have a sense of being in control. Hospitable space offers opportunities to be active and to talk, but also to watch, listen, think and reflect on difficult issues and rehearse how to act differently. While practical considerations such as architecture and furniture matter, psychological space and aspects such as how children feel about themselves and other people and how relationships are formed, routines and rules applied and language used, are more important. These are discussed in more detail later in this chapter and in Part III.

Chapter 4 indicated that engagement and motivation is greater when rewards are not wholly predictable. Without predictability, many children are left confused, but too predictable an environment provides insufficient challenge. And many children thrive on unpredictability, as long as this does not prompt too much anxiety. Young children must build on what is familiar, their existing funds of knowledge and cultural capital, but, as they become more settled, more autonomy and greater challenge is required to sustain and strengthen their sense of agency.

Routines and rituals help to contain anxiety and provide predictability. This matters particularly for young children and those who, because of prior experience, are under stress and/or easily become anxious. The distinction between routines and rituals is somewhat blurred. Routines are regular patterns which help provide predictability and security. Rituals have significance, usually for a group, and help individuals to belong. Two types can be identified

- the more regular, everyday ones such as eating meals, bedtimes, talking or praying as a family or a faith group or listening to a story; and
- the occasional ones which help groups to deal with significant events, such as welcoming new children, naming ceremonies, transitions from childhood to adulthood, marriages and death.

As discussed in Chapter 4, everyday routines and rituals are particularly significant for young children because of their regularity and predictability. However, many children inhabit fragmented and individualized lives, with few predictable routines and relationships which provide a sense of security and belonging. Moreover, even where the more regular rituals happen, these easily slip into being routines and lose their importance as opportunities for the family, or other group, to be, and interact, with each other. However, the rituals which deal with significant events provide the chance for children, as a group and individuals within a group, to process, the powerful emotions, both happy and sad, associated with such events.

The rest of this chapter argues that, in inclusive environments, children are enabled and encouraged to

- regulate their own behaviour and become intrinsically motivated;
- take the lead as much as possible, as they explore their own and other people's identities; and
- be treated fairly, but to participate with other people and treat them respectfully and kindly.

## Becoming intrinsically motivated

Children may prefer it if adults organize their lives, at least in some respects, but they must be expected and encouraged from a young age to take responsibility for their ordinary needs and their actions, if they are to learn to become confident and self-assured. This section considers how children learn to take responsibility for their actions and to develop intrinsic motivation, emphasizing a sense of agency and increasing self-regulation.

Motivation relates to what leads to specific behaviours and is almost always multi-factorial. In other words, people rarely act as they do for only one reason, since they usually have conflicting desires and loyalties. It therefore helps to try and understand what motivates people, especially young children, though understanding why a particular child act as she or he does in a specific context requires adults to be attuned to that child, as discussed in Chapter 7.

The most basic biological motivators are those associated with emotions such as the fear of pain and desire for pleasure. Behind these lie the wish to look after one's self and one's own survival and well-being. Self-interest is natural and why people act altruistically is puzzling when considered only through the lens of rationality. However, even very young children act compassionately, as Bloom (2013) indicates, and part of growing up in any society involves realizing that one cannot do as one wants and that cooperation may be more effective and fulfilling than acting on one's own.

Behaviours are responses resulting from dispositions, attitudes, beliefs and values, as well as biological motivators. Longer-term dispositions depend to some extent on temperament and habit, but are based on values and beliefs, many of which are shaped, and constantly reshaped, by culture and experience. For motivation to change, assumptions, rather than just visible behaviours, must change, though acting differently, regularly can, in the long run, help to alter assumptions, given the power of habituation.

Motivation is hard to categorize neatly, but can be thought of within three main, overlapping categories

- emotional responses, whether positive such as the desire for enjoyment or the wish for approval, or negative such as fear or shame;
- relational reasons such as compassion and rivalry; and
- cognitive ones such as conscience or religious beliefs.

Young children are motivated in rather different ways from adults, partly because their cognitive and self-regulatory functions are less well developed and their emotional ones more influential. Feeling happy and having fun is a significant source of motivation and engagement. However, young children may not distinguish between short-term gratification and a long-term sense of well-being, what the Ancient Greeks called *eudaimonia* – that is sustained flourishing which is not dependent on the ups and downs of everyday life (see Eaude, 2016: 36). Moreover, children – and many adults – may not recognize that, counter-intuitively, happiness is usually achieved not by seeking it directly or through possessions but as a by-product of experiences, relationships, overcoming challenges and helping other people.

Self-determination theory focuses on the psychological need for relatedness. This refers to the connection and sense of belonging with others which provides the emotional security which individuals need to actively explore and is satisfied through the warmth, support and nurturance of significant others. Attribution theory suggests that long-term dispositions are learned from, or modelled on, other people's styles and patterns of acting (see Martin and Dowson, 2009). Both processes seem to operate particularly strongly for young children.

Relationships with those whom they trust and admire provide a strong source of motivation for young children, since they seek to please adults around them in order to be valued, loved and accepted (see David and Powell, 1999 and Trevarthen, 1992). Young children crave attention and connectedness and tend to relate most readily with the people who are closest and most familiar. However, they may not know how to gain approval, especially if they have insecure models of attachment, and may act in ways which gain the attention of, but exasperate, adults, rather than their approval. Indeed, many very young children, notably two-year-olds, are oppositional, testing out the boundaries of acceptability; and disaffected nine- and ten-year-olds can be very disruptive, particularly when they do not respect the adults involved. Moreover, while young children want approval from others, particularly those whom they respect, they are often impressionable, over-trusting and biddable, especially up to the age of seven or eight, though as indicated in Chapter 4, they are less so than many adults assume.

Situational identities and the specific context exert a powerful influence on young children, as they find abstract, rational thinking difficult and are less experienced at knowing the probable consequences of their actions, so that appeals to conscience are less likely to be effective. This changes to some extent as children reach pre-adolescence and their ability to self-regulate and the influence of the peer group become stronger. The fear of missing out, or being excluded, becomes a stronger motivator as children move into pre-adolescence and are more aware of, and concerned about, their place in the peer group.

As discussed in Chapter 3, assumptions that young children's behaviour must be managed largely by the fear of punishment and the promise of reward and lie deep in most cultures. In some cultures, behaviour is regulated strongly by a sense of honour, usually related to the family or group of which a child is part. Many South Asian cultures emphasize *izzat*, family honour, so that how one's actions are seen by others is very important. Religion acts as a strong motivator for many adults and children. Many religions seek to influence behaviour by the promise of salvation or the fear of punishment after death. So, many children will act in a particular way – or say that they do – because of the family and faith community in which they are being brought up. Adults who interact with children from different backgrounds from themselves must recognize the importance of such motivation, even if they find it strange.

Rather than physical punishment, it is now more common, at least in 'Western' societies, to use sanctions such as the withdrawal of adult approval or 'time-out' to try to encourage children to think about, and so to change, how they behave; and tangible rewards such as stickers or money remain a widely used way of encouraging young children to behave appropriately. And even very young children are expected to think about their behaviour in terms of choice and consequence.

Both punishment and tangible rewards may succeed in controlling behaviour in the short term but are unlikely to help building long-term intrinsic motivation; and Deci et al. (2001) suggest that tangible rewards (both material and symbolic ones) undermine it. While Jovanovic and Matejevic (2014) argue that research on the association between rewards and intrinsic motivation is inconclusive, Deci et al. (2001) emphasize that control must be internal if motivation is to be intrinsic. Rogers (1989) indicates the demotivating effect of a high level of external, in this case adult, control. Children easily become over-dependent on tangible rewards, rather than the approval these are intended to symbolize.

As West-Burnham and Huws-Jones (2007: 38) suggest, 'Morality that is based on obedience, compliance and the threat of sanction will always be fragile because it is based on external, negative compulsion.' In the case of physical punishment, children may become resentful, quite apart from learning that hitting other people is acceptable. Fear, especially of failure and the emotional distress which accompanies that, tends to make children become defensive and withdrawn. Guilt may prompt one to act differently in the short term but is a poor basis for enhancing children's long-term motivation, especially for those with low self-esteem. While rivalry, and interpersonal competition, can be a strong motivator, this often leads to inappropriate actions and, as we shall see, results in too many people being excluded.

Intrinsic motivation involves children moving from externally imposed discipline towards self-discipline or self-regulation. Almost everyone would agree that children must learn to regulate how they act and take responsibility for their actions. Harris (1989: 90–1) argues that four- and five-year-olds know about both personal responsibility and standards of acceptability but do not see the relevance of these to their own feelings, whereas by seven or eight years children do, and so have a more cognitive understanding of emotions such as pride and guilt.

Young children's ability to self-regulate only develops slowly and at different ages as those parts of the brain which enable executive function – self-regulation – are not well developed, so that many children may not understand the link between what they did and what happened as a result. This is exacerbated when children are anxious and even more so for children who have experienced regular and/ or severe stress. As a result, young children may be unable to recognize the consequences of their action and be more strongly influenced by the context and their desire for attention. Many young children, particularly boys, find self-regulation and accepting obligations and responsibilities hard, especially when they receive mixed messages from different adults. Those unused to making choices, based on the likely consequences, find doing so particularly difficult. It is easier for children to make appropriate choices if they are used to doing so and expected to discuss and think about their choices. This helps to explain why what Lareau (2011) calls concerted cultivation enables middle-class children to talk about appropriate choices, though this may not always translate into appropriate and kind actions. I vividly recall an extremely articulate eight-year-old girl who had just given a talk at a conference to explain how she would respond – thoughtfully and kindly – when provoked, but whom I saw kicking another child when she thought (wrongly) that she was unobserved.

This section has discussed different ways in which children are motivated to behave, but rather individually, without considering the social aspects. Williams (2000: 27) points out that 'children need to be free of the pressure to make adult choices if they are ever to *learn* how to make adult choices'. Therefore, while children should be encouraged and helped to make appropriate choices, they require supportive environments in which to do so. Such support ideally involves the gradual transfer of agency and control from adult to child, and where possible to the whole group.

## Participating and working together

This section explores further how young children internalize the abstract, often elusive, values and qualities associated with a robust identity, bearing in mind the many pressures which encourage them to act in other ways.

As mentioned in Chapter 3, values such as courage or respect can easily be promoted as abstract ideas which are only vague aspirations. Values have to be lived, not mere statements of intent or parroting what one is supposed to do; and children must learn to decide between competing values, not just in principle but in actual situations. Moreover, one should recall Haydon's (2004) warning that universal values tends to prioritize 'Western', liberal ones and that the values and qualities deemed most important vary somewhat between cultures, with children bringing different identities and assumptions to any situation.

Many of the processes involved in the construction, and reshaping, of children's identities happen tacitly, though not automatically. Values and qualities are internalized mainly by repeated practice, supported by feedback and reflection, incrementally and slowly, over time. Being disposed to act in such ways gradually becomes automatic and spontaneous or 'second nature', which in Young's words (1994: 116) 'is history, culture and personal experience disguised as first nature or biology'.

As NACCCE (1999: 49) suggests, 'Most young people belong simultaneously to a range of cultural groups and communities. They do not develop their ideas and values in isolation. They do so in relation to the groups and communities to which they belong and they express them in the clothes they wear, the stories they tell, the jokes they like and the music they make.'

Through participation in groups, children are socialized into cultural norms and expectations, at least to some extent – but they are frequently brought up at home with different expectations in terms of behaviour from those they encounter in formal settings, especially working-class children and those from many minority ethnic groups. Middle-class children have frequently been encouraged to talk about how they should respond, though a sense of entitlement may mean that they do not easily accept that such norms and expectations apply to them. Some children, whatever their background, appeal to their rights to claim that they need not do as adults say. And many children will have been told to 'hit back', especially those from backgrounds where this response is expected, accepted and even encouraged. Many grow up with, and absorb, attitudes towards women, people of colour or gay people which may be at odds with those expected in formal settings. Such statements do not apply to all children in any group but highlight that

- children may be pulled in different directions and require help to recognize that rights should not be seen entirely in individual terms, but as entailing obligations and responsibilities; and
- many children find managing transitions hard and need to be guided and supported through these.

Cox (2017), drawing on the work of Lave and Wenger and Rogoff, argues that children internalize values and beliefs mainly through guided participation in learning communities. Guided participation, in Rogoff's (1990: 191) words, 'involves collaboration and shared understanding in routine problem-solving activities'. She continues that children adapt their understanding to new situations by adults helping them to structure their problem-solving attempts and assume responsibility for managing problem-solving. Such an approach emphasizes children's agency and the gradual transfer of control from adult to child and highlights the importance of adult expectations. Both are discussed in more detail in Part III, arguing that adult expectations may be made explicit and reinforced through rules or spoken language, but other, less explicit means, notably the example set, exert more influence.

While there will be, in any group, inevitably, a variety of beliefs and attitudes, a broad conformity to standards of conduct is required for the group to function. All groups require rules as norms to define how one is expected to conduct oneself as a member of the group. Such rules can be implicit or explicit. Young children may find it easier if expectations are made explicit, though they tend to see rules as what is prohibited rather than in positive terms. Some situations need definite, non-negotiable rules, such as what to do when a fire breaks out or if a child is badly hurt. However, if children are to exercise judgement, and learn to do so, maxims, more general guides to behaviour, are more appropriate than rules to be followed regardless of context. As Bellous and Clinton write (2016: 20), 'Maxims invite us to stop, think and make a shift. While maxims look like rules, applying them isn't about obedience; it's about reflecting on experience and on the reality of other people, and allowing their reality to influence our own.'

Young children, and those from chaotic backgrounds, may find acting on the basis of maxims more difficult than following definite rules with clear boundaries, since doing so requires that they take account of the context and how others feel. This emphasizes the importance of theory of mind and empathy, which many such children find difficult. The question becomes how flexible rules and boundaries should be and how to create the appropriate level of structure, neither too constraining nor too fluid.

In Ellyatt's words, 'The correct degree of structure … seems essential for the child to make sense of the environment and to provide choices that lie within the ability of the chooser. Too many choices or too few can depress motivation and subsequent achievement' (2016: 4). In particular, children from chaotic backgrounds need more support than others; and those from backgrounds where adult expectations are unpredictable may need clearer boundaries than other children. Those children who most need to be loved may be those whose behaviour is most challenging and the range of choices may have to be limited to enable them to make appropriate choices.

An essential aspect of inclusive environments is that they provide structures within which children can explore their own, without undermining other people's, identities. Nussbaum (2010: 43–4) argues that structures become pernicious when

- those who are less powerful are dehumanized and de-individualized;
- those involved are not personally accountable for their actions; and
- no one raises a critical voice against wrongdoing.

In inclusive environments, both adults and children recognize and respect difference but define people by how they act and interact rather than by their background. To be inclusive does not entail any type of behaviour being acceptable, but involves challenging what excludes some people, for instance by countering discrimination and stereotypes – making assumptions about people on the basis of their appearance and background. Attitudes such as sexism, racism and homophobia, and the behaviours which result, involve relationships of power where other people are seen not only as different but as inferior.

Such attitudes, preconceptions and stereotypes are formed sooner than adults think, often unconsciously. Rowley et al. (2007) conclude that stereotypes have become embedded by the age of nine or ten. However, children soon learn not to express these in front of adults who will disapprove. For instance, I recall when as a head teacher I was talking informally with two eight-year-olds and one made an unthinking comment with a racist overtone. Both immediately recognized that, although they used such terms with their friends, they should not do so with me. Therefore, trying to promote respectful attitudes towards those who are different and to challenge stereotypes by this age is particularly important. The challenge is how to change such views, and the behaviours which accompany them, not just because of adult disapproval but because of a change of beliefs. The interlinked nature of emotion and cognition means that doing so requires accurate factual information – a wide range of experiences to help children understand the world from perspectives other than their own and an environment which discourages anti-social behaviour.

Discrimination is easily normalized through low-level comments, and exclusion is frequently the result of relatively small actions. Those who experience discrimination, especially young children, should not always be expected to be those who challenge this. This is a responsibility for all children and ideally groups move towards a growing sense of collective accountability, rather than regulating behaviour being the responsibility only of adults. Let us think what this might entail in practice, for instance, in relation to name-calling. The names used may vary between different groups and change over time, but name-calling is not just harmless banter when based on factors such as gender, race, class, sexuality or disability. Young children may not know cognitively what the names mean or signify and may say that they are just playing, but they nearly always know that name-calling is a type of bullying that is unkind and designed to exclude. And even if not, name-calling is pernicious because it normalizes 'othering' and putting other children down and must be challenged, if an environment is to be inclusive (see Gaine and George, 1993: 94–5 for a more detailed discussion). While adults should set an example in challenging these, all children must be expected and encouraged to do so, not just those who have been called names.

Restorative approaches to conflict resolution, where children (both perpetrators and those who feel aggrieved) are enabled to reflect together in a non-judgemental and non-confrontational way how individuals could have acted differently help children to understand the implications of their action on other people, and so can help children think about the consequences of their actions, without creating a sense of defensiveness and resentment.

The EPPE project (Sylva et al., 2010) highlighted the importance for young children of what they call 'sustained shared thinking'. This and collaboration in shared activities helps very young children learn to act and interact appropriately, and shared activity and thinking in inclusive environments remain no less important as children get older. While interpersonal rivalry and individual effort may help in achieving some outcomes, especially cognitive ones, the learning associated with the qualities and dispositions associated with global citizenship involve collective, as well as individual, processes. Put simply, robust and compassionate identities are constructed through what we do and believe together, not just what an individual does and believes alone.

## Developing confidence, resilience and empathy

This section focuses on how young children can develop and internalize confidence, resilience and empathy as three key qualities which contribute to robust but flexible identities, as examples of how such qualities can be strengthened. However, it must be considered in the light of Part III, which discusses how adults contribute to, or constrain, how children internalize these and other qualities discussed in Chapter 3.

One complex and contested issue is the extent to which qualities and dispositions are domain-specific or transferable to other contexts. A considerable body of research suggests that knowledge and skills are specific to particular domains. It seems unlikely that knowing how, and being able, to play a musical instrument or an ability to draw a picture or throw a ball accurately helps a child learn to read fluently or conduct a science experiment. And Chapter 4 highlighted the importance of relationships and context in how young children respond and learn. However, there are well known but poorly understood links between domains such as those between music and mathematics.

Underlying qualities seem more transferable than knowledge and skills as long as these help to create and sustain a sense of agency and the confidence to succeed. It may be – and experience suggests that it is – that becoming more confident and successful in one domain, such as making friends or interpreting what one observes, tends to have a knock-on effect in enhancing young children's confidence and self-esteem in other respects. For instance, many children's confidence soars once they can – and are seen to be able to – overcome a new challenge, without much adult support, such as learning to read or complete a task previously beyond them. If so, then strengthening situational identities contributes to making substantive ones more robust, gradually over time.

However, whether confidence is always an asset and how it is built up is complex, especially once children move into formal settings. Confidence is a quality which many children from advantaged backgrounds manifest, and therefore one usually seen as necessary to succeed and desirable for those disadvantaged by factors such as gender, ethnicity, class or a combination of these. But many children's confidence and self-esteem remains low despite success, often as a result of their upbringing. Girls tend to be less confident than boys, even when boys' confidence is misplaced. Many children from minority ethnic backgrounds may not be confident, especially if in the early stages of learning English and if their identities and abilities are not recognized and celebrated. And, as we have seen, middle-class children tend to be more confident than working-class ones in formal settings, for many reasons including familiar expectations, a sense of entitlement and a greater experience of, and facility in using, language. However, one can have too much confidence and self-esteem can be too high. Since what is appropriate lies between two extremes, arrogance or 'cockiness' should be avoided no less than timidity.

The need for children to be equipped to deal with difficult situations highlights the importance of resilience. While what exactly this entails is debatable, it involves the capacity to 'bounce back' and keep going in the face of adversity and disappointment, but also being able to 'recharge' one's resources and to try again. People may appear resilient if they remain calm by controlling, or denying, their emotions, as boys are frequently taught to do, but such resilience may proves to be illusory or brittle in the face of strong emotional demands. Moreover, what may seem like resilience easily becomes obstinacy, unless tempered by flexibility.

Those who have coped successfully with difficulties are usually more resilient than those who have been overprotected. If children are to become resilient, they must be prepared to try new challenges and ways to approach these; and regularly practice overcoming challenges. However, these must be within the range of what a child can manage on his or her own or with support. Children require not only a sense of individual agency but also the willingness and ability to work with other people, because resilience is both experienced and created collectively as well as individually.

These examples emphasize the significance of children's beliefs and self-esteem, especially optimism about whether they can succeed. While it is frequently thought that success and praise builds resilience, Dweck (2000) indicates how success on its own does not create resilience, and may lead to brittleness, unless supported by a growth mindset. This involves the belief that intelligence and ability are not fixed and that achieving what has proved previously too difficult becomes possible with greater effort, experience or support. Lancy (2015: 394) suggests that children who are frequently praised tend to show less motivation and persistence. And, as we shall see in Chapter 7, praise must be authentic if children are not to be submerged in a constant stream of warm words which tends to undermine, rather than promote, resilience.

Qualities such as resilience and confidence are often seen largely in individual terms, whereas these are best strengthened working with other people within supportive communities. Opportunities to try, and succeed in, a wide range of experiences and the approval of those whom they respect, in an inclusive environment which offers appropriate levels of nurture and challenge, are crucial in how all young children's confidence and resilience can be strengthened. Moreover, as argued in Eaude (2016), children must be encouraged to be empathetic and thoughtful towards others, if they are to develop as citizens of a diverse, democratic society.

No one can ever know how someone else feels or thinks with complete accuracy, because we all bring different cultural assumptions, experiences and interpretations to any situation. But gaining a greater understanding of, and empathy for, those who are different is an essential aspect of global citizenship. This is hard since affiliation tend to be stronger towards those who are similar, and closest, to us, especially so for young children, given their tendency to be most attached to those closest to them and the difficulty which they have with abstract, distant ideas. As Haidt (2012: 244) suggests, 'We trust and co-operate more readily with people who look and sound like us. We expect them to share our values and norms.' It is easier to feel empathy for those who are similar, but children (and adults) need also to learn to empathize with those who are different.

The Introduction referred to children building up what Putnam (2000) calls bridging, as well as bonding, capital. This involves respecting the differences, and recognizing the similarities, between people and empathizing, at least to some extent, with those who are different. A sense of belonging can easily be inward-looking and hostile to difference, which makes creating bridging capital difficult, but to do so the tendency to 'other' those who are different must be countered. If children are to learn to respect those from backgrounds and with views that different from their own, they must encounter such views and be helped to understand the people who hold them, and why.

Young children's understanding of themselves and other people tends to be enhanced by taking part in a wide range of activities. While it is often assumed that culture, in the sense of art, music and literature, improves people, such activities do not necessarily make them more humane. Broadening cultural horizons does not, as such, lead to anyone becoming a better person. One need only think of dictators and mass murderers who appreciated culture in that sense, but nevertheless acted with indescribable cruelty. People only seem to be improved, in the sense of being more caring or compassionate, by changes of attitude especially towards other people.

Children must recognize how others feel and respond if they are to learn to act other than in line with their immediate wishes and self-interest. This highlights the importance of, and need to develop, empathy, which is a vaccine against, and antidote to, egocentricity and narcissism. Baron-Cohen (2011: 11) identifies two essential aspects of empathy, namely recognition and response, writing that 'empathy is our ability to identify what someone else is thinking or feeling, and to respond to their thoughts and feeling with an appropriate emotion'. Rather than just recognizing or sympathizing with someone else's feelings, empathy involves trying to see and understand the situation from someone else's perspective in so far as one can, and responding appropriately, especially when the other person requires support and reassurance. Collaborating, and cooperating, with a wide range of other people relies on, and helps to build, empathy, re-emphasizing that children must interact with people who are different from themselves if they are to become outward-looking and sensitive to other people's feelings.

Empathy relies to a considerable extent on intuition. While Bellous and Sheffield (2017: 207) argue, cogently, that 'right feeling undergirds right thinking and right practice', this does not mean that one should rely solely on feelings. Children must think about their actions but unless they take account of other people's feelings, they are unlikely to act appropriately. As Nussbaum (2010: 23) observes, 'It is easier to treat people as objects to be manipulated if you have never learned any other way to see them.' So, to understand the consequences of our actions, we must develop, and use, the ability to feel what it may be like to see the world through the eyes of someone different from oneself.

To do so, and inhabit someone else's persona, helps a child to imagine how others feel and so to enable him or her to become more empathetic. As we have seen, this is enhanced through participating in play, drama and hearing or reading stories. But simple day-to-day interactions with other people, such as being aware, and responding, to their needs by holding doors open, being friendly to those who are lonely or comforting people who are upset, all help children to become more outward-looking and sensitive to other people's feelings and needs, and to both manifest and create empathy.

As we reach the end of Part II, it is worth recalling that, as Robinson and Aronica (2015) suggests, children are natural learners, and their innate curiosity, enthusiasm and creativity (and much else besides) should be respected and supported, but they vary considerably in terms of personality, backgrounds and abilities. Children benefit from a broad range of experiences which engage them and from representing these in different ways, with enacting, drawing and talking assisting particularly those children less capable of, or used to, abstract thinking. Therefore, education should be broad and diverse and children's curiosity and imagination nurtured and encouraged. Moreover, children should not be encouraged, let alone forced, to specialize on a narrow range of activities too early. By too early, I do not mean any specific age, as this may vary between activities and individual children, but rather at any age if this means that opportunities to try new activities and develop existing talents and identities are constrained. Remembering Hare's words at the start of this chapter, children must be both nurtured and challenged if they are to become robust enough to cope with the journey ahead; and finding the correct balance presents considerable challenges for adults, as we shall see in Part III.

Part III

# The Implications for Adults

Part I explored the complex relationship between identities and cultures, arguing that young children require a coherent, robust but flexible sense of identity to thrive and cope with the challenges they face and, where possible, prevent later difficulties. Such an identity involves a wide range of qualities and dispositions associated with global citizenship many of which, such as confidence, resilience and empathy, are common to most cultures, but some are more culturally specific.

Part II started to consider how such an identity is shaped, and the intrinsic motivation and the disposition to manifest the qualities in different situations strengthened. Among the key points are that

- each child must be seen and understood as a whole person but with multiple, interlinked identities;
- young children, right from the start, are trying to make sense of many often-confusing experiences but find it difficult to understand and internalize abstract ideas;
- social and emotional well-being is the bedrock of a robust identity, based on relationships of care and trust and environments which are hospitable and culturally sensitive and provide a sense of belonging;
- constructing such an identity is an active, creative and reciprocal process, with young children strongly influenced by relationships and other people's expectations; and
- much of the knowledge required is procedural and personal/interpersonal and internalized as memes – chunks of cultural information – mainly through example, imitation and repetition, rather than as discrete skills.

One may reasonably say that such ideas are all very well in principle but ask what these entail in practice. Part III considers the implications for adults, recognizing the many different factors which influence young children's identities and trying to avoid sweeping generalizations which ignore cultural differences. Since children receive mixed messages, adults must try to ensure that children are equipped from a young age with a sense of agency to find their own path towards a sense of identity which is sufficiently robust to weather the storms of life, but flexible enough to adapt to change, albeit with guidance and support.

I shall argue that an approach based broadly on virtue ethics, as mentioned briefly in Chapter 3, is the best way to help embed the qualities and dispositions associated with such an identity. This calls for a significant change of priorities, adopting a holistic approach, based on guided participation and apprenticeship, with plenty of opportunities for enjoyment, creativity and challenge throughout children's lives. While such a view sees education more broadly than what happens at school, a rethinking of the current approach in schools is required, emphasizing many different types of knowledge and ways of learning.

One recurring theme is that of power and authority, particularly the asymmetry of power between adults and children. Adults should not idealize childhood as a time of innocence since many children experience it as a time of powerlessness and face greater difficulties than adults realize. The relationship between adults and children is very rarely that of a friend, even though the relationship may be friendly, and adults must consider where, and how, to establish boundaries, not least because they are more experienced and usually responsible for children's well-being. Although the qualities and dispositions which adults require are similar to those discussed in relation to children, differences of power and the roles involved mean that these are not exactly the same.

Many of the implications follow logically from, and echo, the previous discussion, but helping to shape young children's identities is riven with dilemmas and puzzles. For instance, adults constantly have to decide the extent to which they can, and should

- accept children as they are, leaving them free to make choices, or encourage them to try out new, possibly unfamiliar, activities and roles;
- express their own values and beliefs and expect children to adopt these or encourage them to develop and refine their own;
- protect children or expect and enable them to fend for themselves;
- provide predictability and consistency or challenge and flexibility; and
- emphasize similarities between people or highlight differences.

For adults outside a child's immediate family, this is exacerbated by the need to respect the beliefs and practices embedded in his or her culture, while possibly wishing to encourage and enable him or her to challenge some of these.

Part III tries to suggest how these may best be resolved, trying to avoid simplistic solutions. Chapter 7 considers the implications of adopting a holistic approach, recognizing these dilemmas and advocating the idea of apprenticeship. Chapter 8 discusses what this entails for adults outside formal settings such as schools, notably parents/carers, family members and leaders of voluntary groups. While it is usual to refer to parents/carers, I only use this where this is significant, otherwise shortening this to parents. Chapter 9 examines the issues for schools and teachers, suggesting a very different approach from that currently adopted, as described in Chapter 3.

# 7

# Working towards a holistic approach

*Seeing even the infant and the pre-schooler as active agents bent on mastery of a particular form of life, or developing a workable way of being in the world, demands a rethinking of the entire educational process. It is not so much a matter of providing something the child lacks, as enabling something the child already has: the desire to make sense of self and others, the drive to understand what the devil is going on.*

Geertz, 2001: 22

## Balancing conflicting priorities

Part III argues that adults who support children as they strive to construct coherent, robust but flexible identities need to adopt a holistic approach, taking account of Geertz's view, above, that the entire educational process should be rethought. Recalling the discussion of inclusive environments, this chapter explores how adults can help to

- ensure that all children have a sense of belonging and are seen to matter;
- respond appropriately to children's ideas and concerns and create mutually respectful relationships;
- encourage intrinsic motivation and the disposition to act appropriately even when the going gets tough;
- help to dismantle barriers to learning; and
- provide a balance of haven and challenge with appropriate expectations and structures.

Recognizing that how to do so may vary significantly, at home, in voluntary groups and in school and that cultures, families and individuals vary so much that any generalizations must be treated with caution, this chapter outlines some general considerations bearing in mind the need to balance different priorities.

Children are all unique. They share a common humanity, but their needs differ because of temperament, background and prior experience. A holistic approach recognizes that any individual is more than the sum of his or her separate parts; and that the different elements of their identities are all linked and influence each other (see Eaude, 2018b). Therefore, adults should try to consider each child as whole, even when the adult's role relates mainly to one aspect.

A holistic approach must try to ensure that children are fit and healthy both physically and mentally, without which other needs are unlikely to be met. Young children require enough nourishment, activity and sleep and must avoid harmful substances and too great a level of stress. They enjoy and benefit from simple activities such as experiencing the outdoors and playing with other children. And they need love, support and a sense of belonging where they are seen as somebody who matters. This is likely to help them flourish and avoid the sustained unhappiness or loneliness which may lead to later mental health difficulties.

The culture(s) in which children grow up, the experiences they have and the relationships formed exert a profound influence on how their identities are shaped. Identities are constructed as a by-product of such experiences and relationships. Robust identities depend on children being able actively to construct and re-negotiate their own narratives of identity within the larger narratives of the cultures in which they grow up, rather than identities being imposed by adults.

As we have seen, a consumerist culture suggests that happiness is to be found through possessions and markers of identity such as celebrity and fashion. Lancy (2015: 398–9) suggests that adults' wish to keep children happy encourages them to search for fame and celebrity with success presented as based mainly on looks and possessions. Since a more sustained sense of well-being results more from loving relationships, a sense of belonging and thinking of others, rather than possessions and just oneself, adults need to create and sustain environments which enable this.

At the start of Chapter 4, I cited Salmon's words that 'identity ... is forged out of interaction with others. Who we are is inextricably bound up with who we are known to be.' Relationships with trusted adults strongly affect children's level of motivation, self-confidence and willingness to take risks. We have seen that many children grow up in relationships which do not provide a secure basis for their identity, whether because children are not well cared for, or witness such distressing experiences as domestic violence and parents or other family members manifesting behaviours associated with alcoholism, substance abuse and crime. This emphasizes the importance of creating trusting and respectful relationships. Pinker (2014: 74) suggests that 'long-term bonds are forged through a casual exchange of home-baked goods, baby-sitting, borrowed tools, shared expertise and spur-of-the-moment visits'. While referring mainly to adults, this illustrates that relationships of trust are built up and sustained over time, gradually, almost without noticing, through fairly normal actions, interactions and activities. Respect implies trust but, although children crave adult approval and become trustworthy by being trusted, adults frequently over-control children, and are reluctant to trust them, even with relatively small tasks which carry little risk.

Interacting with young children can be enjoyable and fulfilling but also at times exasperating. Relationships with young children entail what Erikson calls 'cog-wheeling', indicating that adult relationships with children are interactive and reciprocal, with children not the only ones engaged in the developmental process (see Kimes Myers, 1997: 7–11). As a result, young children often arouse strong emotional responses in adults who interact with them and evoke the 'child-within', unconscious responses which may have been buried for many years. This frequently occurs when an adult's authority is challenged directly, but even apparently innocuous activities such as play has the potential to evoke the child within us. For instance, I recall feeling a sense of panic and inadequacy when a very troubled four-year-old whom I was supposed to be observing told me, very forcefully, to 'play' with a set of building blocks. In interacting with young children, adults, especially parents and teachers, frequently discover much about themselves, often in uncomfortable and even distressing ways. Some implications of this are explored further in this chapter and the next two.

I shall suggest that the relationships between adults and children which help to create a robust sense of identity are those based on the idea of apprenticeship. This is discussed in more depth in Chapter 8, but three key aspects are

- the feedback the more experienced person gives, based on attunement to the less experienced person;
- the expectations and environments she or he establishes; and
- the example she or he provides.

In reciprocal relationships, these are all interlinked, but what these entail is discussed in the next three sections of this chapter. However, we first consider some of the dilemmas highlighted previously that adults face in supporting children' search for such an identity.

Almost all adults want to influence their children's identities to some extent. While adults may wish to control how children's identities develop, they cannot do so without potentially causing damage. As adults, we can never know definitely what type of person a child will become and so should provide diverse opportunities, while not leaving children to negotiate the complexity of shaping a coherent identity without guidance and reassurance. Recalling the idea of culture as husbandry, a vital aspect of adults', especially parents', role is to enable children to understand and value their 'roots'. However, education also entails creating new 'routes' which open up new possibilities beyond what children believe, and their background might suggest, is achievable.

Adults can enable or constrain how young children develop and exert influence by offering guidance and support. In doing so, they have to balance often-conflicting priorities such as

- providing a mixture of structure and freedom, predictability and uncertainty, exploration and reassurance;
- helping him or her to decide when to accept and when to challenge what she or he finds unfair; and
- being prepared to hold on and recognizing when to let go, rather like helping a toddler who is just learning to walk, gradually changing who is in control,

though the extent to which, and how, adults should do this depends on individual children's needs, wishes and the context, recognizing that the gulf between adults' and children's experience and worldviews is wide.

How any adult should act depends on their beliefs and values and what they hope to achieve. Inevitably, we all believe that some practices are better than others and that some, even though allowed or encouraged in some cultures, are inappropriate, or even abhorrent. As Bruner (1990: 30) writes, 'Open-mindedness is the keystone of what we call a democratic culture', continuing that this implies 'a willingness to construe knowledge and values from multiple perspectives, without loss of commitment to one's own values'. This calls for adults to adopt an open-ended approach. But I suggest that one should be wary of assuming that one's own practices and the assumptions and values which lie behind them are necessarily better than those of other cultures.

Williams (2000: 51) argues for adults to protect what he calls the imaginative space of childhood – providing opportunities for children to play, to explore, to enquire, to imagine, to question and to be silent, and not propel children into the adult world too soon. Williams suggests that 'the protection of the imaginative space of childhood obviously needs a background of security, adult availability and adult consistency' (2000: 51). However, as we have seen, children, especially those from chaotic families, need to feel secure and safe, but also to be challenged. Children benefit from consistency but must be able to cope with unpredictability and learn to fend for themselves. While adults are frequently advised to be consistent to avoid giving mixed messages, I suggest that this is only partly true, and that a diversity of approaches is inevitable and may be valuable, especially as children approach adolescence.

Adults tend to underestimate what young children can do, in the right context, and so risk infantilizing them. For instance, many children take on considerable responsibilities, especially where parents cannot or do not fulfil these; and even very young bi- or multi-lingual children know which language to use in talking to different adults and can switch rapidly and fluently between these. Young children are in some ways vulnerable, but to treat them as incapable may undermine their resilience. To help create and sustain a sense of agency and a robust identity, adults must try to avoid children acquiring a sense of learned helplessness and to find ways of guiding and facilitating without imposing or forcing. While adults need at times to scaffold children's learning, such scaffolding must be temporary, if children are to avoid becoming dependent on it.

While young children must be protected, in some respects, and most adults wish to do so, there is a danger of overprotecting them. For instance, children have to decide how to respond when they experience unkindness or discrimination, whether against themselves, or someone else, although as we have seen a supportive environment makes it much easier to do so. Children must be protected from what is likely to be damaging, but also equipped to cope with situations which they, and adults, may find confusing or painful. In my view, young children should be protected, where possible, from pornography and violence and the more corrosive aspects of consumerism. The latter may be a losing battle, but adults can help children at least to recognize how such influences affect their choices and their emerging identities.

## Becoming attuned to, and interacting with, young children

Most children, especially as they approach adolescence, want to be left alone when they're alright, but supported when uncertain or in trouble. To work out when to intervene, and how, and when to back off, adults must try to be attuned to each individual child, given that children's temperaments, personalities, cultures and backgrounds differ so much.

Adults who interact with young children need to know about, and be sensitive to, their background, experiences and personal characteristics. In how much detail this is necessary will depend on the adult's role. Everyone usually needs to know things such as the child's name, medical conditions and allergies, home language, religion, if any, position in the family and the level of the child's experience in the activity. Close family members may know most of this, but other adults may not. Adults must recognize, and take account of, the challenges children face, and take their concerns seriously, if they are to enable children to cope with them. Examples of such challenges are responsibilities such as caring for other family members or difficulties within their local community or peer group or issues such as neglect or abuse or incidents such as a bereavement or serious bullying. While their importance may seem obvious, it is remarkable how often some adults do not know these, or even recognize the need to do so.

Knowing such information helps adults understand the child and how best to interact with him or her, quite apart from showing respect for the individual. However, attunement entails much more than this. Being attuned to a young child involves being aware of, and responsive to, a child's actions and feelings and empathizing with how she or he feels and thinks, with this operating more intuitively than cognitively.

Complete empathy with young children – or any other person – is impossible, but adults should be attuned in so far as they can, without assuming they can know how a child feels or projecting their own emotions or wishes on to him or her. In particular, adults should acknowledge that young children have a complex range of emotions, and help them to process and respond to these, rather than expecting children always to be happy, when they may have good reasons to be sad or angry. Adults must try to see and understand the world through the child's eyes and try to enter, at least to some extent, the child's mental world. This involves adults interpreting what a child does to try and realize why she or he responds in a particular way, especially when she or he seems anxious or unsure.

In thinking how adults can become attuned to young children, it helps to recognize that, as Hattie (2009) points out, much of the most valuable feedback is that which adults receive by watching and listening to children, learning from their insights and questions and interpreting both verbal and non-verbal cues, rather than talking at them. This enables adults to understand, to some extent, how a child feels, and so to be more attuned to, and have some awareness of, how the world looks from his or her perspective.

In interacting with young children and enabling their search for a coherent identity, the feedback which adults provide to children, whether consciously or otherwise, is important. Feedback is not just, or primarily, what is said, but depends on subtle aspects such as tone of voice, body language and gesture. Subliminal messages are often the most influential ones and much of the most valuable feedback non-verbal (see Jackson et al., 1993). Feedback to children – both non-verbal and verbal – helps to

- show approval or disapproval and reinforce appropriate, and discourage inappropriate, actions;
- provide guidance, support and reassurance; and
- make explicit expectations and pose new challenges.

Hattie and Timperley (2007) argue that feedback to children is most useful when it is specific, addresses achievable goals and does not carry high threats to self-esteem. Negative perceptions of self, based on the views of other people, may be particularly strong in children, given the asymmetry of power. Adults undermine children's identities more easily than strengthen them and must avoid helping to create, or reinforce, a child's identity as someone who is incapable, a naughty boy or a little princess, identities which may last for a long time. Adults should be aware of the emotional cost of failure which makes children scared and defensive, and must not, especially in public, humiliate or put down children who misbehave, take risks and ask questions, however foolish or naive their comments. One of my most uncomfortable moments as a teacher was witnessing a ten-year-old boy being berated aggressively for his constant misbehaviour in front of the whole school. The maxims that adults should tell children off in private and praise them in public and distinguish a child's actions from his or her substantive identity as a person have a great deal of force.

Self-esteem is built up gradually and to some extent by reassurance and praise, but praise should be for real achievements, rather than a constant stream of warm words for what may reasonably be expected. In Alexander's words, 'Praise may not be what it seems. For one thing, it becomes devalued if it is used too often and without discrimination; for another the use of overt praise may be at variance with other messages about children's work which a teacher is conveying and which children readily pick up' (1995: 206). While Alexander was referring to teachers, this applies to all adults. Feedback from adults to young children works best when it is authentic and immediate, either to an individual or to a group, and combines honesty with sensitivity. Young children are sensitive to when adults are not being genuine, even if they may not be able, or prepared, to articulate this in words.

Adults should encourage and praise behaviours such as effort and perseverance rather than those associated with performance, if they are to foster a growth mindset and, with it, greater resilience. Performance (outcome or ego-driven) goals must not dominate, or exclude, learning (or process) goals (see Dweck, 2000). If adults are to tell off or criticize children, as inevitably they must, at times, the focus should be on their behaviour rather than visible features or the child as a person. The latter tends to suggest (however unwittingly) that ability is innate and unchanging.

Demonstrating ways of acting and interacting, and encouraging children to act in a similar way, is more influential than relying on language and on cognitive processes. However, adults can influence children's attitudes to some extent through the language they use, the questions they ask and answers they give, but must be careful about what they say and how they say it, given the uneven power relationship between adults and children. For instance, adults can use language to encourage children to explore and to imagine, whereas too often they use it to tell and provide answers to questions that children may not have even considered and which often make little sense to them. To stop children from asking questions or to answer them too definitely makes it less likely that children will retain their curiosity and exercise their imagination. And when a child has misbehaved and is worried, it is usually more helpful to ask him or her to explain what happened, rather than asking why she or he did it. He or she probably doesn't 'know', can't explain or just wishes she or he had not. Asking a child to think about how someone else would feel about a situation can help him or her to shift the focus from herself or himself and perhaps create a sense of empathy, but to expect a young child to do so when worried or confused is expecting a great deal.

As discussed in Chapter 4, language is usually best used reciprocally, with children taking the lead where possible. From an early age, children should be encouraged to use words not only to say what they want, but to ask questions and to express their feelings. Conversation and dialogue provide opportunities for adults to listen and respond to children and to model how to listen and respond to other people (see Mercer, 2000: 134–8). Adults can model dialogue by doing all of these respectfully

- listening carefully;
- building on what they have heard and seen;

- questioning;
- offering alternative interpretations; and
- not always knowing the answer.

In this way, children can be helped to explore questions and ask new ones, while maintaining their sense of agency and control.

The influence of adults operates both consciously and at a level below consciousness, with the latter often having more effect. Much of what helps to fill what I have called the well of memory on which children can draw in later life is not the result of intentional actions. This re-emphasizes the importance of the environments – the micro-cultures – in which young children grow up and which adults help to create and sustain through their expectations and their actions. Since micro-cultures help to determine what behaviours are acceptable and otherwise, or at least affect and influence these, it may help to think of adults more as creators of environments and micro-cultures than as direct shapers of identities.

## Establishing expectations and reducing the barriers to learning

This section focuses on adults' expectations and how these can contribute to creating and sustaining inclusive environments. Adult expectations matter because these affect children's behaviour and beliefs about themselves, their self-esteem and their aspirations, and influence young children particularly strongly because of the asymmetry of power and children's respect for adults' (supposedly) superior knowledge. Adults must seek to widen children's perspectives, especially those of children who are absorbed in their own concerns, and offer, and support, alternative narratives of who a child can become. Broad expectations can help extend the horizons of possibility and enable children to understand perspectives other than their own. Narrowing the opportunities available tends to restrict young children's aspirations, which is particularly damaging for those with already limited aspirations, or facing apparently impossible barriers, for whatever reason. However, adults must also not raise children's aspirations and hopes unrealistically.

Education is frequently described as helping children to fulfil their potential, but everyone has the potential for ill as well as for good. It is hard to imagine that anyone would wish a child to become a criminal or a drug addict. Apart from this, views of what constitutes success vary according to several factors, many of which relate to gender, ethnicity and class backgrounds. While many parents will wish their children attend college, others may prefer them to become farmers, builders or join the armed forces. However uncomfortable it may be to articulate this, most middle-class parents would prefer their child to become a doctor or a business person than a hairdresser or a labourer. Those who have migrated from other countries usually want children to achieve jobs with higher status, and financial reward, than they themselves have done. This may result in some parents putting on enormous pressure to succeed by becoming professionals such as doctors or accountants. Others may see success more in terms of marriage and having children, especially for girls. Whatever one thinks of whether such expectations are appropriate or realistic, children have to negotiate a route towards a coherent identity, taking account of the different expectations which they encounter.

Adult expectations are manifested in many ways, in terms of attainment and conduct, tacitly and explicitly, both long and short term, and vary according to factors such as gender, ethnicity and class. However, to help children create robust, flexible identities, expectations must be broader than those which encourage high academic attainment or compliant behaviour. They must be ambitious but realistic and not tied too closely to adults' – especially parents' – own, sometimes unfulfilled, hopes. For those in settings outside the family, expectations should take account of, rather than be dismissive of, a child's family and culture, while helping to ensure that these are not too limiting.

As Good and Brophy (1990: 443) suggest,

> Expectations tend to be self-sustaining. They affect both *perception*, by causing teachers to be alert for what they expect and less likely to notice what they do not expect, and *interpretation*, by causing teachers to interpret (perhaps to distort) what they see so that it is consistent with their expectations. Some expectations persist even though they do not co-incide with the facts' (emphasis is in the original).

Good and Brophy were referring to teachers, but this statement applies more widely and points to two related dangers: confirmation bias and unconscious bias (see Nickerson, 1998; Moule, 2009).

An assumption that those who are apparently similar to us think like us – and that those who are apparently different think differently – may easily mislead us. Confirmation bias refers to the (often unconscious) tendency to see, and take notice of, what we expect and look to ignore what does not confirm to our expectations and preconceptions, including our prejudices. Likewise, unconscious bias results from an assumption which makes a judgement about ability or character based on one or more unrelated features, whether visible or otherwise.

Examples of unconscious bias include assumptions about individuals on the basis of visible elements such as skin colour, language and physical ability. These may involve ignoring talents or falsely assuming interests or abilities. For instance, I did not know about the sporting ability of one boy I taught until he later became a professional footballer, although we recognized and celebrated other children's similar achievements. I suspect that this was in part because he was black and neither voluble nor a show-off. My experience suggests that many South Asian boys are keen on cricket and middle-class girls on fashion. However, one must be careful about such generalizations and seek to work out consciously whether these have any basis in particular cases, to avoid stereotyping individuals. Though I am ashamed to say it, many of my assumptions about girls and boys of Pakistani heritage, as being quiet and compliant or boisterous and good at cricket, respectively, were based on unconscious bias and only partially and slowly altered by examples to the contrary. No less worrying was my tendency to find middle-class, articulate, cerebral pupils, especially white boys, particularly interesting to teach – even if at times their level of self-esteem bordered on arrogance.

Quite how deep some of our assumptions and consequent actions lie is illustrated by the following story. When I was a head teacher, a group of six- and seven-year-old boys kept misbehaving. Several warnings and sanctions had no obvious effect. Normally, I would have called in their parents straightaway, but I delayed because I was worried that they would be punished severely, as all the families were of Pakistani or Bangladeshi heritage. When, eventually, I did, the parents were supportive and grateful but, understandably, asked why I had not contacted them sooner.

I have emphasized that adults must try to remove or reduce barriers which undermine children's agency and sense of identity. Doing so can help children escape from a poverty of aspirations, experience and relationships, which act as barriers to constructing a robust identity and which children from all backgrounds may experience. While adults can help to minimize children's insecurity and self-consciousness, they must also try to reduce structural barriers. Such barriers may be

- societal, such as discrimination on the grounds of gender, race, socio-economic background and disability;

- situational, such as the lack (or the cost) of a broad range of opportunities; or
- attitudinal and motivational, such as a low level of confidence and negative feelings about education.

Societal barriers are often subtle and invisible to those who do not face them or at least very hard to see, let alone to dismantle. What is hidden, especially to the powerful, is all too evident to others. Each barrier may on its own be small, but they operate cumulatively to make success – and the qualities associated with that – hard to achieve. While adults can help to address attitudinal and motivational barriers, and to some extent situational ones, for individuals, it is hard to do so for societal ones, except in the long term by challenging stereotyping and discrimination and encouraging children to do so in an inclusive environment.

Creating an inclusive environment involves trying to avoid stereotypes based on perceptions of culture and background, without ignoring children's backgrounds. Adults must try to challenge and work against unconscious and confirmation bias and stereotypes. To help children avoid judging or objectifying people on the basis of appearance, adults must try to do so themselves. Changing one's behaviours is hard, and assumptions particularly so, as we are creatures of habit and find altering these unsettling. To change how one acts involves looking out for, acknowledging and working consciously against one's own, often unconscious, prejudices, and being very wary of making assumptions about individuals based on a limited knowledge of the child's background. Doing so usually requires other people's assistance over a long time, rather than being an individual endeavour.

It is tempting to say that one should treat all children the same. However, those who consider disadvantaged groups (e.g. Skelton, 2001; Hirsch, 2018), suggest that adults should not ignore factors such as gender and race, as these lead adults to underestimate such factors. Doing so is sometimes called being 'gender-blind' and 'colour-blind', though I would add that one should not be 'class-' or 'disability-blind'. While adults should have expectations of children broadly similar in terms of outcome, what they do to strengthen their identities must vary for children of different backgrounds, because they come from different starting points. For instance, children may often have to be prompted to participate in activities not associated with a particular group identity. This may entail adults encouraging children to listen to unfamiliar types of music and to join in types of activity in which they may be reluctant to do so, such as boys joining a choir or a dance class, or girls doing electronics or taking part in sports usually associated with boys. It may also mean providing, or looking out for, specific opportunities to build confidence in girls and to encourage boys to listen and care for others. With children from backgrounds with restricted aspirations more emphasis may be needed on widening the horizons of possibility, whereas those from relatively sheltered, middle-class backgrounds may need to be helped towards a greater understanding of, and sympathy for, a diversity of beliefs and practices.

As discussed in Chapter 6, an essential aspect of creating inclusive environments is to provide hospitable space and structures within which children can explore their own, without undermining other people's, identities. Adults should recognize and respect children's rights, and enable children to do so, but also expect children to recognize, and fulfil, their responsibilities towards other people. Adults must be supportive rather than punitive, proactive as well as reactive, and enable children, in groups, increasingly to take collective responsibility, trying to ensure that children respect those who are different and do not misuse their power in relation to other children, by excluding or scapegoating children seen as less powerful than themselves.

Those who nurture young children have a responsibility to counter stereotyping and so help reduce the likelihood of them acting in discriminatory ways, in an increasingly diverse world. Let us take the example of verbal bullying, recalling the discussion in Chapter 6 of how name-calling does not just involve harmless banter. While it may seem easier to ignore hurtful comments or small unkindnesses, especially with children who may not realize the impact of their comments or actions, doing so normalizes such actions.

Addressing particular incidents may involve discussion of what bullying is, how it makes the child herself or himself and other children feel and strategies which the bully can adopt – such as ignoring the bullying, tell the bully to stop and seeking help from an adult. So, for instance, when bullied, children must learn to say no and be assertive, but also to seek help where necessary rather than suffer in silence. However, adults must where possible involve, and deal with, the bully not just the child who has been bullied, which may be difficult outside formal settings and particularly upsetting when the bully is one's own child. And a proactive response involves encouraging and enabling other children not to be passive bystanders but to take responsibility for intervening and challenging such behaviour.

Creating and sustaining an inclusive environment is not easy as it frequently entails recognizing and challenging one's own, and other people's, assumptions in ways that may be unsettling. Success may be only partial and take a long time, so that adults must be patient and keep going. Doing so involves establishing expectations by relatively ordinary actions such as listening carefully to children and providing positive role models with whom a child can identify. The next section discusses why setting a good example matters and highlights the qualities adults require to support children in constructing robust but flexible identities.

## Providing positive role models

As James Baldwin wrote (1991: 60), 'Children never have been very good at listening to their elders but they have never failed to imitate them.' The example which adults set and how expectations are manifested in normal interactions are key aspects of how children are guided in constructing their identities. Who adults are, and how they act and interact, matters more than what they say and what they know.

Children mostly internalize cultural norms and assumptions implicitly. Small, apparently trivial, actions are more significant in embedding good habits than adults tend to recognize, through regular, day-to-day routines, drip-feeding rather than in large, indigestible chunks. For instance, a young child learns how to take turns mainly by immersion and receiving positive feedback when she or he does so, and being regularly reminded. Abstract ideas and qualities, such as respect or resilience, are internalized by a child seeing what these entail by watching someone else and performing these repeatedly over time. Much of what is involved consists of relatively unremarkable actions, such as listening carefully, saying please and thank you, helping people who require assistance and persevering in the face of difficulties.

If young children are to learn to act and interact in these ways, adults must model how to do so. Doing so is more complex than it may appear. Expectations, values and beliefs are often implicit but children may need help by someone making explicit what is required, rather than just relying on imitation. As a trivial example, I recall that many children copied my foibles and mannerisms rather than what I was trying to demonstrate as a hockey coach. More seriously, when adults model how a boy or a girl or a member of a family or a faith community should act, they may have to point out, and reinforce, salient points – what matters. But since adults cannot, and must not, control children's identities, emphasizing only what is essential, and leaving scope for children to explore and find out for themselves, may have a greater long-term effect in qualities and dispositions being internalized.

While role modelling matters for all children, how it operates seems to depend partly on factors such as gender, ethnicity and class. Children may identify with and emulate a range of different people, and not always those who set a good example. Many boys, in particular, who manifest anti-social behaviour, have little experience of predictable and sensitive male role models. If boys are to be enabled to express and regulate a wide range of emotions and be more reflective, rather than responding through anger, they will benefit from seeing men acting in caring and nurturing roles which are different from those associated with traditional approaches to masculinity, particularly those manifested by denial of emotion and/or violence. Such an example matters particularly where no adult male is present at home – or only those who manifest undesirable models of masculinity. Similarly, many girls are socialized into roles where they are not expected to be assertive and to limit their aspirations to what has traditionally expected of girls. Therefore, if they are to explore and adopt other identities, girls benefit from seeing a range of women acting confidently and successfully in activities and roles not traditionally associated with femininity, such as mathematics and science.

Similar considerations apply in relation to ethnicity, social class and (dis)ability. However, role modelling is not simply about people of particular genders, ethnicities, classes or physical abilities demonstrating how such identities should be manifested. Who does the role-modelling matters, especially for children from historically disadvantaged groups, but how alternative identities (and narratives of identity) are modelled matters even more than who does the performing. If stereotypes based on such factors are to be broken down, all children need to see a range of people occupying roles usually associated with a different group, such as black women succeeding in business, white men listening and cooperating in groups and disabled people fulfilling roles which others may have thought beyond them.

While celebrities or sports stars may provide positive role models (or often not), these are idealized and distant. As argued in Chapter 6, more immediate ones, and those who manifest desirable qualities frequently, whether adults, older children or the peer group, seem likely to exert more influence in the long term with young children. In a task as complex and lengthy as constructing robust but flexible identities, all children benefit from seeing a diverse range of people demonstrating how to act and interact, rather than just those of a particular gender, ethnicity, class or ability doing so. Ideally, all will give broadly similar messages, but manifest qualities and values in different ways, depending on the context and nature of the activity.

Jackson et al. (1993: 286–7) write that the teachers with whom they worked did not use the term 'role model' much, suggesting that perhaps it seems too 'heroic'. They spoke of 'humbler virtues' such as

- showing respect for others;
- demonstrating what it means to be intellectually absorbed;
- paying close attention to what is being said;
- being a 'good sport'; and even
- showing that it is okay to make mistakes and to be confused.

While this refers to teachers, similar considerations apply to other adults. The necessary qualities are relatively ordinary and no adult can, or should, be expected to be perfect all the time. Usually, it is more realistic to be 'good enough', to borrow Winnicott's term.

Though no list of qualities will command universal agreement, I suggest that those highlighted in Table 2 are helpful for adults in interacting with young children so that children are enabled to strengthen the qualities identified in Chapter 3, remembering that adults

- have to exercise judgement and often balance contrasting qualities, such as firmness with flexibility and optimism with realism; and
- require patience and resilience to strengthen children's long-term dispositions and intrinsic motivation, given that doing so takes time and is not easy.

The interpersonal ones, such as empathy, compassion and sensitivity are particularly important, given the reciprocal nature of learning and the need for adults to be attuned to young children. One should not underestimate the extent to which adults must be optimistic and enthusiastic. However, young children frequently enable adults to remain optimistic and enthusiastic, since these tend to be contagious, as long as adults are relaxed in children's company and allow them where possible to take a lead. The rest of this section considers briefly some of these qualities, especially those on the bottom line, which are harder for adults to model than they may appear.

**Table 2** Desirable qualities for adults in supporting how children construct their identities

| Fairness | Flexibility | Firmness | Resilience | Patience |
|---|---|---|---|---|
| Empathy | Sensitivity | Compassion | Optimism | Enthusiasm |
| Respect | Trust | Playfulness | Confidence | Humility |

Playfulness and humour can be useful tools in enhancing children's learning about themselves and other people. Jokes, analogies and metaphors can enable children to move away from a binary view and adults should encourage and capitalize on children's playfulness rather than restrict or prohibit it (see Engel 2005: 190). However, adults must be careful about how humour is used. For instance, using cartoons, or exaggeration, can make it easier to engage children's attention and help them make particular ideas or qualities more comprehensible, but adults must take care not to reinforce stereotypes through what may be intended as a joke. And adults should avoid, and stop people from, using sarcasm or trivializing or mocking what may matter profoundly to other children, because such actions are abuses of power and undermine children's self-esteem.

Children need to be loved and feel secure, valued and respected as individuals, however they behave. Rogers's idea (1951) of unconditional positive regard emphasizes children being respected for who they are, rather than this depending on what they do or avoid doing. This implies respecting all children whatever their background or ability to succeed in a particular context or only in ways determined by adults, but also being sensitive to individual and cultural difference, for instance recognizing that the practices associated with a faith community, and for most South Asians of *izzat*, family honour, matter a great deal to children and their families, and may entail children avoiding certain types of food and, especially for girls, wearing modest clothing. Yet, too many adults, especially in formal settings, are not good at respecting children, their background and their views and seem, however deliberately, to make respect conditional on success, or at least compliance, and seek to standardize, rather than encourage divergence and creativity. Adults in formal settings should be more prepared to adapt what they do rather than expect children always to do so.

Although children may expect adults to be confident, confidence is frequently non-reciprocal, given the asymmetry of power. If children are to cope with ambiguity, complexity and not-knowing, adults must model this. So, for an adult, especially a parent or teacher, to manifest too much confidence may reduce rather than enhance young children's confidence – and consequently undermine their sense of agency. Adults should avoid being too certain if young children are to be encouraged to enquire and explore.

One of the more surprising qualities in Table 2 may be humility. Since children's identities are constructed constantly through small steps, adults must try to model these qualities particularly in everyday activities. It is impossible to do so the whole time, but adults should do their best and be humble enough to admit and apologize when they fall short.

This chapter has outlined some dilemmas and paradoxes which adults face in helping children to construct a coherent, robust but flexible sense of identity, and some broad considerations in how to do so. The next two consider specific implications of a holistic approach for different groups of adults: in Chapter 9 those who work in formal settings and schools; and in Chapter 8, those in other roles.

8

# Considering the implications for adults outside schools

*School, more than we have realized, competes with myriad forms of 'anti-school' as a provider of agency, identity and self-esteem – no less at the middle-class suburban mall than on the ghetto streets.*

Bruner, 1996: 38

## Adopting a holistic approach

As we have seen, children's identities are constructed and shaped in many contexts, such as the family, immediate community, faith group (for some), choirs, sports teams and other voluntary groups and more formal settings such as nurseries and schools. The home, family and immediate community exert the earliest and the deepest influence. Formal settings are influential sources of identity, but, as Bruner suggests in the quotation at the start of this chapter, many competing influences and messages, notably from the media and the peer group, affect children and how their identities are shaped. This chapter explores further what a holistic approach based on the idea of apprenticeship entails and the implications for adults who interact with children outside formal settings such as schools.

I have emphasized the importance of trusting and respectful relationships especially for children who have had little, or no, experience of such relationships elsewhere. Such relationships act as a buffer against stress and anxiety, and can enable children to take risks, for instance in asking questions and being critical of other people, including adults.

Relationships between adults and children may be involuntary or voluntary and be

- permanent, as with parents and other family members;
- relatively long term, as with a teacher or leader of a voluntary group; or

- short term, as with an adult leading a one-off session or short programme.

The processes and practices involved in an apprenticeship approach will vary depending on individuals, the group and the context, but these relationships affect how adults and children should interact in ways explored in this, and in the next, chapter.

Rogoff (1990) uses the term 'apprenticeship' to describe an approach based on a relationship where a more experienced person provides an example and guidance, while those who are less experienced learn primarily by watching, listening and imitating, over time. Those who are less experienced are incorporated into what Lave and Wenger (1991) call a community of practice, where ways of working and values as well as skills are passed on and internalized.

The relationship between a more experienced person and the less experienced one is at the heart of an apprenticeship approach with the more experienced person

- taking the lead initially and remaining in control, while ensuring a gradual change over time of who takes the initiative;
- showing how more than talking at; and
- expecting and enabling those who are less experienced to act with increasing levels of self-regulation, individually or as a group.

An apprenticeship relationship treats the learner as-if-capable, though inexperienced, and requires of the more experienced person subtle skills such as facilitation, feedback and mentoring more than direct instruction and imposition. The less experienced person is expected to watch and listen, but also to act and to question; and the more experienced one trusts and respects the less experienced one, even when she or he may make mistakes, and provides constructive feedback.

Recognizing the difference of experience between adults and young children, one might think that adults should be expected always to take the lead and say what to do and demand automatic respect. However, in this context, trust and respect does not mean that adults or children should be unchallenging or uncritical, but that either can do so, in a way that remains respectful of the other person, whatever their level of experience or status – and indeed mindful of this. Adults need to model appropriate responses and to provide reassurance and formative feedback, and increasingly to follow a child's lead, as much as possible, to maintain his or her agency.

The apprenticeship relationship is usually seen as one-to-one and adult-to-child but it can be one-to-many, and be from a more experienced child to a less experienced one – and in some cases child to adult. This highlights the benefit of mixed-age and intergenerational groups and of children taking the lead and adults encouraging them to do so.

Let us think what an apprenticeship approach entails in terms of behaviour and motivation. Chapter 6 emphasized reinforcing what a child does that is appropriate, rather than focusing on what she or he does wrong, and avoiding dependence on tangible rewards, if intrinsic motivation is to become embedded. Enabling children to exercise agency and judgement implies that boundaries must be managed with some flexibility and children encouraged to act increasingly on the basis of maxims rather than inflexible rules. But most young children love tangible rewards and some, especially those from backgrounds where they have not experienced supportive boundaries, find making choices and judgements hard and stricter, less negotiable rules easier to handle.

While young children must learn to make appropriate choices and decisions, they are often expected to do so by thinking about the consequences and find this difficult, particularly those unused to make choices or who are anxious. Since making choices is easier when one is used to doing so, adults must provide opportunities and support and reinforce children's ability to do so and understand the possible consequences. Encouraging children's agency and enabling them to make appropriate choices, sometimes, paradoxically, entails limiting the choices available – hence the need, at times, to narrow the parameters of choice in ways that may frustrate and upset some children, especially those who find it hard to self-regulate and control their responses. While 'time out' often helps a child to calm down and self-regulate, this should usually be brief and be seen by a child as disapproval of a particular behaviour rather than a rejection of him or her as a person, if self-esteem is not to be undermined. But she or he also must be able to think about, and make, choices free of the fear of the consequences, especially the emotional ones, of failure. Empowering a child to do so involves helping him or her to think together with other people, individually or as a group, about the context, recognize the possible consequences of their actions and consider other possible courses of action.

The construction of identities has been presented as a constantly changing narrative, building a child's self-esteem, without encouraging too great an emphasis on herself or himself. Sources of a young child's self-esteem are varied, with many seeming relatively mundane such as the first time when she or he

- used the potty;
- overcame a difficulty with speech or a particular movement;

- tied his or her own shoelaces;
- performed in public on his or her own; or
- managed to read a book independently.

Some of these are to do with cognition. However, many of those most significant in terms of identity and self-esteem are related to social and emotional development, whether providing a sense of private achievement or public recognition. And some may refer to aspects of a child's life which adults, especially parents, may find painful or be reluctant to talk about.

The education of the whole child is a collective endeavour, for all adults who interact with him or her, even though different cultures and individuals will have varying views of childhood, how children should be brought up and the roles of different adults. For instance, many cultures and societies see the school's role as mainly related to cognitive development and academic attainment, with religious, moral and character education the responsibility of the home and faith community. Inevitably, adults have different roles, interests and strengths, with parents having the first, and usually the most significant, influence, and often knowing most about their own child, especially those with disabilities. Teachers and other professionals bring particular expertise. A holistic approach entails adults in different roles collaborating and supporting, rather than blaming, each other.

One area where collaboration is particularly valuable is in helping children to cope with transitions. Transitions matter because children may be uncertain about what to expect and what is expected of them; and they may not, initially, feel a sense of belonging. Settling into a new environment is easier where expectations are familiar, so that middle-class children are more likely to have the necessary cultural capital. But, while moving into a new context may be confusing for children and for some particularly so, children are usually far more capable and resilient than adults, particularly middle-class ones, tend to think. For example, many children who have experienced considerable difficulties as a result of migration settle remarkably quickly into a new environment, especially if they experience predictable relationships. However, transitions are harder for those who find making friends difficult and those who experience contrasting values and expectations at home, in their community and at school.

Therefore, adults, especially parents, have to support children to manage transitions to new settings and deal with new, possibly unfamiliar and conflicting, expectations. Some of this can be done beforehand by children meeting the adults involved, enabling him or her to ask questions and the adults providing reassurance, whether in the environment with which the child is familiar or the new one. It may be best not to overload the child in advance with information as this may create anxiety, but it usually helps where expectations are made explicit, for instance about

- practical matters such as clothing and lunches; and
- how children are expected to behave, both in terms of what is allowed and forbidden, and more subtly to what extent children are encouraged to say what they think and to ask questions.

Adults, especially parents, may need to make clear to children that different types of behaviour and response are required in a new context and that children may find this difficult; and then support and reassure children once they have started in a new context for longer than adults may expect.

If children are to be seen and supported holistically, adults need to support and complement each other. This can be hard, especially where different groups of adults have conflicting beliefs and expectations. To try to do so, adults must be aware of, and sensitive to, the challenges which other adults face; and we now turn to this.

## Figuring out how parents/carers can help young children's search for identity

This section considers how parents – including where appropriate carers – can help strengthen children's identities and build their self-esteem and resilience. It does not claim to be a definitive guide on how to parent young children. However, the discussion so far indicates that parents/carers have a crucial role in

- preparing the ground in which identities are constructed;
- scaffolding a range of emerging identities; and
- guiding, supporting and accompanying their child on the journey,

rather than forcing a particular identity on to him or her.

Most parents want their children to enjoy good health, physical and mental, and to be happy, and not to suffer or be estranged from their family. However, beyond that, what parents want for their children and how to achieve this vary, as discussed previously. Chapter 3 highlighted Lareau's distinction between concerted cultivation and the accomplishment of natural growth, associated, broadly, with middle-class and working-class parenting styles, respectively. While my middle-class assumptions mean that I tend to favour an approach based on concerted cultivation, important lessons can be learned from enabling natural growth, for instance in allowing children space to play on their own and interact with other children and in not scholarizing childhood – or children.

Chapter 4 emphasized the influence of models of attachment and primary and secondary socialization in how children learn to act and interact. The home is the most significant influence for very young children, with the approach of parents vital in how children's identities are constructed and shaped. In discussing attachment, we saw how babies and toddlers learn to regulate their response to emotion in socially appropriate ways. The interaction between baby and prime carer, usually the mother through gazing, smiling, talking, touching – the list is endless – is how babies learn to make sense of experience and to regulate their emotions. Rogoff (1990: 75–83) emphasizes how a parent works with, and steers, a child's pre-existing focus of attention through joint attention in developing inter-subjectivity. Social skills and emotional regulation, which are the bedrock of learning, are developed gradually through interactions, initially between parent and child, and then with other people.

Parents have a long-term and intimate, but not necessarily a smooth, relationship with their children. They almost certainly know the child better than anyone else and have a life-long commitment to him or her. As a result, parents have a key role in nurturing and guiding children and providing stability, positive role models and ongoing support. There are exceptions and many parents find providing a safe, secure home environment impossible and many children grow up in homes with no suitable role models, especially in relation to masculinity.

Parents help children to internalize values and attitudes and strengthen intrinsic motivation mainly by their expectations in terms of appropriate behaviours and responses, by modelling the qualities involved and helping children to articulate and practice what these involve. Through primary socialization, and thereafter, parents establish expectations. Expectations may be as varied as what, and how, children are expected to eat, the clothes they wear, how to talk to their parents and other adults and who children are allowed to play with. The nature of what a child sees as constituting success – and therefore his or her aspirations in this respect – is likely to depend on socialization within the family and immediate community. As we have seen, parenting is imbued with judgements about what is valued and expectations are likely to be based at least partly on a child's gender, ethnicity and class. For instance, these are often manifested in girls being assigned to caring roles and boys expecting to be looked after. And parents usually encourage, or discourage, particular activities or behaviours dependent on culture and background.

While some parents may wish to discourage their children from playing with certain toys, such as guns, or encourage them to play with others, such as dolls, in order to avoid gender (or other) stereotyping, the other influences on children from friendship groups and the media may be too strong for this to have much long-term influence. Trying to influence a child's behaviours and attitudes seems more important and fruitful than trying to change his or her interests, though these are often linked.

If a child's identity is to become robust, parents must not impose or try to force him or her into a particular identity, especially one which reflects who parents are – or would have wished to become. Such an imposition easily creates unrealistic expectations and may create considerable anxiety and stress. Children, especially as they approach, and during, adolescence, frequently reject the advice which parents offer and rebel against an imposed identity, especially if they sense they are being controlled or harangued. Despite this, parents must continue to love and remain alongside their children and encourage a broad range of interests and the self-esteem which may be associated with these but learn to let go. An appealing metaphor is that of providing an anchor but with a long, loose chain to keep children safe while giving them scope to enable movement and exploration.

We have seen that helping children construct robust identities involves many dilemmas. Among those for parents are that they have to provide security, be available and be consistent, but to offer challenge and flexibility. They cannot always be available, not least because they have to manage their own lives and those of other members of the family; and children must be equipped to cope with problems without becoming overdependent. Parents must also show interest but know when to respect children's privacy and back off to allow them to deal with things for themselves; and make mistakes. This often entails leaving children alone when they are alright, but, especially as children approach adolescence, being there to provide support when they are, or may be, in trouble. For parents to listen to and take seriously children's concerns, however trivial these may seem, helps children make sense of these, even if parents do nothing visible as a result.

The relationship between parent and child is not that of friends and equals. Parents must provide boundaries which are predictable but not inflexible, to equip as well as to protect and to offer stability, support and reassurance. Parents must exert authority without misusing their power. For example, managing sibling rivalry can be very demanding when one child thinks that she or he is being treated unfairly. But, while parents must try to be fair and to justify what they do, they must be prepared to stand their ground if their authority is not to be undermined.

If a child is to maintain a sense of agency, and not be overprotected or infantilized or develop too great a sense of entitlement, she or he must take on responsibilities, and so must be given responsibility and meaningful tasks, such as looking after their possessions or having, and caring for, a pet or helping with what needs doing. To strengthen a child's sense of agency over time implies a gradual transfer of responsibility. Let us take the example of how long children should spend watching television or playing computer games. Parents will usually determine how long very young children are allowed to spend on such devices – and discuss and negotiate this as they get older and, hopefully, more responsible. Similarly, young children may be told what they have to eat, but as they grow older children must be encouraged and allowed to make choices where possible, if they are to take responsibility for their own health, though parents will probably continue to monitor and control the amount of sugar or junk food they eat.

Children, especially when they are very young and those in large families, benefit from having the sustained attention of one or both parents for some of the time. Since young children learn about themselves and other people through reciprocal activities, especially those which they enjoy, parents need to provide opportunities for these, such as hearing stories and rhymes, singing songs and talking with an adult. Lancy (2015: 35) suggests that dinner-table conversations are one vital way in which children can learn social conventions through example and discussion. Children benefit from doing things with their parents – and other adults – such as eating, playing games, watching television programmes, visiting places or other activities which they both enjoy. But children must also have space and time to entertain themselves, rather than always be occupied or entertained, and to play and do things on their own and with their friends.

This discussion highlights the importance of routines and rituals such as meals, bed time stories and (in some families) prayers, and collective rituals such as celebrations of birthdays which help children gain a sense of belonging. However, in many families, such discussions between adults and children happen less than previously as families are more fragmented, family life is less routinized and children's lives more individualized. And children, as they approach adolescence, may be more reluctant to participate in such rituals as they become more independent.

So far, I have not distinguished between mothers and fathers, though we have seen that women do far more childcare than men and the value of diverse role models, from men and women, which provide different ways for children to see what acting as a male or a female entails. However, the positive example provided by strong, supportive mothers is often significant in whether children succeed and thrive, particularly those from disadvantaged backgrounds, especially working-class girls and those from Afro-Caribbean backgrounds (see Reay, 2017; Wright, 2013). The absence or inability of a father, or other male – whether the absence is real or because of disengagement – to provide a positive role model and a continuity of support seems to contribute to many boys, particularly those from disadvantaged backgrounds, getting into trouble. Although the reasons for such outcomes are complex and easily oversimplified, there is little doubt that all children need at least one parent or close adult with a long-term commitment to provide support and guidance as they negotiate their identities in the face of societal pressures which offer attractive, but potentially damaging, images of success.

Parents and carers can help children in constructing their identities looking both back and forward to understand their life narrative better. For children to be helped to think about the milestones they have achieved and the hurdles they have crossed successfully provides a source of self-esteem and hope. Moreover, for parents to talk about themselves, and other family members, as children and the experiences, wishes and problems which they encountered – and how they resolved these – can help children to recognize that their own experiences and problems are not unique.

Most parents are well placed to help children to some extent to prepare for the turbulence of puberty and adolescence, but embarrassment or lack of knowledge may mean that parents do not feel able to, or do not, do so very well. Other adults, whether professionals or other family members or friends, may be better placed to do so in these and other respects. This highlights the importance of the extended family and friends, as discussed in the next section.

## Thinking about the role of the extended family and family friends

One significant aspect of identity is where an individual child fits into a larger family narrative. This relates not only to their place as a son or a daughter and as a sibling, but how they are placed in the family as an older, middle or younger sibling or only child. These are likely to affect how she or he has been brought up and the relationships and expectations which result. For instance, a first child or an only child may have been treated as particularly important; and an older child with several young siblings may be expected to take on responsibility for these.

One should not overlook the role which older siblings can fulfil, especially in large families, where parents may have less time to attend to children. In some cultures, and big families, older siblings play an important role in bringing up and supporting younger children. For instance, Rogoff (2003: 122–5) provides many examples of how, in different cultures, older siblings, especially pre-adolescent girls, have fulfilled significant caring roles with younger siblings. This is in contrast to modern Western societies where this does not occur, especially in middle-class families and young children are looked after almost exclusively by adults or by older girls acting as babysitters. Gregory (2000) highlights how older siblings or cousins were crucial in helping younger children to learn to read in Bangladeshi families in East London. This relationship also illustrates the mutual benefit of children teaching other children, where the more experienced one may have to simplify a task and so think about it deeply and the less experienced one sees how someone who is closer in age and experience than an adult approaches the task.

Children's identities are affected not only by the immediate family but also by the extended family and their values and assumptions, for instance in relation to gender and religion. While the extended family has always been a significant influence in some cultures, and especially in working-class communities, this has become less strong as families have become more dispersed. But the extended family's influence remains strong and may matter particularly for children with dual or multiple heritage and those whose family has migrated from a different culture. However, in such cases, the values and expectations between generations may be markedly different.

The role of older family members, such as grandparents and uncles and aunts, is in some respects similar to that of parents, in supporting and guiding a child, but their relationship with children is usually less emotionally intense because they usually have more time and are not so caught up, emotionally, with him or her. While the relationship is usually long-term, and from within a similar cultural background, such family members are with a child only for some of the time. This can enable them to provide another perspective for parents and children alike, though in different respects. For instance, parents/carers may overreact to, or ignore, their child's worries about friendships, bullying or progress at school and family members can provide a more measured view.

Through their relationship with a child, other family members can help him or her to make sense of what parents do and why – for better or worse – and provide continuity where this is, or feels as if, missing.

Understanding their life story and how they fit into larger groups, especially the family, is interesting for most children but likely to be particularly significant for those who

- are of dual or mixed heritage; or
- have experienced dislocation or disruption, such as children who have been adopted or are in public care.

Helping such children to understand this may require considerable sensitivity, but following the child's lead in terms of the questions she or he asks and using artefacts, pictures and stories is likely to be helpful. Although, as adults, we tend to avoid difficult questions, especially those which unsettle and disturb us, children usually want their questions about their life story answered, honestly at an appropriate level – and it is all too easy for parents/carers to avoid doing so for whatever reason. Other family members may be able help a child to understand his or her place in the wider family narrative and culture.

Grandparents can help reinforce messages, supplement what parents do and compensate to some extent for what children do not get at home or at school by

- treating children more as individuals in ways that may be impossible when the whole family is together;
- doing activities with children which parents may not be able to do or entirely approve of or which schools do not offer, especially in relation to opportunities for play and aspects of learning not covered at school;
- providing 'treats' or taking children to enjoyable places and activities they might otherwise not visit, for whatever reason, such as financial considerations or time;
- talking and interacting with children about topics which parents/carers may find difficult;
- offering alternative safe spaces for children to talk about their concerns such as parental arguments in ways that may be impossible, or at least difficult, with parents;
- helping children believe in themselves and create greater self-esteem, especially where parents/carers cannot, or do not, do so; and
- enabling a child to create alternative versions of events and so change how she or he understands these.

One group whose importance is underestimated is that of close family friends or neighbours, often friends of parents. Like grandparents, they have an emotional distance but the length of their relationship with the family often means that they know the child well and the milestones of his or her life story such as

- their first words,
- the first time they rode their bike on their own;
- when they started to read independently; and
- when they first performed in public or made their first communion (or similar ritual marking new ways of belonging in a faith community),

as well as more difficult times, such as parental disputes and separation, and personal, smaller events which may seem unimportant to an outsider but matter profoundly to a child. Moreover, family friends may be more closely aligned with the parents' values than other members of the family, especially if the latter disapprove of how a child is being brought up.

Members of the extended family and family friends tend to know the child well over time and have seen how they develop, enabling them to offer a longer perspective and provide stability over time. Such relationships may help children and parents understand each other better and to reduce tension between parents and children, especially as the latter approach adolescence. This may surface, for instance, in relation to expectations in terms of gender or religion, such as what children should wear, whether and why their parents want them to attend religious services, or more generally in terms of having a phone or use social media. These relationships may be particularly helpful for children whose lives are disrupted such as when a parent is absent or where parents cannot support their children, for whatever reason.

Children tend to think of their parents as they are now, not how they were previously. Members of the extended family and family friends may be well placed to share memories of events when a child's parents were not present or before she or he was born. For instance, for a child to know how his or her mother or father or were as a child and the challenges they faced can help him or her to understand the family narrative and perhaps to recognize that his or her own experiences and worries are not abnormal.

Grandparents may be much better at parenting, at least in theory, than they were themselves as parents – or at least think that they are. As a result, they can have fun with children without having constantly to stick rigidly to parents' expectations and perhaps subvert these to some extent, in ways that may help a child to explore his or her own identity. However, problems frequently occur if grandparents have different views of how children should be brought up, especially where there is a clash between the parents' and grandparents' values and expectations. Therefore, there is a considerable danger of grandparents interfering and undermining the parents – or being seen to do so, so that sensitivity and the ability to keep quiet and bite one's lip, and not offer unsolicited advice, are essential.

Since parents are usually in an intense and long-term relationship with their children, a child may listen to, and internalize, some messages more when hearing these from another family member, a family friend or a professional. Family friends may help parents to reframe what professionals are saying, for instance in relation to health or lack of progress at school. Their distance from, but knowledge of, a child can make it for them easier to persuade parents to

- adopt a wider perspective or a less controlling approach;
- encourage and enable children to try new activities, or to do less; and
- focus on the positive when children – or parents – are finding things difficult.

Members of the extended family and family friends may be able to help to some extent to counter adverse influences from the media or a child's peer group. They may be better placed than some parents to help boys to talk about their vulnerabilities and so encourage them to extend their emotional repertoire; and likewise to encourage less confident girls to take part in activities which enable them to be more assertive and confident. Similarly, children may find it easier to discuss sensitive or troubling issues related to culture or religion with such adults than with their parents.

The roles described in this section can be carried out in family gatherings and other formal events, or more informally in one-to-one conversations. While members of the family and friends can exert a strong and positive influence, children's identities, especially as they approach adolescence, are increasingly shaped in other groups, as discussed in the next section.

## Reflecting on how other significant adults can help strengthen children's identities

This section discusses briefly how adults who are not family members or teachers can support young children's search for a coherent identity. Among such adults are those providing childcare, professionals, leaders of faith communities, those with expertise in sport, drama, dance or music – sometimes called 'creatives' – and leaders of voluntary groups.

Children often act differently at home, at school and in other contexts and may be likely to listen and be more deferential to other adults, whom they respect and trust, than to their own parents. Paradoxically, the emotional distance, linked to expertise in a particular area and lack of a close relationship, may help in getting across messages to a child, or parents/carers, as long as the relationship is one of respect. For example, children frequently take more notice of exhortations to work hard or be punctual when these are given by someone other than their parents, such as the leader of a voluntary group.

Groups such as faith communities, sports clubs and scout groups may exert a positive influence by adults building different types of relationship with children and creating spaces which are enjoyable and welcoming, providing a sense of belonging. Such groups may be able to compensate for difficulties in the home and help to broaden children's cultural horizons. Those where participants are of different ages can provide opportunities where a young child can learn from an older and more experienced one and take a lead with those who are younger.

Given that many very young children spend a great deal of time in childcare, those providing such care fulfil an important role in helping the child and in supporting parents. As long as these are nurturing, and children are given enough attention, such relationships can help children to have a greater, and enriching, diversity of experience. They can provide a different environment – either more or less structured – and alternative role models and types of interaction from those which children encounter at home. By liaising closely with parents, those providing childcare can enhance parents' understanding of their children in ways similar to those outlined in the previous section.

Professionals such as paediatricians and social workers usually interact with young children when they are having difficulties related to health, learning or family circumstances. They bring specific expertise but usually without being in a position to build a long-term relationship, making it important that they draw on the insights of those who know a child well, including him or her as appropriate. A holistic approach to assessment implies finding out as much as possible which is relevant about the child's background and life story, being curious, without being too intrusive, and involving the child and parents and other significant adults, where possible.

In offering advice to parents/carers – and their children – and suggesting suitable provision, professionals must recognize cultural sensitivities and expectations and the difficulties that families may have in following such advice and accessing such provision, and provide support where possible. Professionals should be sympathetic in considering the age and experience and level of ability of many parents, without abdicating their responsibility if there are serious concerns. Professionals must recognize how difficult it is to parent young children, especially for those who are unsure because of inexperience, isolation and difficulties related to such factors. This is exacerbated by the need to juggle the demands of other children, of work and home and other priorities.

Most parents want the best for their children, though what they understand by this may differ, as does their ability to provide a secure, predictable and caring environment which enables children to thrive. Most provide love and some security, though many may find this hard, and some do not manage to do so for whatever reason. Sometimes, this may be because they don't know how or can't, possibly because of the models of parenting which they learned from their own parents or because of external factors such as poverty, mental health difficulties or addiction. Many of these difficulties are not the result of personal choice and professionals should in such cases seek to avoid blaming parents/carers – and certainly their children, though it is easy to do so.

While I am wary of suggesting how faith leaders should work with young children, not least because I am not a member of a faith community, many of the considerations discussed in Chapter 7 apply if children are to create a strong, lasting religious identity. This view is supported by the articles in Lifelong Faith (2015) and Wimberley and Parker (2010) which explore from two different Christian perspectives the rationale for, and practical implications of, how children's faith can best be nurtured.

Separating children from adults to take part in activities designed to be at the children's level may be appropriate at times, but risks offering simplistic messages. Images, symbols and rituals can all be understood at different levels of sophistication, but rely on regular exposure to, or involvement in, these. Expecting agreement with abstract ideas which young children do not understand may lead to disengagement and in the long term to a brittle identity. Activities such as Godly Play and hearing, and discussing, the stories of faith help children to relate the messages of a religious tradition to their own experience. Creating a robust faith identity should involve incorporation into the practices of a religious tradition, but also requires children being enabled to question some of the messages and assumptions of the prevailing macro-culture, and to search for answers with the guidance of people who are more experienced. Even very young children can start to understand the practices of a faith tradition by participating in, and sometimes taking a role in leading, worship, though, as

Yust (2017) argues, the types of worship may have to be adapted. Moreover, this can provide opportunities for adults to learn from young children, particularly in terms of simplicity.

Supplementary schools are popular with many parents dissatisfied with what the formal school system offers, especially for some ethnic minorities, sometimes for religious reasons but often because they are unhappy with low expectations and an often-tacit racism. Such schools usually provide strict discipline and high expectations in terms of attainment and children listening to adults and doing what they are told. The danger is that, while children may behave well in that context, they, especially boys, often find situations where the rules and expectations are more fluid, and they are expected to make decisions, difficult to handle, since motivation is largely dependent on extrinsic control. This is true to some extent in school, but particularly so outside, especially where peer group pressure exerts a strong influence and sexism, racism and homophobia may be common.

Whether children are participating in a group on a voluntary basis or not is likely to be significant in whether and how children are engaged. Voluntary groups can be helpful for children who find a sense of belonging difficult elsewhere. Let us take three examples where children's participation is usually voluntary and enjoyable

- 'creatives', usually arts professionals who may not have a teaching qualification but have a particular expertise in areas such as dance, drama, art or music;
- sports coaches, who similarly are often not qualified teachers but are skilled in, often, one or more sports; and
- leaders of cubscouts, brownie, or similar, groups.

Some of these groups have requirements such as uniforms which may help to foster a sense of group identity and make it less likely that children will be seen to be different on the basis of culture and class. While, inevitably, such groups will usually contain children of similar interest and backgrounds, they may provide a greater mix in terms of gender, ethnicity and class than other groups. This presents scope for children to associate and cooperate with those who are different and so to create bridging capital.

The effect on children's self-esteem and identities usually depends on the relationships created. The enthusiasm and encouragement of adult leaders frequently helps children to learn new skills, to develop latent talents and to feel included. In all of these groups adults will, inevitably, focus mainly on the activity with which they are most concerned and the child's situational identity, but can also contribute to a broader, substantive sense of identity. Therefore, as well as providing a source of children's enjoyment, and identity-as-an-artist (or whatever), such activities can help to build self-esteem and strengthen children's motivation to act and interact in thoughtful ways, and offer alternative role models to those which many children may see at home and which most see in the media.

Activities such as painting, pottery, music, dance and drama lessons provide opportunities for children to enjoy themselves and develop the skills associated with the activity. Structure and rules are often implicit in such activities, making it easier for children to be creative. For instance, a group session of singing or drama requires those participating to cooperate enabling children to do so without embarrassment. However, those leading drama groups, especially, may work on sensitive themes, especially as children approach adolescence, and it may require considerable expertise to run such a session so that all children feel safe, remain engaged and are able to experiment with different identities.

Sport provides an important source of enjoyment and identity for many children, especially boys. Sport is often associated with particular class backgrounds and assumptions, with some encouraging a particular style of masculinity based on competitiveness and aggressive behaviour. The issues for sports coaches are in many respects similar, in terms of relationships and rules, to those discussed previously, with the nature of the activity determining what is expected. One difference is that many children from a young age – and their parents – enjoy competition between individuals and teams. Sport tends to be based on performance and competition and being part of, and competing as, a team is often what attracts many children, and adults, to sport, as it did, and does, for me. However, I suggest that, especially with young children, sports coaches should emphasize, and try to develop, non-sport-specific qualities such as

- managing one's emotions;
- a commitment to fair play;
- perseverance; and
- learning to win and lose gracefully.

In particular, while competition between teams and/or individuals is inherent in sport, coaches should discourage hyper-competitiveness and training too hard from a young age.

Groups such as cubscouts or brownies usually have a less specific focus, but enable children to take part in enjoyable activities such as playing games as a group, hearing stories and enjoying the natural world. Many children enjoy a clear structure of expectations in a more relaxed atmosphere than is usually possible at school and the sense of identity symbolized by the uniform. The continuity of relationships over several years, with the adults and other children, may offer the chance for a child both to learn from older children and to provide a positive example to younger ones.

This section has considered, albeit in general terms, some of the challenges and opportunities for adults working outside schools, arguing that they have a responsibility in relation to the whole child which extends beyond situational identity in that particular context. It is time to consider the implications for those who work in formal settings and schools.

# 9

# Reviewing the implications for schools and teachers

*Children bring to school very particular family identities, identities which facilitate some kinds of learning, but inhibit others. Social relationships with other young people, and participation in school culture, act to produce new dimensions in the sense of self, which frame the meaning of pupils' classroom conduct and closely govern what they may and may not do.*

Salmon, 1995: 62

## Rethinking the aims of schooling

Chapter 3 highlighted that schools currently tend to emphasize cognitive attainment, in a narrow range of subject areas, at the expense of other types of achievement, and that discussion of aims, and what it is to be an educated person, has been stifled by the assumption that success is measured largely in terms of test scores.

While school is only one of many influences on children's identities, schools (and particularly teachers) matter, especially for children who do not experience caring relationships and appropriate expectations elsewhere, and as one of the few places where children of different backgrounds regularly mix. While I refer to teachers, most of what is said applies to all who work in schools. Support staff may be especially significant as they often spend more time with children, especially those with learning difficulties, as individuals or in small groups.

The aims of schooling are, inevitably, influenced by a society's beliefs and values (see Alexander, 2000), but, as argued in Eaude (2016), these must include a moral element, in the sense that education is intended to improve children, even though there may be disagreement about what improvement means and the practical implications. Chapter 7 suggested that seeing children as active meaning-makers requires a radical reassessment of the aims of education and how to meet these. This chapter explores the implications for schools and dilemmas such as whether, and to what extent, teachers should

- adopt a broad curriculum as opposed to focusing on 'the basics';
- challenge, and seek to change, children's assumptions; and
- encourage divergence or expect conformity;

but argues that

- a holistic education should promote children's physical and mental health, recognize and celebrate diverse identities and intelligences and concentrate on procedural and personal/interpersonal as well as propositional knowledge; and
- there should be more focus than at present on the kind of person a child is and will become – and on the qualities that this entails.

Schools influence not only what children are expected to learn but also how they are expected to, and do, learn about themselves and other people. In Bruner's words (1963: 33):

> A curriculum reflects not only the nature of knowledge itself but also the nature of the knower and the knowing-getting process. …We teach a subject not to produce little living libraries … but rather to get the student to think mathematically … to consider matters as an historian does, to take part in the process of knowledge-getting. Knowing is a process, not a product.

Educating the whole child involves extending children's knowledge and skills and strengthening qualities, dispositions and intrinsic motivation across, and beyond, the formal curriculum. Seen like this, education is more about the sort of person a child is, and will become, than about transmitting knowledge or covering the syllabus.

As Salmon suggests, at the start of this chapter, the context of school, and the acquisition of new identities as readers, mathematicians and artists, and as people operating in a new social context, affects profoundly how children see themselves and how they act and interact. Since children's beliefs about themselves are so important, teachers must encourage them to see identities as changeable and strengthen what Dweck (2000) calls a 'growth mindset', where children see themselves as capable of change, with help and support where necessary. Teachers should seek to reinforce behaviours which manifest qualities such as courage or resilience, but encouraging children not to see such qualities as innate. To do this, teachers must try to avoid such a view themselves, especially when referring to children who have restricted levels of experience or are unused to interacting with other children and adults. Moreover, teachers must avoid presenting the growth mindset so that children feel blamed for their shortcomings.

In Stenhouse's words (1967: 1), 'Sociologists commonly conceive the function of education as the transmission of culture from generation to generation.' Alexander (2000: 164) points out that 'schools and classrooms are both cultural channels and micro-cultures in their own right'. As cultural channels, they influence, though they do not determine, the attitudes and beliefs which children internalize. As micro-cultures, they convey messages about what, and who is valued, and can help filter and modify the messages heard elsewhere. But, as Bruner suggests (1996: 27), 'school curricula and classroom "climates" always reflect inarticulate cultural values as well as explicit plans; and these values are never far removed from considerations of social class, gender, and the prerogatives of social power'.

Brooker (2002: 168–9) draws on an understanding of culture as based on shared experiences of learning and constantly remade together as individuals, families and communities, rather than a collection of artefacts, beliefs and practices. From this, she argues that teachers should recognize, and engage with, the language and perspectives which children from different backgrounds bring and encourage shared experiences of learning, rather than adopt the children's, or their families', practices or values. However, teachers must be sensitive to the latter. At one level, this involves

- being aware of religious festivals, dress and food and the significance which children and their families may ascribe to these;
- taking account of some religious groups' disapproval, or forbidding, of some types of music or artistic representation, such as images of God being forbidden in Islam and Judaism;
- ensuring that the materials available which children reflect cultural diversity; and
- encouraging children to be aware of the contribution of other cultures in disciplines like mathematics, science, literature, art, music and architecture.

However, cultural sensitivity implies more than 'a steel drums, saris and somosa' approach, where other cultures are seen, somewhat tokenistically, as exotic. Teachers must seek to value, rather than erase, children's existing cultural identities and recognize, and try to dismantle, the barriers which many children face. This involves trying to create inclusive, welcoming and hospitable environments, which

- are sensitive to the language and practices which children bring to a new setting;
- value children's cultures, backgrounds, interests and abilities and build on these;
- celebrate a wide range of achievements; and
- strengthen, but do not rely on, cognitive processes.

A child's home language is a vital aspect of his or her identity, even though children for whom this differs from that spoken in school may be reluctant to speak it when they are unsure whether this is acceptable. As the Bullock report (HMSO, 1975: 287) stated over forty years ago, 'No child should be expected to cast off the language and culture of the home as he (or she) crosses the school threshold, nor to live and act as though school represent two totally separate and different cultures which have to be kept firmly apart.'

Bibby, describing the (quietly expressed but obvious) excitement of two Somali girls at hearing a greeting in Somali during a song, and how the teacher told them off, comments that 'we just need to notice the ease with which moments of potential recognition and joining can be missed and devalued' (2011: 66). This illustrates how easy it is for teachers to be unaware of relatively small but important issues, and that teachers must not only take account of children's culture and interests but also have the ability and sensitivity to do so unexpectedly and quickly. Teaching is a relationship-based profession and, given the asymmetry of power, teachers should be acutely aware of the influence they wield in what they say and do. Bibby's (2011: 43) insight that 'comments, judgements, are never neutral, they are always infused with extra meanings from the positions we occupy' helps to explain why teachers' comments about, and judgements of, children are so significant in building, or undermining, self-esteem and identity.

We have seen that all children need a sense of belonging. Creating an inclusive environment is particularly important, but difficult, with children with disrupted lives and unpredictable relationships, such as those who have been rejected or unloved or come from chaotic or stressful homes. Doing so entails all children, including these, being loved and cared for and challenged appropriately. To achieve this, schools, in Noddings's words (1991: 161),

> should become places in which teachers and students live together, talk to each other, reason together, take delight in each others' company. Like good parents,

teachers should be concerned first and foremost with the kind of people their charges are becoming. My guess is that when schools focus on what really matters in life, the cognitive ends we are now striving towards in such painful and artificial ways will be met as natural culminations of the means we have widely chosen.

However, as discussed in Eaude (2014), it is hard to create hospitable space in the very competitive climate of schools.

The formal curriculum (usually in reality more like a syllabus) is only one element of the curriculum. The informal and the hidden curriculum often matter more in how children construct their identities, with the subliminal messages which schools and teachers give, sometimes without conscious thought or intending to do so, the most influential ones (see Jackson et al., 1993). Recognizing that, in a holistic education, curriculum, pedagogy and assessment are mutually reinforcing, in meeting the aims set out previously, the next three sections discuss the implications for each, in relation to young children's identities.

## Striving towards a broad, balanced and inclusive curriculum

This section considers what a broad, balanced and inclusive curriculum for young children entails, in contrast to the narrow, restricted curriculum which many experience in a climate of performativity.

All people have a range of abilities and talents, though young children's may be not yet discovered or well developed. Therefore, as Reed (2001: 122) writes, 'even the youngest children should be exposed to a broad and ambitious curriculum in the hopes of identifying one or more areas at which each child excels or is motivated to learn'. Of course, children must learn English (or the main language) and mathematics, but they require a richer, broader curriculum than one focused mainly on content knowledge and decontextualized skills. The idea of the 'horizon of possibility' suggests how new experiences can help open up previously invisible possibilities and territory which may have appeared distant and unattainable becomes accessible. Moreover, while studying mathematics or geography should strengthen children's identities as scientists or geographers, if well taught such subject disciplines help to encourage children's sense of agency and strengthen the qualities and dispositions associated with a robust, but flexible, identity. For instance, physical education is concerned not only with health, specific skills and organized games and sport, but with fostering qualities such as persistence and teamwork. Similar considerations apply for any subject or activity.

A balanced curriculum does not over-emphasize one or more subject areas or types of knowledge. All Our Futures (NACCCE, 1999: 52–3) argues for balance

- between different fields of study and disciplines;
- within all disciplines, between tradition and innovation; and
- the teaching of different values and traditions, reflecting and responding to cultural diversity.

In any curriculum, or syllabus, choices have to be made about what should be prioritized, and to what extent schools should concentrate on children learning canonical knowledge or build on their existing funds of knowledge. The question of who – politicians, administrators or teachers – should make such choices is, and always will be, a matter of debate. However, children will learn little of value if they are not engaged and challenged – and young children's behaviour soon becomes disruptive if they are bored. Therefore, even if one's aim is for children to learn a body of canonical knowledge, meaningful and engaging activities must be the foundation for this.

An inclusive curriculum seeks to engage all children and foster a sense of agency. While schooling involves initiation and acculturation into unfamiliar groups and types of knowledge, doing so should take account of children's pre-existing knowledge, assumptions and values. Yet, many schools, unwittingly, exclude de facto many children, and have always done so, because schools are competitive and often unfamiliar or alienating cultures for them. A lack of respect for what children value and are good at, tends to lead to disengagement. If a child is very skilled at computer games or has a deep knowledge of his or her religious heritage, but these skills and this knowledge are not valued in school, she or he soon recognizes this.

Activities related to learning outside school often provide a considerable source of success and self-esteem. For instance, I remember two ten-year-old girls asking me, their classroom teacher, if they could show the class their disco-dancing. To my shame, I did not even know that they went to dancing lessons, let alone that they entered, and won, competitions. Yet this was an important, though largely unrecognized, aspect of their identities. Needless to say, their performance was superb. Likewise, many young children find activities such as cooking and making music more engaging, and learn more sophisticated skills associated with such activities, than in their school learning. Children from disadvantaged backgrounds frequently have a depth of cultural capital and funds of knowledge which are not valued in schools. While teachers must try to find out about, value and draw on these, it is easy to overlook them in the busyness of classroom life.

Part II highlighted the importance of perception in how young children learn and of the images they see, and the impact of indirect means of learning such as stories. So, teachers must consider carefully which images, books and stories to present. Having a diverse range of these available helps to extend children's horizons and to interest children who may otherwise be disengaged from school learning. For instance, I recall two ten-year-old boys who were good, but reluctant, readers, both of whom loved a book called 'The Balaclava Boys', largely because they identified with the situations described and characters similar to themselves. While environments and relationships are vital, the content of the curriculum makes a significant difference in the extent to which children are motivated, especially those less engaged with school learning.

In helping all children to be engaged and feel included, a key issue is which types of knowledge, language, stories and role models and whose history, music, art and literature are emphasized and valued. Considering the experience of women, people of colour, those with disabilities or those living in difficult circumstances, provides different perspectives on the world from one which concentrates mainly on the experience of the powerful. Where the images, examples and stories presented are all, or mostly, of prosperous white men, children of different ethnicities, socio-economic backgrounds and girls do not see their own cultures reflected; and it is understandable if they feel excluded.

The books available should take account of, and reflect, different children's experience and cultural sensitivities in terms of ethnicity, gender and class and celebrate the diversity of societies, worldwide, not just children in the class. All children benefit from toys, pictures, stories and other materials which reflect many different backgrounds, cultures and abilities. This helps those from historically disadvantaged backgrounds to see that people like them – and by extension they and their families – matter; and it enables other children to recognize that not only people like themselves matter and so welcome, rather than be afraid of, difference and diversity.

Teachers must try to enable all children to access a common cultural heritage, such as through stories from history and religion without which a nuanced understanding of poetry and literature is difficult. A key question is whose history and which artefacts and stories are highlighted and valued. If children are to understand and celebrate diversity, the curriculum should include not only the heritage of the dominant culture but also other heritages, and to some extent popular, as well as high, culture. If children are to respect different cultures, albeit critically, teachers must introduce these and highlight their contribution for instance in science and the arts. In a globalized world, all children benefit from such an approach, not just those from cultures and backgrounds different from the culture of the majority.

The cultural capital valued in school includes sustained use of reciprocal language and references to 'high culture' which children from working-class backgrounds may not have experienced, as a result of poverty or parents not realizing what will be valuable in school (see Lancy, 2015: 355–7). Teachers should try to enable all children to experience a wide range of opportunities, remembering also that children living in poverty need economic capital – that is, money – so that they can participate in the experiences which wealthier children may take for granted (see Reay, 2017).

For young children to experience a broad curriculum, what they study should include not only subjects traditionally studied in school, including at least one additional language, which can help children to understand a different culture, but also areas such as design, construction and architecture, photography, philosophy and astronomy. Many of these are enjoyable and engaging and can help to build confidence and self-esteem in children, especially those who are less academically successful.

All Our Futures (NACCCE, 1999: 160) sees creative and cultural education more like a general function of education, rather than occurring only in certain subject areas or types of lesson, or through specific programmes, though the latter may be helpful and some subjects and disciplines seem to offer more opportunities than others. Identities are not explored and strengthened only in lessons called personal and social education, social studies or citizenship. Rather, enabling children to be creative and learn about themselves and other people must be integral to how the curriculum is organized and taught. As with what in England is called spiritual, moral, cultural and social (SMSC) development, understanding oneself and other people and issues of identity and belonging underlie every area of learning.

Bruner (1996: 42) argues that 'a system of education must help those growing up in a culture find an identity within that culture. Without it they stumble after meaning. It is only in the narrative mode that one can construct an identity and find a place in one's culture.' Yet, as Bruner points out (1996: 40), most schools tend to treat the arts of narrative, such as song, drama and fiction, as decorative rather than necessary. As discussed in Chapter 5, play, drama and story and the humanities and the arts occupy an important place in how children's identities are constructed, and help to create a more robust sense of identity, not least because these enable children to explore people and how they respond in different situations. In particular, the humanities, well taught, help children to explore complex questions with no simple answers, to make inferences and to apply critical thinking skills. By encouraging a recognition of the complexities of culture and why people act as they do, the humanities can help to avoid bigotry and reduce the danger of radicalization.

An inclusive curriculum provides an entitlement for all children, but is not constrained by too much content or limited by artificial boundaries. Play, drama and story cross disciplinary boundaries and subjects should be seen as contexts for how children learn rather than as separate silos. For instance, children must learn to apply propositional knowledge and skills, and those associated with literacy can be taught and internalized through the humanities or science, rather than just in lessons called English. Indeed, whether discrete subject boundaries, as opposed to broad areas of study, are helpful when working with young children is questionable (see Eaude, 2018a, chapter 5).

A holistic education introduces children to unfamiliar ideas and musical and artistic traditions and enables them to see ideas and situations from perspectives other than their own. To do this, children must learn to recognize that knowledge is contestable and interpreted through the lens of particular cultures. This may sound rather grand for young children, but in practice entails them learning to question what they hear and to see and understand situations from perspectives other than their own.

The approach which I am advocating has similarities to that of *Bildung*, a term usually used only with older children and adults. *Bildung* refers to the German tradition of self-cultivation where philosophy and education are linked in ways that refer to both personal and cultural maturation. As a result, selfhood and identity are achieved within the broader society through personal transformation, shaping human beings and taking account of their humanity as well as intellectual skills. Fulfilment is achieved through practical activity that promotes the development of one's own individual talents and abilities which in turn lead to the development of one's society. This involves a challenge to each individual's accepted beliefs and requires individuals to have the freedom and agency to develop a wide variety of talents and abilities. *Bildung* does not simply accept the sociopolitical status quo, but encourages students to engage in a critique of society. While this may sound ambitious for young children, I suggest that they can, and should, be equipped with the foundations of such an approach, characterized more in terms of qualities and dispositions than of (propositional) knowledge.

## Unpicking the implications for pedagogy

Alexander's (2000) detailed study of pedagogy in primary and elementary schools in five systems highlights how deeply rooted traditions and assumptions are embedded in how schools and curricula are organized, and teachers teach, usually reflecting long-standing cultural beliefs and national identities and priorities. For instance, many societies in South East Asia are highly competitive and encourage children to work hard and defer to their teachers more than in England. Children in England and the areas of the United States studied tend to work as individuals or in small groups, whereas in Russia and France there is a greater emphasis on whole class discussion. Alexander's research provides a warning against being too specific about advocating particular types of pedagogy and assessment procedures and policy borrowing. Moreover, the needs of different age groups and classes vary. However, this section explores some pedagogical implications of the argument that a holistic education requires teachers to work in new, unfamiliar ways.

Fransson and Grannäs (2013: 7) use Honig's idea of 'dilemmatic spaces' to argue that dilemmas are not specific events or situations but ever-present in classrooms. Teaching inherently involves multiple, sometimes-conflicting, aims and dilemmas and, therefore, entails compromises, though the nature of these will vary between teachers and for individuals at different times. For instance, a wish to encourage children's creativity and breadth of experience may be hampered by the demand to meet short-term targets; and the perceived need to cover a full curriculum may restrict opportunities for reflection.

As Alexander (1995) observes, comparing gardens to jungles as metaphors for primary classrooms, a garden has to have some structure imposed on it, if it is not to run wild. For the teacher to establish routines helps to provide young children with structures which contain anxiety and encourage a sense of belonging. But such structures must have some flexibility if they are not to be constraining.

In Pollard with Filer's (1996: 91) words, 'It is essential that (children) exercise a significant degree of control of the (learning) process so that they can build on intrinsic motivation where that exists.' Otherwise, without a sense of agency, children are likely to become passive, dependent and disengaged. Teachers must exert their authority without misusing their power. This involves regulating the classroom climate, like constantly adjusting a thermostat, and may require the teacher to do what some children may dislike. For instance, enabling sustained shared thinking, in groups, and giving a voice to the voiceless, entails encouraging children who are quiet or less confident to find their voice and express themselves, and therefore ensuring that other children do not interrupt or dominate discussions.

Chapter 4 emphasized that tasks must be sufficiently challenging, but not too difficult, that is, within the child's Zone of Proximal Development (ZPD). In Olson's words (2001: 113), 'Discovery provides a large problem space; expository teaching a more delimited one. Each has its risks. Too large a problem space and a child may never hit on a solution; define it too narrowly and a student may simply memorize a solution.' This makes the task of structuring knowledge, so that it is matched to the children's level of understanding, both important and demanding, and highlights the close link between pedagogy and assessment.

To teach reciprocally, teachers must be attuned to how children feel and try to look through the lens of childhood, as far as possible, to understand how young children see the world and why they may have misconceptions or interpret the world in the ways that they do. As Hattie (2009) indicates, feedback *to* the teacher enables him or her to understand a child or group more accurately. This involves teachers watching, and listening to children, far more than telling them, and is essential both to enable sensitive teaching and to provide the basis for accurate feedback *from* the teacher.

Teachers require a wide repertoire of pedagogies to present material and encourage children to represent their experiences in a variety of ways. Stories, images, analogies and metaphors are essential components of the teacher's toolkit in every subject area. Telling is only one tool, and often a rather blunt, ineffective one, especially with young children (see Reed, 2001), although many children and parents may prefer it. As Engel (2015: 103–6) suggests, schools and teachers tend to discourage curiosity. The age when children start to be taught formally may be more influential in their curiosity and creativity being restricted than is usually thought. In Katz's words (2003: 368), 'If formal instruction is introduced too early, too intensely and too abstractly, the children may indeed learn the instructed knowledge and skills, but they may do so at the expense of the disposition to use them.' Therefore, teachers should be wary of using formal instruction with very young children rather than providing extensive opportunities to play, to explore and to be curious. For teachers to maintain young children's sense of agency and voice requires an approach based more on apprenticeship and facilitation than direct instruction – on showing, encouraging, guiding and reassuring more than telling. Such an approach is time consuming and difficult particularly in the busy world of the primary classroom in a culture of performativity.

While there is a danger of expecting too much of children too soon, teachers must also avoid infantilizing them by having low expectations of what they can do or seeing expectations only in relation to the standards agenda and conforming behaviour. If children are expected to take risks, to listen carefully to each other, to speak out and to discuss and challenge each other and the teacher, this must be explicitly encouraged. If children are expected to manifest a sense of agency, they must be allowed to try their own approach and make mistakes. Encouraging children to persevere requires challenging tasks which take time to complete, and developing teamwork must involve children regularly working cooperatively in groups. To enable this, teachers must provide time, space and opportunities for activity and exploration and for discussion, reflection and silence.

Teachers must differentiate if children's individual needs are to be met. However, differentiation is far more subtle than placing children into groups of similar ability or attainment. While children are frequently grouped by ability – or teachers' perceptions of this – and are likely, given the choice, to work mainly with their friends, there is a strong argument to group children in a variety of ways, such as with mixed abilities and backgrounds and sometimes single sex groups, dependent on what a teacher hopes to achieve. For instance, mixed groups may be less popular with children but provide a context for them to interact with those from different backgrounds, and so for ideas and stereotypes to be challenged and bridging capital to be created.

If the contribution of different cultures is to be celebrated and teamwork developed, children must have frequent opportunities to work and cooperate in groups with those who are different, not just with their friends. If children are to learn not to see themselves, and those like them, as normal and others as strange, and increasingly to recognize what is taken for granted in their own culture, they need to compare and contrast, but difference should not be overemphasized, and it is likely to be more fruitful to start by looking for similarities than differences.

Altering teachers' pedagogy requires a change of beliefs and attitudes. How teachers understand young children in the early stages of learning English as an additional language provides one example. Such children must not be regarded as, or grouped unthinkingly with, children with cognitive difficulties. Teachers must treat such children as capable, but inexperienced, learners, for instance supporting their emerging command of English by using visual cues and allowing each child time to rehearse his or her responses.

Adopting an apprenticeship approach involves altering the dynamics of the primary classroom (see Eaude, 2018a, chapter 2 for a fuller discussion of what follows). For teachers actually to change how they teach and embed such changes is hard partly because this involves breaking deep-rooted habits, but also because structural reasons and intrapersonal ones militate against such change.

One obvious feature of most primary classrooms is the number of children, all with different backgrounds, personalities and interests. Among the consequences for children are delay, denial (i.e. not being able to do what they want), interruption and social distraction (see Pollard, 1985: 41–2). And, as Jackson (1968) indicates, classrooms are inherently competitive places, where comparisons are constantly made. For many young children, joining and being part of a large group is hard, not least because they receive adult attention less, and less immediately, than they are used to. The desire to belong easily leads to a wish to gain attention or to disappear into the crowd. And young children find it hard to regulate their responses. As a result, behaviour which may seem funny or disrupts the class tends to encourage other children to copy it; and the fear of embarrassment leads many children to avoid taking risks.

As Pollard (1985, 1996) indicates, many implicit rules operate in the primary classroom to ensure that children and the teacher remain within their comfort zones and avoid the anxiety which accompanies significant challenges to their identities as learners and teachers. To summarize Pollard with Filer's argument (1996: 90–1), pupils and teachers interact to produce taken-for-granted understandings and rules about behaviour in classrooms, a working consensus, the product of an often-implicit negotiation between children and teacher, though usually the teacher controls the explicit rules. Such a consensus determines, for instance, who is in charge of the talk and the amount of work that is acceptable, and is not easily altered.

Bibby indicates (2011: 2) that teachers experience conflicting emotions, mostly unconsciously, and struggle to hold together the love and the hate, the desire and the fear they feel. She calls teaching an 'impossible profession', arguing (2011: 6) that

- our actions are influenced by a dynamic unconscious which we can never access directly or know completely;
- we are defended subjects in the sense that we all have to – and do – erect defences, often unconscious, to manage the anxieties we face; and

- society and culture help to shape our unconscious – that is, we are psychosocial beings.

This, especially the unconscious aspect, which exerts influence all the time, makes it hard for teachers to change how they teach. For instance, while teachers must seek to provide emotional stability, teaching young children often sets off emotional triggers, bringing out the 'child within', especially when working with a demanding class. As a result, teachers tend to over-control. To avoid this but provide emotional stability, teachers must be aware of what triggers their own emotional responses, so that they can try consciously to avoid over-reacting.

Given the importance for young children of example who teachers are, and how they act, matters more than what they know. Teachers must demonstrate qualities and dispositions such as patience, resilience and humility, and manifest respect, passion and enthusiasm to encourage these in children. They must be prepared to encourage children to take risks, and reflect on and learn from their mistakes, and to do so themselves. However, while teachers need to exercise informed judgement and have the confidence to do so, they must, if children are to remain curious, creative and critical, avoid too great a certainty and adopt a stance which Claxton describes as 'confident uncertainty'.

## Reviewing approaches to assessment and planning

As discussed, children from a young age are categorized, and judged, mainly on how well they can perform in tests of reading, writing and mathematics – and by their behaviour. Adopting a holistic approach has significant implications for assessment, both in making assessment methods more appropriate and culturally sensitive and in what is assessed, to take account of the whole child and his or her identities and achievements.

Let us distinguish between assessment and testing. The shaping of identities and cultural development are not testable meaningfully, though such processes can be assessed. Holistic assessment is not simply concerned with testing how well information has been memorized. As Bruner argued, (see Nurse and Headington, 1999: 15), children should be judged on what they can generate from what they know – how well they can leap the barrier from learning to thinking, that is as active and creative learners. A holistic approach does not ignore data, but is not data driven and focuses on wider aspects such as what a child has achieved and who she or he is, and may become.

The lack of reliability of current assessment procedures, especially for young children, where the context of a task may be unfamiliar to some groups and results are skewed disproportionately to disadvantage children according to their gender, ethnicity and especially class is well established. As well as ensuring that assessment procedures must be fairer and subtler, a holistic approach demands that assessment is predominantly used formatively, to indicate what a child has to do to improve, not only in relation to attainment but more broadly (see Black and Wiliam, 1998 and Eaude, 2018a: 121–6 for more detailed discussions of formative assessment). Moreover, how teachers teach must be constantly informed by ongoing assessment of children's current level of understanding and therefore whether the activity should be altered. This is essential if teachers are to create the pedagogical content knowledge necessary to structure knowledge appropriately and to enhance children's learning (see Eaude, 2018a: 104–8).

In Gipps's (1999: 383) words, 'Passing responsibility for assessment to the student is crucial as it helps them to develop as self-monitoring learners.' While very young children may find this tricky, teachers can establish the expectation that children will think about what they can do well, find hard and should do to improve, not just in terms of school work but more broadly – and support them as they do so.

Teachers should be cautious of labelling young children by ability, especially those children who are unfamiliar with the expectations and demands of schools. Diagnoses and labels frequently depend to a large extent on the school's, and the teacher's, assumptions about children's backgrounds. While labels can help to explain children's strengths and difficulties, they too easily limit those who are labelled and become self-fulfilling. Labelling children is detrimental when this, however unintentionally, encourages in children the belief that their abilities or identities cannot be changed or leads them to identify themselves based mainly on how they have been labelled.

Chapter 6 raised the question to what extent qualities and dispositions are context-specific or transferable from one context to another. Many are, to some extent, transferable. For instance, becoming more confident as a writer, or more reflective about other people's responses, may help a child to be more confident or reflective in other activities. This is not always the case, but to help children develop and strengthen such qualities teachers have to discover strengths on which to build and areas where a child needs additional support. A holistic approach seeks to assess strengths and weaknesses, children's existing funds of knowledge and what they can do, as well as their misconceptions and what they find difficult. Understanding the barriers which a child faces must not be an excuse for low attainment or poor behaviour but can help explain why a particular child may find some aspect of learning or behaviour difficult, or may be confident in one area but not in another. Doing so can help teachers to recognize how children's existing identities facilitate some kinds of learning and inhibit others – and what to do about it.

Sometimes, such assessment may make it clear what adults should do. At others, it may indicate that adults should back off and allow the child to explore his or her emerging identity. For example, I recall a six-year-old boy whose parents were understandably worried that since he wore girls' clothes and behaved flamboyantly he would be teased and bullied. After discussion, we left the decision in his hands – and he soon adopted more conventional clothing. However, if he had been forbidden to dress like that, a different outcome might have resulted. Such judgements are usually best made on the basis of collective discussion.

To reveal what may be hidden, or far from obvious, assessment should take place mainly in contexts familiar to the child, over a long period of time. If children are to be enabled rather than constrained, assessment needs to be divergent rather than convergent – that is, focused more on what children can, or may be able to, do rather than on the curriculum or what the teacher requires. For example, portfolios of work, collected over time, are frequently far more revealing than just looking at test scores.

Holistic assessment requires teachers, and other adults, to be aware of individuals' backgrounds and previous experience. Teachers must try to avoid careless assumptions about children's families, given the number of families where children do not live with both parents, are part of reconstituted families, have parents of the same gender or were adopted or born following IVF. At the least, teachers need to know these and some facts such as the child's place in the family, first language and physical and mental health, where she or he has lived previously, whether his or her family has migrated and if so, to which generation after migration the child belongs. More sensitive information about domestic arrangements and family difficulties may help in understanding a child better – and so are aspects to be considered in assessing the whole child.

Much assessment is integral to teaching and continuous. However, in assessing a child with complex needs or who is puzzling, the involvement of a wide range of people who know him or her helps to ensure that different aspects of a child's history in terms of health and development, physically, linguistically and in other ways are known. But schools are associated by many parents with failure or they may not know what is expected or feel excluded or blamed. Many parents may not understand the school's approach, or disagree with it, or be too scared to ask or challenge professionals. Therefore, including such parents is vital but requires sensitivity.

One group for whom holistic assessment is particularly revealing is children whose first language is not English. This should usually involve the parents/carers, and possibly another adult who speaks the first language, support staff and other professionals involved and if possible the child herself or himself. I recall one six-year-old who spoke very little English and was not making progress. For some months, we assumed that he was finding it hard to settle and waited to see if he would do so. However, when we were still puzzled as to whether he had learning difficulties, separate from his poor command of English, discussion between his parents and teachers, including bilingual staff, revealed that he had travelled between countries frequently and had not gained a secure command of any language. As a result, he did not have a secure linguistic basis on which to build a secure grasp of English and was making little progress and confused about the whole experience and expectations of school. While overtly related to his language development, this collective assessment illuminated why he was confused more generally and enabled his teachers to adopt a more appropriate approach. This illustrates the importance of involving parents and other professionals and, where necessary and possible, those who speak the child's (and often the parents') first language to explore what has happened previously and cultural assumptions.

The implications of a holistic approach for teachers' planning follow logically from the previous discussion. Among them are that children must be enabled and encouraged to take part in a broad range of meaningful experiences and activities where their imagination and creativity is not tightly constrained. As Engel (2015: 190) suggests, teachers should fill classrooms with the kinds of complexity that invites inquiry and provide children with interesting materials, seductive details and desirable difficulty.

Children must have some choice and agency in what they do, with opportunities to work on their own and with other children and to discuss in both small and large groups, and must be encouraged, and given time and permission, to think and to challenge each other and the teacher. This implies that planning must be open-ended and long-term, with broad objectives related to the qualities and dispositions teachers wish to strengthen. For instance, children must work with others if cooperation and teamwork are to be encouraged and in mixed groups if they are to recognize and celebrate difference. In short-term planning, of individual lessons, a considerable degree of flexibility must be included if teachers are to respond promptly to children's comments and questions.

This chapter has argued that helping to strengthen all children's identities and to combat the historic disadvantage experienced by many groups calls for an approach which

- is sensitive to such disadvantage without allowing this to become an excuse;
- adopts a holistic, formative and divergent approach, which takes account of, and draws on, children's existing funds of knowledge, recognizing their knowledge has to be extended into new, often unfamiliar, areas; and
- provides a broad range of opportunities which encourages children's agency within an inclusive and supportive learning community.

Having reached the end of Part III, it is time to draw together the argument of the whole book.

# Conclusion

## Reflecting on identities, cultures and belonging

This book has wound its way through complicated and difficult terrain. The range and complexity of the issues discussed means that many are inevitably matters of debate and it has been impossible to consider some in great depth. But how young children construct robust but flexible identities, and are best helped to do so, is profoundly important and too often overlooked.

Inevitably, I have not managed to escape entirely from my own assumptions, but have explored and challenged many of these, and encouraged you to question your own, including some which may seem obvious. In emphasizing that young children should take risks, I have done so myself and tried to encourage readers to do so.

I have argued that the world is, and will be, one of constant change and is harder for children to navigate than in the past. Social and cultural changes have led to most people having more fragmented identities and split loyalties than previously, with many of the structures which provided and supported a sense of identity no longer available. While social attitudes have altered to some extent in recent years, many of the assumptions and structures which lead to, and reinforce, discrimination remain and are deep-rooted.

Although many of the crude stereotypes common when I was a child – about women, black-skinned people, foreigners and the disabled – are less evident, young children still live in a world where

- women, people of colour, those from socio-economically disadvantaged backgrounds and those with disabilities are often portrayed in stereotypical ways or not visible enough; and
- those from such backgrounds remain disadvantaged, especially when one or more of these factors intersect.

For instance, attitudes towards children with a range of disabilities have improved dramatically in the last fifty years, so that such children are much more visible and included outside the home and in mainstream classrooms. However, underlying, unconscious bias easily leads adults to overprotect children with disabilities and to have low expectations of what they can achieve. Similarly, stereotypical, often unconscious, assumptions about girls, children of colour, and those from working-class backgrounds, are still common. However, these assumptions often remain hidden especially to those who do not experience the discrimination which results. Individualism and competitiveness may equip some children to succeed in many respects but at the risk of those children becoming brittle and uncaring and other children, especially those already disadvantaged, being left with a feeling of failure and exclusion. The outcomes highlighted in Chapter 1 suggest that it is the behaviour and attitudes of the powerful, especially those of white men, and current models of masculinity, and the structures which perpetuate disadvantage, which most need to change.

In most 'Western' societies, the influence of organized religion has diminished with increasing secularization. However, globalization has led to a greater diversity, with religious affiliation remaining a central element of identity for a significant minority. The view in secular societies of religion as a largely private matter is not shared across all cultures but discourages public manifestations of religious affiliation. As a result, those children for whom religion forms an important aspect of their identity may feel split between the private world of home and faith community and the more public world of school and the street; and those with little knowledge or experience of religion may come to see people of faith as odd and possibly 'other', especially if such impressions are reinforced at home and not countered elsewhere.

People are not all the same, though we share many commonalities. We all have multiple, intersecting and often conflicting identities, some personal and private, some more public and open to the gaze, admiration or scorn of other people. These identities are influenced by factors such as gender, race, home language (and dialect and accent), class and religion, as well as upbringing and the macro-culture, and the assumptions which underlie these. Such factors do not determine identities, but they affect how children are perceived and how they feel about themselves – and therefore their sense of self. While some aspects of any individual's identity depend on genetics and temperament, most are learned and open to change, at least in some respects.

Chapter 1 highlighted that culture is normative, passing on what is deemed to be of value, but not static. Culture both reflects and influences how people think and act. Therefore, culture, broadly understood, is potentially an agent of both individual and social change and the medium in which identities are constructed and influenced. Who we are, and become, as individuals, is shaped partly by the micro-cultures and communities to which we belong. We are not independent, completely autonomous beings, but interdependent ones, bound together, but also separated, by practices and underlying beliefs and assumptions associated with, and reinforced by, the cultures we inhabit.

I have argued that to cope with, and flourish in, a world of constant, unforeseeable, change, and to contribute to creating a more just and sustainable world, all children

- must develop coherent and robust identities and a sense of agency to be able to respond flexibly to new situations;
- have a sense of belonging and an increasingly deep understanding of themselves, their own cultures and other people and cultures; and
- develop and strengthen the values, qualities and dispositions and the motivation to exercise these in unfamiliar contexts, even when the going gets tough,

and that such identities can, and must, be nurtured from an early age.

While recognizing that which values and qualities are prioritized will vary to some extent between cultures, I have suggested that children require those associated with global citizenship if their identities are to be robust but flexible. As discussed in Chapter 3, these include compassion, respect for other people, confidence, resilience and the ability to work cooperatively. To strengthen such qualities, children must have a sense of personal agency, the belief that change is possible, but also a sense of belonging, if they are not to feel isolated and rudderless.

Constructing such identities is difficult for many children in a world characterized by fragmentation of many of the structures which have traditionally provided a sense of belonging, the insecurity which accompanies this and the seductive messages about success and belonging presented through the media and on the street. It is especially hard for those from backgrounds characterized by unpredictability and historic disadvantage – or both – who grow up without the support provided by relationships of love and care, those children described as unanchored ships.

In writing this book, I have been struck by how similar the construction of young children's identities is to how they learn to understand and use language. Facility in using language, whether heard or spoken, is picked up naturally, by using words to communicate without much direct instruction, through a reciprocal process where children hear particular forms of spoken language, with variations of use, tone and accent. From this, and the feedback to reinforce or correct what they do, children learn to rehearse and to replicate what they say as a way of communicating their wants and ideas, but often with subtle changes and new mannerisms, and sometimes an accent or a stammer. Gradually, children's repertoire and confidence grows, along with an awareness of when to speak in one way, when in another, but such awareness is often tacit or only partly conscious.

Identities are constructed in similar ways, individually but reciprocally. Identities depend on feelings about who one is, influenced by who one is seen to be, rather than who one 'is'. We are always in the process of becoming. Identities do not develop predictably or evenly through a linear, stage-related process, but are constructed – and constantly reconstructed, as children explore, shed old identities and graft or overlay new on to existing ones. While true throughout the life cycle, this is particularly evident and significant in childhood and adolescence.

The micro-cultures in which children grow up, especially the home and immediate community, exert the strongest influence on how their identities are shaped. While the home and formal settings remain influential, the peer group becomes increasingly so as children approach adolescence, given their wish for a sense of belonging. The fear of embarrassment, especially in public, comes to matter more, leading to children being strongly motivated by how they are perceived within their peer group.

Chapter 3 highlighted how children are influenced by the macro-culture, especially through the media, with unkind, and sometimes violent, behaviour condoned and even celebrated. Despite recent social and cultural changes, the macro-culture in most societies continues to provide a strongly genderized and racialized view of identities. Images of success are based mainly on looks and possessions, encouraging the belief that these will lead to happiness, rather than long-term happiness and a secure sense of self resulting from a broader, less individualistic, sense of well-being.

One change with considerable implications is the impact of technology, so that children will have to adapt to new technologies such as the increased use of robotics and artificial intelligence. Technologies have great potential for good, especially in broadening children's horizons and most children are more adaptable than adults assume. However, the immediacy of responses expected may discourage sustained attention, except when children are strongly motivated. The addictive quality of technology is likely to be harmful to some children. Moreover, children may easily become more risk averse if relying on technology, when other pressures also encourage this.

Identities are not just a matter of individual choice, however much that message may be given. Choice appears to be on offer, though young children are often ill-equipped to exercise such choice appropriately. The influence of television, advertising and social media, the powerful, seductive messages about success and consumerism and the constant comparison with other people and how they look can easily encourage children – and adults – to focus on themselves and their image and to become narcissistic and brittle. Adults should steer children away from a wish always to be perfect. The individualism, obsession with oneself and constant comparison with others which the macro-culture promotes militate against children developing robust identities.

## Unravelling the implications for young children

Children construct and reshape their identities as a constantly changing narrative from very early childhood, through pre-adolescence and beyond. This happens incrementally over a long time, involving many small steps as each child tries to make sense of what she or he experiences to find his or her place in the world and creates a coherent narrative, of who she or he is, and may become. The process is more like a marathon than a sprint.

Constructing new identities is a natural part of growing up, though at times a puzzling one. Children are, and must be allowed to be, active creators of their own identities, trying to make sense of who they are and where they fit in. However, many of the deepest, most enduring patterns of behaviour and response are formed in early childhood. These patterns are more influential than is sometimes recognized and, to some extent, survive the turmoil of adolescence. For instance, the models of attachment formed in infancy and the behaviours and expectations associated with gender, race and class are learned early and hard to change thereafter. Moreover, remembering the importance of self-esteem and how other people's perceptions affect this, what may seem to an adult superficial and transient – such as size, wearing glasses, characters on TV or imaginary friends – and what these signify about whether, and where, one belongs may be very significant to young children.

Identities are, and become, fragile for many reasons, depending to some extent on adult expectations related to race, gender, class and ability, though even more so by the reality of not being cared for and of poverty and discrimination. Children's self-esteem and identities are more easily damaged and undermined than built up, especially those from backgrounds with a history of insecurity, discrimination or exclusion. Children – and adults – must recognize that characteristics such as intelligence and ability are not fixed but can be strengthened by perseverance and trying again, possibly with a different approach or additional support.

As the quotation from Geertz at the start of Chapter 7 indicates, seeing very young children as active learners demands 'a rethinking of the entire educational process'. No one doubts that children need to become literate and numerate, and understand science and technology, but a holistic approach aspires to far more than this. In particular, it calls for a greater emphasis, both in schools and more widely, on

- physical and mental health;
- aspects of personal growth such as what in England is called spiritual, moral, cultural and social development;
- behaviour being based on intrinsic motivation rather than the promise of reward or the fear of punishment;
- practical activity and procedural knowledge; and
- a broad and balanced range of opportunities.

Young children require enough sleep and a diet which will keep them physically healthy. They must feel safe and be protected from excessive stress, though not overprotected, if they are not to become what Hare described as 'emotional toffees'. Anxiety must be contained, if children's creativity is to flourish and they are to exercise a sense of agency. Children benefit from being active and having the time and space to play on their own and with other children. They need plenty of opportunities to relax and enjoy each other's, and adults', company and to question and reflect.

Each child benefits from being respected for who she or he is and to be loved and cared for. However, this does not entail them being left unchallenged, or wrapped in cotton wool. All children require both haven and challenge, though some more of one than the other, with these needs varying over time and according to the context, as well as individually. For instance, while boys and girls have similar needs, these vary somewhat. Both may need encouragement to take part, and persist, in activities not traditionally associated with their gender – such as reading fiction or singing for boys and science and some sorts of sport for girls. Boys tend to require more help to listen and take turns, to express their emotions and to extend their emotional repertoire, and girls encouragement to be assertive and more confident. And while all children require opportunities to care for others, boys, who are frequently less used to doing so, benefit particularly from such opportunities and so gain a greater empathy for other people.

Similar considerations apply to children of different ethnic groups and social backgrounds. Those from socio-economically disadvantaged backgrounds may need encouragement to be confident if they are to gain a sense of agency and avoid becoming disengaged, and possibly disaffected. Children from historically advantaged groups must learn to be respectful of unfamiliar cultures and children from varied backgrounds if they are to avoid a sense of superiority or automatic entitlement. Each child is an individual with needs that vary, depending on their background and previous experience.

Part II emphasized the extent to which young children rely more on emotional than cognitive processes. However, they must learn to regulate their behaviour and to create an extensive emotional repertoire – which many boys in particular find hard because of early socialization and adult expectations. This book has advocated an approach where children learn to conduct themselves and manifest the qualities associated with global citizenship based on intrinsic motivation – acting and interacting appropriately when unobserved by others, despite pressures to do otherwise. Since identities are constructed mainly in spaces to which adults have limited access, children must be motivated intrinsically to enable them to deal with uncertainty and to cope with the difficulties they encounter, both now and subsequently. Encouraging children's agency and intrinsic motivation involves them learning to act on the basis of values and reflection, rather than self-interest and impulse, and their behaviour being based increasingly on general maxims and rules of thumb, though very young children, and those who find it difficult to recognize how other people feel, may require more definite rules.

Most children benefit from a broad range of experiences and activities. This does not necessarily make them more compassionate or empathetic, though it may help to do so. But for a child to have several areas where she or he feels secure and confident helps to make his or her identity more robust, like a table with several legs. Emphasizing one element of identity to the exclusion of others tends to lead to brittleness.

If children are to be open to, and develop, new ideas, without following the latest fad, they require creativity, curiosity, imagination and the habits and dispositions associated with critical thinking. These encourage children constantly to question and challenge what they may have learned to take for granted, in a world where information is readily available, but its veracity often questionable, and respond appropriately and sensitively. Moreover, children must learn that information, however factual it may appear, is open to question and interpretation and to be respectful but not uncritical towards adults, which many young children may find difficult.

All children, especially those from disadvantaged backgrounds, benefit from their cultural horizons being extended, to build up the cultural capital necessary to succeed in different contexts. Experiences which enable this may include visits to the theatre, museums and places of interest, but also to the park and the seaside – experiences which many privileged children and adults may, wrongly, take for granted. Moreover, a breadth of experiences makes it more likely that all children will welcome diversity and create bridging capital.

The idea that identities are just caught or taught is simplistic. Much of what helps in constructing robust identities is learned indirectly and subliminally, as if by osmosis, without conscious awareness, through participation in communities of practice. A holistic approach emphasizes aspects such as example, relationships and environments in how children make sense of experience, and are helped to do so, more than what children are told or taught explicitly. However, since children learn by example to a large extent without conscious thought, they may imitate what is undesirable, and not pick up what matters most. So, their attention frequently has to be drawn to what to practice – and so internalize – and when they act appropriately this needs to be reinforced.

Children need time and space to watch, listen, copy and reflect if they are to make sense of the mixed messages they receive. A sense of agency helps them to do so from an early age. However, this does not mean that children should be allowed to do as they wish or that adults should not seek to exert influence and provide support and guidance. For instance, children's actions and views must be challenged when they are unkind or hurtful and when they objectify other people on the basis of appearance. But it is no less important that when they act appropriately – such as courageously, generously or thoughtfully – adults express their approval to reinforce this.

## Exploring the challenges for adults

Structures and boundaries are necessary to enable creativity to flourish, but these must have some flexibility if they are not to become constraints. Boundaries, structures, routines and rituals help to establish collective expectations, but tight structures easily become limiting and oppressive. Being able to manage these flexibly calls for adults who are attuned to particular groups and individuals and sensitive to their varied cultures and backgrounds, and not too controlling. Since the boundaries between early childhood and pre-adolescence are fluid, adults must be aware of individual children's likely responses and their capacity to cope with the unexpected.

Such considerations have led to my advocacy of an apprenticeship approach, with adults' roles mainly that of steering and guiding, where children, right from the start, are treated as if capable, but supported as necessary, with a gradual transfer of control and agency.

While helping children negotiate the construction of their identities may seem, and is, complex, adults must not be paralysed by the complexities. Many of the implications are surprisingly simple, such as that loving, and caring for, children and the sorts of people they become matter more than pressurizing them to succeed academically at the expense of the latter. Adults should avoid, or alleviate as much as possible, children being under too much stress, especially those who experience chronic or intense stress in other parts of their lives. Adults need to encourage children's sense of agency and provide guidance and support, rather than impose their own assumptions or create a sense of dependence.

There is no guarantee that adults can ensure that children will develop robust but flexible identities, but they can try to establish the foundations. Such foundations must be broad, as no one knows how any individual will turn out – and many different possibilities should remain open. An approach based on virtue ethics, which emphasizes the sort of person a child is and will become, and focuses on qualities and dispositions, seems most appropriate to equip children for a changing world.

The most significant influence is that of the home, with parents occupying a central role in how children's identities are constructed and shaped, remembering primary socialization. Individuals and societies inevitably differ on what the role of the home, faith and other groups and schools should be, but Chapter 8 emphasized that adults must work together and outlined some of the challenges in doing so. A holistic approach involves a range of adults collaborating to try to minimize the often-hard-to-see barriers both in schooling systems and more widely. These barriers include discrimination based on factors such as gender, race and socio-economic background, the lack (or cost) of opportunities and a low level of confidence and negative feelings about formal education. In some respects, adults can compensate for what children miss out on elsewhere. This is not just a case of school compensating for home, but also those outside schools compensating for what children do not experience at school.

Adults, especially teachers, must seek to value, rather than erase, children's existing cultural identities and take account of differences but not be 'blind' to children's gender, colour or socio-economic background. Trying to treat everyone the same ignores existing patterns of discrimination and in so doing helps, however unintentionally, to perpetuate these. Adults must support those who are discriminated against and work to change the behaviour and attitudes of those doing the discriminating. For instance, sexist, racist and homophobic views must be challenged, particularly in formal settings, as these may be reinforced elsewhere. In particular, young children must be encouraged to focus less on themselves and to build up empathy, and consideration, for other people, so helping in the long term to avoid bigotry and extremism.

Much of what I have written suggests that adults should be, to some extent, counter-cultural in the current culture of materialism and consumerism, in that children should be encouraged and enabled to question and challenge received wisdom – and what they may take for granted. This may involve questioning ideas such as that success is achieved by becoming a celebrity or having good looks rather than by persistence and practice, and helping children to recognize that much of what is most worthwhile in life cannot be measured. It may entail helping boys and girls to consider different ways of being masculine or feminine from those with which they are familiar. Similar considerations apply in relation to race, class and religion, recognizing that such issues may have to be handled with great sensitivity. However difficult this may be, gradually changing these, and the structures which limit children's opportunities, is necessary if the status quo is not to remain as it is.

Chapter 7 explored how unconscious bias affects attitudes, and so behaviours, without individuals necessarily being aware of this. Adults must try to avoid, and help children avoid, stereotyping individuals based on crude preconceptions and generalizations about their backgrounds and the assumptions which accompany this, such as that all, or most, people in Africa are seen as poor or that anything other than a tiny minority of Muslims are terrorists. Apart from being inaccurate, such views help to create and perpetuate stereotypes.

Adults must examine, challenge and sometimes try to change their own assumptions. Given that other societies and cultures have differing views of childhood, and how children should be brought up, from that current in 'Western' societies, adults should be wary of believing that their own assumptions and those of their own culture are correct. In many respects, the approach adopted in WEIRD (Western, educated, industrialized, rich democracies) societies, especially in how young children are expected to respond to adults, is not self-evidently beneficial, for instance in overprotecting and over-controlling children. Despite the benefits of 'concerted cultivation' and an environment where discussion is encouraged, children must also be allowed time and space to develop naturally without too much pressure from adults. Children learning to watch, listen and wait, rather than always being the centre of attention, or having lives which are not always fully occupied, is something that many middle-class parents can learn from other cultures. Such considerations should act as a warning against complacency and a call to humility.

Many children find it hard when adult expectations, and ways of trying to ensure that children meet these, including teaching methods, are different at home or in religious settings and at school. For instance, rules may be strict in the former, with children expected to conform and punished if they do not; whereas at school the same children may be expected to make difficult decisions and choices when they are less used to doing so. The result can often be confusion, which, when combined with feelings of resentment and adult stereotyping, can easily lead to children becoming disaffected. Adults must be aware that young children may find adapting to different approaches and expectations hard, and help them manage transitions between settings, while also enabling to cope with new challenges.

The types of environment and expectation which adults create and the qualities and dispositions they manifest and model really matter. As Jackson et al. (1993) indicate, what is valued is manifested by what people do far more than what they say. In working with young children, adults must be positive and optimistic, though also realistic, and be sympathetic to children's difficulties and concerns. If children are to learn to be compassionate, considerate and respectful, they must be treated in such ways. If children are to celebrate diversity and create bridging capital, adults must do so. Adults must try to 'walk the talk', though none of us can do so all the time.

Children often take more notice of what other trusted or respected adults say and do than of their parents. Opportunities for intergenerational and informal learning, in groups such as those associated with places of worship and sports clubs, have the potential to provide valuable role models, exert influence on how children respond to the messages promoted in the media and mitigate the pressure to be popular with one's peer group. In an increasingly diverse world, all children benefit from seeing a range of adults with different types of expectation and manifesting such qualities, rather than only those of a particular gender, ethnicity, class or ability doing so.

This discussion has raised several puzzles where adults have to balance different priorities and exercise judgement in deciding how to respond. For instance, adults have a responsibility to protect children, also to try and ensure that they are equipped to deal with difficulty and uncertainty and to protect themselves in ways other than through aggression. Children, especially those backgrounds of unpredictable and confusing responses, benefit from predictability, but not too safe an environment. Adopting an apprenticeship approach requires sensitivity, judgement, time and patience.

## Summarizing what a holistic education implies for teachers, schools and policy

I have argued that education has the potential to transform both individuals and society, but that a holistic approach calls for rethinking the aims of education, particularly those associated with schooling, and radical changes to the curriculum, pedagogy and assessment. This does not entail adding new subjects or programmes to the formal curriculum, but for how schools operate to change so that teachers are encouraged to be more sensitive to differences of background and culture and draw on, and extend, children's existing funds of knowledge. If all children are to experience learning as meaningful and engaging, teachers must take more account of children's and families' cultural capital and the extent to which those from historically disadvantaged backgrounds may feel out of place, and therefore consider how schools can adapt and become more inclusive.

The qualities and dispositions associated with global citizenship are strengthened through a wide range of opportunities and experiences. Play, drama and stories are vital in how children come to understand themselves and the world they inhabit. The humanities and the arts, well taught, are essential, not just desirable, in the education of the whole child and the shaping of coherent identities. Becoming confident users of language, able to engage in dialogue with other people, helps children to understand themselves and other people. Children benefit from being introduced to a wide and diverse range of music, art and literature, not just those deemed to be 'high culture' or from Western sources. While true for all young children, such a curriculum matters especially for those from backgrounds where their experience has been limited for whatever reason.

If children are to understand and respect diverse views and abilities, and to learn to work cooperatively with those who are different, they must work in groups with those with a range of backgrounds and aptitudes, not always with those who are broadly similar, whether in terms of gender, ethnicity, background or (perceived) ability.

Given that many parents associate school with failure and that worries about teaching methods and issues such as food and clothing create significant anxiety, schools and teachers must strive to create environments which are hospitable and welcoming to parents as well as children. Environments must be adapted to take account of such concerns to some extent, rather than expecting children and parents always to adapt to the school environment. Moreover, teachers must strive to

- be self-reflective to try and avoid unconscious bias and avoid deficit models where children are judged by their backgrounds rather than their behaviours and achievements;
- be aware of, and resist, institutional racism and genderism, such as where low expectations are created by how children are grouped and low aspirations and attainment reinforced; and
- discuss such issues regularly with other colleagues, as countering unconscious bias on one's own is so hard.

Classroom teachers are well placed to lead on a holistic education, though they must work in collaboration with other adults. Classroom teachers are influential in helping shape each child's identities not just as a mathematician, historian or reader but more broadly as a learner and as a person, given the long and close relationship which can be created over time. They can help create and sustain hospitable environments in which children feel safe and are treated with respect and encouraged to build relationships which are trusting but not over-trusting. But they must encourage imagination and creativity across the whole curriculum, and try to create environments which discourage intense interpersonal competitiveness, if children are to become resilient, empathetic and compassionate.

Since, as Alexander (2010: 308) argues, 'pupils will not learn to think for themselves if their teachers are expected to do as they are told', teachers must exercise their initiative and even be on occasion bloody-minded, not just compliant deliverers. Such a view requires the teacher's role to be rethought. In Hargreaves (2003: 161) words, 'Teachers are not deliverers but developers of learning.' Those who focus only on teaching techniques and curriculum standards ... promote a diminished view of teaching and teacher professionalism that has no place in a sophisticated knowledge society.'

Adopting an approach based more on facilitation than didactic instruction is not easy. The discussion in Chapter 9 of the dynamics of the primary classroom, as well as the constraints imposed by policy, indicate why it is so hard for teachers to change their habits. Teachers must be aware, and take account, of the asymmetry of power between themselves and children and be careful not to misuse their power, while retaining their authority and asserting this firmly but flexibly. They should be careful not to impose their views, but rather try to demonstrate how to act and interact appropriately.

Teachers must be attuned, as far as possible, to individual children and be aware of beliefs and practices within the family and the communities in which children have grown up, and adopt broad, divergent and culturally sensitive approaches to assessment. They must take account of many factors in understanding and assessing young children. An individual's actions may be understood somewhat differently when viewed through different lenses such as those of gender, race, class and physical ability, and how these intersect with each other. But trying to understand why a child may be finding life hard must be used to decide how best to support him or her rather than as an excuse for underachievement or low expectations.

While it is hazardous to make recommendations in relation to educational policy, since this is frequently system-specific, as Alexander (2000) argued, some comments in relation to the international trends outlined in Chapter 3 may be appropriate.

Given the importance of diverse role models, and that most adults who work in primary schools are female, middle-class and white, more teachers, and other adults, from other groups should be recruited, not least because this is likely to help discrimination and bias to be recognized and challenged. However, the qualities which adults manifest are ultimately more important than their physical characteristics.

A narrowly focused educational system affects both individuals and societies adversely in preparing for an unknown future. A change of what one hopes to achieve implies a change of how young children are taught and what is emphasized. The construction of robust but flexible identities calls for a broad and balanced curriculum. While learning to be a confident reader, writer and mathematician is important, a schooling system in which performance in tests of literacy and numeracy become the main criterion of success institutionalizes low aspirations. Propositional knowledge and skills matter but the qualities and dispositions which affect the sort of person a child is, and will become, even more so.

The notion of standards based on what can be measured in tests of some aspects of English and mathematics and the marginalization of the humanities and the arts must be changed. Assessment must be more holistic, culturally sensitive and appropriate for young children; and inspection be used to encourage the education of the whole child, with more trust placed in teachers and their judgement, rather than to ensure performativity and compliance.

However, moving away from a performativity culture in schools is a significant challenge in the current outcome- and data-led context. Following Nussbaum, and others, I have suggested that a narrow, instrumentalist curriculum limits children's ability to become the active and engaged citizens essential to participation in a democratic society. Since primary classrooms are 'dilemmatic spaces', teachers must be allowed to exercise professional judgement if they are to meet the varying needs of a group of young children. If children are to be creative, and take risks, teachers must be permitted and encouraged to do so, without the fear of being punished for making mistakes. And if learning is to be enjoyable, teachers must be allowed to enable this and to enjoy children's company, as discussed in Chapter 9.

You may think the picture which I have painted in unduly gloomy. Changes in recent years in attitudes towards gender, race and disability – and the growing recognition that discrimination on the basis of these is unacceptable – are sources of optimism. However, such changes may be less profound than is frequently thought – and there is a long way to travel if a more humane and just society is to be created.

In the end, we cannot, as adults, control children's identities, or impose them, however much we may wish to. Children are often caught between two or more cultures and have to construct, and constantly re-negotiate between, different identities, for themselves, especially as they get older and encounter new uncertainties. But adults can help foster a sense of belonging and agency so that children are enabled to steer a route confidently through the turbulences of adolescence and adulthood, and are equipped to see themselves and other people as responsible and interdependent citizens of a changing world with all the challenges and possibilities that this presents.

# Glossary

**Accomplishment of natural growth** an approach to bringing up children associated with working-class parenting, which emphasizes parents expecting children to do as they are told and allowing them to act without constant adult supervision (as opposed to concerted cultivation).

*Bildung* an educational tradition where philosophy and education are linked in a manner that refers to both personal and cultural maturation.

**Bonding capital** what links people to those who are similar.

**Bridging capital** what links people to those who are different.

**Calibration** where learning occurs through completing an action rapidly and so internalizing how the correct action feels by practice rather than through deliberate adjustment.

**Concerted cultivation** an approach to bringing up children associated with middle-class parenting, which emphasizes parents encouraging children to speak up for themselves and controlling children's leisure activities (as opposed to accomplishment of natural growth).

**Cultural capital** the often unspoken knowledge of a culture or group's beliefs, practices and ways of interacting which enables one to fit into that culture or group.

**Essentialism** the belief that aspects of people such as identity and character are fixed and do not change.

**Fixed mindset** the idea that intelligence is innate and not open to change.

**Funds of knowledge** those types of knowledge which are not valued in school learning, especially those associated with children who have been historically disadvantaged.

**Growth mindset** the idea that intelligence is fluid and open to change.

**Intersectionality** the idea that two or more different factors such as gender, race and class combine in terms of how they influence constructs such as identity or personality.

**Meme** an element of culture or behaviour passed on or learned by non-genetic means, especially by imitation, often as a whole activity.

**Performativity** the idea, in this context, that education is mainly about measurable outcomes and that children and teachers should concentrate on these.

**Schemata** explanatory structures which codify disparate bits of information and through which we make sense of experience.

**Social capital** the idea that social relationships and networks are central to how influence is exerted for a common good, with transactions marked by reciprocity, trust and cooperation (though the idea that this is always for a common good is disputed).

**Theory of mind** the recognition that other people see and understand the world differently from how a child does him or herself.

# Bibliography

Abbott, D. (1998), *Culture and Identity*, London: Hodder and Stoughton.
Adler, P. A. and P. Adler (1998), *Peer Power: Preadolescent Culture and Identity*, New Brunswick: Rutgers University Press.
Adler, P. A., S. J. Kless and P. Adler (1992), 'Socialisation to Gender Roles: Popularity Among Elementary School Boys and Girls', *Sociology of Education*, 65 (3): 169–87.
Alexander, R. (1992), *Policy and Practice in Primary Education*, London: Routledge.
Alexander, R. (1995), *Versions of Primary Education*, London: Methuen.
Alexander, R. (2000), *Culture and Pedagogy: International Comparisons in Primary Education*, Oxford: Blackwell.
Alexander, R. (ed.) (2010), *Children, Their World, Their Education - Final Report and Recommendations of the Cambridge Primary Review*, Abingdon: Routledge.
Alexander, R. J. (2004), 'Still No Pedagogy? Principle, Pragmatism and Compliance in Primary Education', *Cambridge Journal of Education*, 34 (1): 7–33.
Anning, A. (1997), *The First Years At School*, Buckingham: Open University Press.
Arendt, H. (1970), *Men in Dark Times*, London: Cape.
Arnold, M. (1869), *Culture and Anarchy: An Essay in Political and Social Criticism*, London: Smith Elder.
Bailin, S., R. Case, J. R. Coombs and L. B. Daniels (1999), 'Common Misconceptions of Critical Thinking', *Journal of Curriculum Studies*, 31 (3): 269–83.
Baldwin, J. (1991), *Nobody Knows My Name*, Harmondsworth: Penguin.
Baldwin, P. (2012), *With Drama in Mind: Real Learning in Imagined Worlds*, London: Continuum.
Ball, S. J. (2003), 'The Teacher's Soul and the Terrors of Performativity', *Journal of Education Policy*, 18 (2): 215–28.
Baron-Cohen, S. (2011), *Zero Degrees of Empathy: A New Theory of Human Cruelty*, London: Allen Lane.
Bateson, G. and M. C. Bateson (1988), *Angels Fear*, London: Rider.
Bauman, Z. (2000), *Liquid Modernity*, Oxford: Polity.
Bellous, J. and J. Clinton (2016), *Learning Social Literacy*, Edmonton: Tall Pine.
Bellous, J. and D. Sheffield (2017), *Conversations that Change Us: Learning the Arts of Theological Reflection*, Edmonton: Tall Pine.
Benjmain, S. and T. Wrigley (2013), 'The Struggle for Justice: A Focus on Students in Poverty', in L. Beckett (ed.), *Teacher Education through Active Engagement: Raising the Professional Voice*, 141–54, London: Routledge.
Berger, P. and T. Luckmann (1967), *The Social Construction of Reality*, London: Allen Lane.

Best, R. (2014), 'Spirituality, Faith and Education: Some Reflections from a UK Perspective', in J. Watson, M. de Souza and A. Trousdale (eds), *Global Perspectives on Spirituality and Education*, 5–20, New York: Routledge.

Bibby, T. (2011), *Education - An 'Impossible Profession': Psychoanalytic Explorations of Learning and Classrooms*, Abingdon: Routledge.

Black, P. and D. Wiliam (1998), 'Assessment and Classroom Learning', *Assessment in Education: Principles, Policy and Practice*, 5 (1): 7–74.

Blakemore, J. E. Owen, S. A. Berenbaum and L. S. Liben (2008), *Gender Development*, New York: Psychology.

Blakemore, S.-J. and Frith, U. (2005), *The Learning Brain: Lessons for Education*, Oxford: Blackwell.

Bloom, P. (2013), *Just Babies – The Origins of Good and Evil*, London: The Bodley Head.

Bloom, P. (2018), *Against Empathy: The Case for Rational Compassion*, London: Vintage.

Bourdieu, P. (1986), 'The Forms of Capital', in J. Richardson (ed.), *Handbook of Theory and Research for the Sociology of Education*, 241–58, New York: Greenwood Press.

Bourn, D., F. Hunt, N. Blum and H. Lawson (2016), *Primary Education for Global Learning and Sustainability – A Report for the Cambridge Primary Review Trust*, Cambridge: CPRT.

Bowlby, J. (1965), *Child Care and the Growth of Love*, London: Penguin.

Brantlinger, E. (2003), *Dividing Classes: How the Middle Class Negotiates and Rationalizes School Advantage*, London: Routledge.

Bronfenbrenner, U. (1979), *The Ecology of Human Development*, Cambridge, MA: Harvard University Press.

Brooker, L. (2002), *Starting School—Young Children Learning Cultures*, Buckingham: Open University Press.

Brown, W. (2013) 'Introduction', in T. Asad, W. Brown, J. Butler and S. Mahmood (eds), *Is Critique Secular? Blasphemy, Injury and Free Speech*, New York: Fordham University Press.

Bruner, J. (1963), *The Process of Education*, New York: Random House.

Bruner, J. (1990), *Acts of Meaning*, Cambridge, MA: Harvard University Press.

Bruner, J. (1991), 'The Narrative Construction of Reality', *Critical Inquiry*, 18 (1): 1–21.

Bruner, J. (1996), *The Culture of Education*, Cambridge, MA: Harvard University Press.

Bruner, J. S. (2006), *In Search of Pedagogy: The Selected Works of Jerome S. Bruner (2 volumes)*, Abingdon: Routledge.

CBI (Confederation of British Industry) (2012), *First Steps- a New Approach for Our Schools*. Available online: http://cbi.binarydev.net/first-steps/The_story.html (accessed 26 June 2019).

Champagne, E. (2009), 'Editorial', *International Journal of Children's Spirituality*, 14 (1): 1–3.

Claxton, G. (1997), *Hare Brain, Tortoise Mind: Why Intelligence Increases When You Think Less*, London: Fourth Estate.

Claxton, G. (2002), *Building Learning Power*, Bristol: TLO Ltd.

Claxton, G. (2007), 'Expanding Young Children's Capacity to Learn', *British Journal of Educational Studies*, 55 (2): 115-34.

Claxton, G. and M. Carr (2004), 'A Framework for Teaching Learning: The Dynamics of Disposition', *Early Years*, 24 (1): 87-97.

Connolly, P. (2002), *Racism, Gender Identities and Young Children: Social Relations in a Multi-Ethnic, Inner City Primary School*, London: Routledge.

Cornwall, J. (1999), 'Pressure, Stress and Children's Behaviour at School', in T. David (ed.), *Young Children Learning*, 90-106, London: Paul Chapman.

Cox, S. (2017), 'Developing Values in Primary Classrooms and the Place of the Humanities', *Education 3-13*, 45 (3): 375-85.

Cowan, N. (2012), 'Working Memory: The Seat of Learning and Comprehension', in S. Della Sala and M. Anderson, *Neuroscience in Education: The Good, the Bad and the Ugly*, 111-27, Oxford: Oxford University Press.

Craft, A. (2009), 'Changes in the Landscape for Creativity in Education', in A. Wilson (ed.), *Creativity in Primary Education*, 5-21, Exeter: Learning Matters.

Craft, A., B. Jeffrey and M. Leibling (eds), (2001), *Creativity in Education*, London: Continuum.

Craft, A., T. Cremin, P. Burnard, T. Dragovic and K. Chappell (2013), 'Possibility Thinking: Culminative Studies of an Evidence-based Concept Driving Creativity', *Education 3-13*, 41 (3): 538-56.

CRC (Convention on the Rights of the Child) (2013), *General Comment 17: The Right of the Child to Rest, Leisure, Play, Recreational Activities, Cultural Life and the Arts (Art.31), UNCRC/C/GC/17*, Geneva: CRC.

Cross, G. (2004), *The Cute and the Cool: Wondrous Innocence and Modern American Children's Culture*, New York: Oxford University Press.

Cupitt, D. (1995), *What Is a Story?* London: SCM Press.

David, T. and S. Powell (1999), 'Changing Childhoods, Changing Minds', in T. David (ed.), *Young Children Learning*, 204-19, London: Paul Chapman.

Davie, G. (2012), Westminster Debates. Available online: faithdebates.org.uk/wp-co ntent/.../1335084386_Davie-Westminster-debates-copy.pdf (accessed 26 June 2019).

Deci, E. L., R. Koestner and R. M. Ryan (2001), 'Extrinsic Rewards and Intrinsic Motivation in Education: Reconsidered Once Again', *Review of Educational Research*, 71 (1): 1-27.

Demos (2010), *Born Creative*. Available online: https://www.demos.co.uk/files/Born_ Creative_-_web_-_final.pdf (accessed 26 June 2019).

De Souza, M. (2016), 'The Spiritual Dimension of Education - Addressing Issues of Identity and Belonging', *Discourse and Communication for Sustainable Education*, 7 (1): 125-38.

Donaldson, M. (1982), *Children's Minds*, Glasgow: Fontana.

Donaldson, M. (1992), *Human Minds - An Exploration*, London: Allen Lane.

Dorling, D. (2015), *Inequality and the 1%*, London: Verso.

Dunn, J. (1988), *The Beginnings of Social Understanding*, Oxford: Blackwell.

Dunn, J. and J. R. Brown (2001), 'Emotion and Pragmatics in Pre-school Years', in D. Bakhurst and S. G. Shanker (eds), *Jerome Bruner: Language, Culture, Self*, 88–103, London: SAGE.

Dweck, C. S. (2000), *Self Theories: Their Role in Motivation, Personality and Development*, Philadelphia: Psychology Press.

Eagleton, T. (2000), *The Idea of Culture*, Oxford: Blackwell.

Eaude, T. (2008), *Children's Spiritual, Moral, Social and Cultural Development – Primary and Early Years*, Exeter: Learning Matters.

Eaude, T. (2011), *Thinking through Pedagogy for Primary and Early Years*, Exeter: Learning Matters.

Eaude, T. (2014), 'Creating Hospitable Space to Nurture Children's Spirituality-Possibilities and Dilemmas Associated with Power', *International Journal of Children's Spirituality*, 19 (3/4): 236–48.

Eaude, T. (2016), *New Perspectives on Young Children's Moral Education – Developing Character Through a Virtue Ethics Approach*, London: Bloomsbury.

Eaude, T. (2017), 'Humanities in the Primary School - Philosophical Considerations', *Education 3-13*, 45 (3): 343–53.

Eaude, T. (2018a), *Developing the Expertise of Primary and Elementary Classroom Teachers: Professional Learning for a Changing World*, London: Bloomsbury.

Eaude, T. (2018b), 'Addressing the Needs of the Whole Child: Implications for Young Children and Adults who Care for them', *International Handbook of Holistic Education*, 61–9, Abingdon: Routledge.

Eaude, T., G. Butt, S. Catling and P. Vass (2017), 'The Future of the Humanities in Primary Schools – Reflections in Troubled Times', *Education 3-13*, 45 (3): 386–95.

Ecclestone, K. and D. Hayes (2009), *The Dangerous Rise of Therapeutic Education*, London: Routledge.

Eisner, E. (2002), *The Arts and the Creation of Mind*, New Haven: Yale University Press.

Ellyatt, W. (2016), *The Unique Child, the Impact of Culture and How We Foster Human Wellbeing*. Available online: https://www.savechildhood.net/wp-content/uploads/2016/10/The-Unique-Child-Wendy-Ellyatt-WATCH-paper-March-2016.pdf (accessed 26 June 2019).

Engel, S. (2005), *Real Kids: Creating Meaning in Everyday Life*, Cambridge, MA: Harvard University Press.

Engel, S. (2015), *The Hungry Mind: The Origins of Curiosity in Childhood*, Cambridge, MA: Harvard University Press.

Erikson, E. H. (1995), *Childhood and Society*, London: Vintage.

Erikson, E. H. (2000), *The Erik Erikson Reader*, London: WW Norton.

Erricker, C. (1998), 'Journeys Through the Heart: The Effect of Death, Loss and Conflict on Children's Worldviews', *Journal of Beliefs and Values*, 19 (1): 107–18.

EYLF (2019), *Belonging, Being & Becoming - The Early Years Learning Framework for Australia*. Available online: https://www.education.gov.au/early-years-learning-framework-0 (accessed 26 June 2019).

Fransson, G. and J. Grannäs (2013), 'Dilemmatic Spaces in Educational Contexts – Towards a Conceptual Framework for Dilemmas in Teachers' Work', *Teachers and Teaching*, 19 (1): 4–17.

Gaine, C. and R. George (1993), *Gender, 'Race' and Class in Schooling: A New Introduction*, London: Falmer.

Galton, M., L. Hargreaves, C. Comber and D. Wall with A. Pell (1999), *Inside the Primary Classroom: 20 Years on*, London: Routledge.

Gardner, H. (1991), *The Unschooled Mind: How Children Think and How Schools should Teach*, London: Fontana.

Gardner, H. (1993), *Frames of Mind: The Theory of Multiple Intelligences*, London: Fontana.

Geertz, C. (1993), *The Interpretation of Cultures*, London: Fontana.

Geertz, C. (2001), 'Imbalancing Act: Jerome Bruner's Cultural Psychology', in D. Bakhurst and S. G. Shanker (eds), *Jerome Bruner: Language, Culture, Self*, 19–30. London: SAGE.

Gerhardt, S. (2004), *Why Love Matters: How Affection Shapes a Baby's Brain*, Hove: Brunner Routledge.

Giddens, A. (1991), *Modernity and Self-identity: Self and Society in the Late Modern Age*, Cambridge: Polity Press.

Gillborn, D. and H. Mirza (2000), *Educational Inequality: Mapping Race, Class and Gender a Synthesis of the Research Evidence*, London: Ofsted.

Gilroy, P. (1997), 'Diaspora and the Detours of Identity', in K. Woodward (ed.), *Identity and Difference*, 301–43, London: SAGE.

Gipps, C. (1999), 'Socio-cultural Aspects of Assessment', *Review of Research in Education*, 24 (1): 55–392.

Goldberg, S. (2000), *Attachment and Development*, London: Hodder Arnold.

Gonzales, N., L. Moll and C. Amanti (2005), *Funds of Knowledge*, Mahwah, NJ: Lawrence Erlbaum.

Good, T. L. and J. E. Brophy (1990), *Educational Psychology: A Realistic Approach*, London: Longman.

Goswami, U. (2011), *The Wiley-Blackwell Handbook of Childhood Cognitive Development*, Malden: Wiley-Blackwell.

Goswami, U. and P. Bryant (2010), 'Children's Cognitive Development and Learning', in R. Alexander (ed.), *The Cambridge Primary Review Research Surveys*, 141–69, Abingdon: Routledge.

Graham, L. J. and R. Slee (2008), 'An Illusory Interiority: Interrogating the Discourse/s of Inclusion', *Educational Philosophy and Theory*, 40 (2): 277–93.

Gregory, E. (2000), *City Literacies: Learning to Read across Generations and Cultures*. London: Routledge.

Haidt, J. (2012), *The Righteous Mind: Why Good People Are Divided by Politics and Religion*, London: Penguin.

Hales, A. (2018), 'The Local in History: Personal and Community History and Its Impact on Identity', *Education 3-13*, 46 (6): 671–84.

Halstead, J. M. (1996), 'Values and Values Education in Schools', in J. M. Halstead and M. J. Taylor (eds), *Values in Education and Education in Values*, 3–14, London: Falmer.

Hare, D. (1995), *Skylight*, London: Faber and Faber.

Hargreaves, A. (2003), *Teaching in the Knowledge Society – Education in the Age of Insecurity*, Maidenhead: Open University Press.

Harris, P. L. (1989), *Children and Emotion*, Oxford: Blackwell.

Harris, P. L. (2012), *Trusting What You're Told: How Children Learn from Others*, Cambridge, MA: Harvard University Press.

Harris-Britt, A., C. R. Valrie, B. Kurtz-Costes and S. J. Rowley (2007), 'Perceived Racial Discrimination and Self-Esteem in African American Youth: Racial Socialization as a Protective Factor', *Journal of Research in Adolescence*, 17 (4): 669–82.

Hattie, J. (2009), *Visible Learning: A Synthesis of Over 800 Meta-analyses Relating to Achievement*, London: Routledge.

Hattie, J. and H. Timperley (2007), 'The Power of Feedback', *Review of Educational Research*, 77 (1): 87–112.

Haydon, G. (2004), 'Values Education: Sustaining the Ethical Environment', *Journal of Moral Education*, 33 (2): 115–29.

Heath, S. B. (1983), *Ways with Words: Language, Life and Work In Communities And Classrooms*, Cambridge, MA: Cambridge University Press.

Hirsch, A. (2018), *Brit(ish): On Race, Identity and Belonging*, London: Jonathan Cape.

Hirsch, E. D. (1987), *Cultural Literacy: What Every American Needs to Know*, Boston: Houghton Mifflin.

HMSO (1975), *A Language for Life* (the Bullock Report), London: HMSO.

Holland, D. C., W. Lachicotte, D. Skinner and C. Cain (2003), *Identity and Agency in Cultural Worlds*, Cambridge, MA: Harvard University Press.

Howard-Jones, P. (ed.) (2010), *Education and Neuroscience: Evidence, Theory and Practical Application*, London: Routledge.

Hyde, B. (2008), *Children and Spirituality: Searching for Meaning and Connectedness*, London: Jessica Kingsley.

Hyde, B. (2009), 'Dangerous Games- Play and Pseudo Play in Religious Education', *Journal of Religious Education*, 57 (2): 37–46.

Inglis, F. (2000), *Clifford Geertz: Culture, Custom and Ethics*, Cambridge: Polity.

Jackson, P. W. (1968), *Life in classrooms*, New York: Holt, Rinehart and Winston.

Jackson, P. W., R. E. Boostrom and D. T. Hansen (1993), *The Moral Life of Schools*, San Francisco: Jossey Bass.

Jacober, A. (2014), 'Adolescent Identity Development', in S. Nash and J. Whitehead (eds), *Christian Youth Work in Theory and Practice: A Handbook*, 97–112, London: SCM.

James, A. (1998), 'From the Child's Point of View: Issues in the Social Construction of Childhood', in C. Panter-Brick (ed.), *Biosocial Perspectives on Children*, 45–65, Cambridge: Cambridge University Press.

Jarvis, P., S. Newman and L. Swiniarski (2014), 'On 'Becoming Social': The Importance of Collaborative Free Play in Childhood', *International Journal of Play*, 3 (1): 53–68.

Jenkins, R. (2014), *Social Identity* (4th Ed.), London: Routledge.

Jovanovic, D. and M. Matejevic (2014), 'Relationship between Rewards and Intrinsic Motivation for Learning – Researches Review', *Procedia - Social and Behavioral Sciences*, 149: 456–60.

Kagan, J. (1994), *Galen's Prophecy*, London: Free Association Books.

Katayama, K. (2004), 'The Virtue Approach to Moral Education', in J. Dunne and P. Hogan (eds), *Education and Practice - Upholding the Integrity of Teaching and Learning*, 61–73, Oxford: Blackwell.

Katz, L. (2003), 'Current Issues and Trends in Early Childhood Education', in T. S. Saraswathi (ed.), *Cross Cultural Perspectives in Human Development: Theory, Research and Application*, 354–82, London: Sage.

Kimes Myers, B. (1997), *Young Children and Spirituality*, London: Routledge.

Krause, I.-B. (ed.) (2012), *Culture and Reflexivity in Systemic Psychotherapy: Mutual Perspectives*, London: Karnac.

Lancy, D. F. (2015), *The Anthropology of Childhood: Cherubs, Chattel, Changelings*, (2nd Ed.), Cambridge: Cambridge University Press.

Lansdown, G. (1994), 'Children's Rights', in B. Mayall (ed.), *Children's Childhoods: Observed and Expressed*, 33–44, London: Falmer Press.

Lareau, A. (2011), *Unequal Childhoods: Class, Race and Family Life*, Berkeley: University of California Press.

Lave, J. and E. Wenger (1991), *Situated Learning: Legitimate Peripheral Participation*, Cambridge: Cambridge University Press.

Lifelong Faith (2015), *Children's Faith Formation*. Available online: https://www.lifelongfaith.com/journal.html (accessed 26 June 2019).

Macintyre, A. (1999), *After Virtue*, London: Duckworth.

Marano, H. E. (2008), *A Nation of Wimps*, New York: Broadway Books.

Martin, A. J. and M. Dowson (2009), 'Interpersonal Relationships, Motivation, Engagement, and Achievement: Yields for Theory, Current Issues, and Educational Practice', *Review of Educational Research*, 79 (1): 327–65.

Maslow, A. (1998), *Toward a Psychology of Being*, New York: Wiley.

Mayall, B. (2002), *Towards a Sociology of Childhood: Thinking from Children's Lives*, Buckingham: Open University Press.

McAdams, D. P. and K. C. McLean (2013), 'Narrative Identity', *Current Directions in Psychological Science*, 22 (3): 233–8.

McCann, J. J. (2016), 'Is Mental Illness Socially Constructed?' *Journal of Applied Psychology and Social Science*, 2 (1): 1–11.

McMahon, L. (1992), *The Handbook of Play Therapy*, London: Routledge.

Meek, M. (1991), *On Being Literate*, London: The Bodley Head.

Mercer, J. A. (2005), *Welcoming Children: A Practical Theology of Childhood*, St. Louis: Chalice Press.

Mercer, N. (2000), *Words and Minds – How We Use Words to Think Together*, London: Routledge.

Modood, T. (1997), 'Culture and Identity', in T. Modood, R. Berthoud, J. Lakey, J. Nazroo, P. Smith, S. Virdee and S. Beishon, *Ethnic Minorities in Britain*, 290–338, London: Policy Studies Institute.

Morpurgo, M. (2011), 'I Long for the Day When Amnesty Is Needed No More', *The Guardian*, 29 May 2011. https://www.theguardian.com/commentisfree/2011/may/29/michael-morpurgo-amnesty-international.

Moule, J. (2009), 'Understanding Unconscious Bias and Unintentional Racism', *Phi Delta Kappan*, 90 (5): 320–26.

NACCCE (National Advisory Committee on Creative and Cultural Education) (1999), *All Our Futures: Creativity, Culture and Education*, Sudbury: DfEE.

Nagel, T. (1986), *The View from Nowhere*, Oxford: Oxford University Press.

Nickerson, R. S. (1998), 'Confirmation Bias: A Ubiquitous Phenomenon in Many Guises', *Review of General Psychology*, 2 (2): 175–220.

Noddings, N. (1991), 'Stories in Dialogue: Caring and Interpersonal Reasoning', in C. Witherell and N. Noddings (eds), *Stories Lives Tell: Narrative and Dialogue in Education*, 157–70, New York: Teachers' College Press.

Noddings, N. (2013), *Caring – A Relational Approach to Ethics and Moral Education*, Berkeley: University of California Press.

Nurse, A. D. and R. Headington (1999), 'Balancing the Needs of Children, Parents and Teachers', in T. David (ed.), *Young Children Learning*, 13–31, London: Paul Chapman.

Nussbaum, M. (2010), *Not for Profit: Why Democracy Needs the Humanities*, Princeton: Princeton University Press.

Nussbaum, M. (2017), 'Martha C Nussbaum Talks about the Humanities, Mythmaking and International Development' *Humanities*, 38 (2): 4.

Ogbu, J. (1974), *The Next Generation: An Ethnography of Education in an Urban Neighbourhood*, New York: Academic Press.

Olson, D. R. (2001), 'Education- the Bridge from Culture to Mind', in D. Bakhurst and S. G. Shanker (eds), *Jerome Bruner: Language, Culture, Self*, 104–15, London: SAGE.

O'Keeffe, G. S., K. Clarke-Pearson and Council on Communications and Media (2011), 'Clinical Report: The Impact of Social Media on Children, Adolescents, and Families', *Pediatrics*, 127 (4): 800–5.

Palmer, S. (2006), *Toxic Childhood*, London: Orion Books.

Pepper, D. (2008), *Primary Curriculum Change: Directions of Travel in 10 Countries since 2005*, London: QCA.

Pinker, S. (2014). *The Village Effect: Why Face-to-Face Contact Matters*, London, Atlantic Books.

Pollard, A. (1985), *The Social World of the Primary School*, London: Cassell.

Pollard, A. with A. Filer (1996), *The Social World of Children's Learning*, London: Continuum.

Putnam, R. D. (2000), *Bowling Alone: The Collapse and Revival of American Community*, New York: Simon & Schuster.

Reay, D. (2017), *Miseducation - Inequality, Education and the Working Classes*, Bristol, Policy Press.

Reed, E. S. (2001), 'Towards a Cultural Ecology of Instruction', in D. Bakhurst and S. G. Shanker (eds), *Jerome Bruner: Language, Culture, Self*, 116–26, London: SAGE.

Renold, E. (2006), '"They Won't Let Us Play ... Unless You're Going Out with One of Them": Girls, Boys and Butler's "Heterosexual Matrix" in the Primary Years', *British Journal of Sociology of Education*, 27 (4): 489–509.

Richardson, R. and A. Wood (2000), *Inclusive Schools, Inclusive Society: Race and Identity on the Agenda*, Stoke-on-Trent: Trentham.

Robinson, K. and L. Aronica (2015), *Creative Schools: The Grassroots Revolution That's Transforming Education*, New York: Viking Press.

Rogers, C. (1951), *Client-centered Therapy: Its Current Practice, Implications and Theory*, London: Constable.

Rogers, C. (1989), 'Early Admission, Early Labelling', in C. Desforges (ed.), *Early Childhood Education*, 94–109, Edinburgh: Scottish Academic Press.

Rogoff, B. (1990), *Apprenticeship in Thinking - Cognitive Development in Social Context*, Oxford: Oxford University Press.

Rogoff, B. (2003), *The Cultural Nature of Human Development*, New York: Oxford University Press.

Rowley, S. J., B. Kurtz-Costes, R. Mistry and L. Feagans (2007), 'Social Status as a Predictor of Race and Gender Stereotypes in Late Childhood and Early Adolescence', *Social Development*, 16 (1): 150–68.

RSA (Royal Society of Arts) (2014), *Schools with Soul: A New Approach to Spiritual, Moral, Social and Cultural Education*. Available online: https://www.thersa.org/globalassets/pdfs/reports/schools-with-soul-report.pdf (accessed 26 June 2019).

Russell, J. (2007), *How Children Become Moral Selves – Building Character and Promoting Citizenship Education*, Eastbourne: Sussex Academic Press.

Salmon, P. (1995), *Psychology in the Classroom - Reconstructing Teachers and Learners*, London: Cassell.

Sanders-Phillips, K., B. Settles-Reaves, D. Walker and J. Brownlow (2009), 'Social Inequality and Racial Discrimination: Risk Factors for Health Disparities in Children of Color', *Pediatrics*, 124 (Supplement 3): 176–86.

Savage, M. (2015), *Social Class in the 21st Century*, London: Pelican.

Skelton, C. (2001), *Schooling the Boys: Masculinities and Primary Education*, Buckingham: Open University Press.

Stenhouse, L. (1967), *Culture and Education*, London: Nelson.

Sylva, K., E. Melhuish, P. Sammons, I. Siraj-Blatchford and B. Taggart (eds), (2010), *Early Childhood Matters - Evidence from the Effective Pre-school and Primary Education Project*, Abingdon: Routledge.

Tassoni, P. and K. Hucker (2005), *Planning Play and the Early Years*, Oxford: Heinemann.

Taylor, C. (1989), *Sources of the Self: The Making of the Modern Identity*, Cambridge: Cambridge University Press.

Thompson, R. A. (2009) 'Early Foundations: Conscience and the Development of Moral Character', in D. Narváez and D. K. Lapsley (eds), *Personality, Identity and Character: Explorations in Moral Psychology*, 159–84, Cambridge: Cambridge University Press.

Thorne, B. (1993), *Gender Play; Girls and Boys in School*, Buckingham: Open University Press.

Timimi, S. (2005), *Naughty Boys: Anti-Social Behaviour, ADHD and the Role of Culture*, New York: Palgrave Macmillan.

Tizard, B. and M. Hughes (1984), *Young Children Learning - Talking and Thinking at Home and at School*, London: Fontana.

Todd, S. (2015), *The People: The Rise and Fall of the Working Classes*, London: John Murray.

Tommerdahl, J. (2010), 'A Model for Bridging the Gap between Neuroscience and Education', *Oxford Review of Education*, 36 (1): 97–109.

Trevarthen, C. (1992), 'An Infant's Motives for Speaking and Thinking in the Culture', in A. H. Wold (ed.), *The Dialogical Alternative: Towards a Theory and Language and Mind*, 99–137, Oslo: Scandinavian University Press.

Troyna, B. and R. Hatcher (1992), *Racism in Children's Lives*, London: Routledge.

UNCRC (United Nations Convention on the Rights of the Child) (1989). Summary. Available online: https://www.unicef.org.uk/what-we-do/un-convention-child-rights/ (accessed 26 June 2019).

UNESCO (2014), *Global Citizenship Education. Preparing Learners for the Challenges of the 21st Century*, Paris: UNESCO.

UNICEF (2007), *Child Poverty in Perspective: An Overview of Child Well-Being in Rich Countries: A Comparative Assessment of the Lives and Well-Being of Children and Adolescents in Economically Advanced Nations*, Florence: Unicef Innocenti Centre (Innocenti Report Card 7). Available online: https://www.unicef-irc.org/publications/pdf/rc7_eng.pdf (accessed 26 June 2019).

UNICEF (2013), *Child Well-being in Rich Countries: A Comparative Overview*, Florence: Unicef Innocenti Centre (Innocenti Report Card 11). Available online: https://www.unicef-irc.org/publications/683-child-well-being-in-rich-countries-a-comparative-overview.html (accessed 26 June 2019).

Vygotsky, L. S. (1978), *Mind in Society: The Development of Higher Psychological Processes*, Cambridge, MA: Harvard University Press.

Wall, J. (2010), *Ethics in Light of Childhood*, Washington: Georgetown University Press.

West-Burnham, J. and V. Huws-Jones (2007), *Spiritual and Moral Development in Schools*, London: Continuum.

Westerlund, K. (2016), 'Spirituality and Mental Health among Children and Youth – A Swedish Point of View, *International Journal of Children's Spirituality*, 21 (3–4): 216–29.

Wilkinson, R. and K. Pickett (2009), *The Spirit Level – Why More Equal Societies Almost Always Do Better*, London: Allen Lane.

Wilkinson, R. and K. Pickett (2018), *The Inner Level – How More Equal Societies Reduce Stress, Restore Sanity and Improve Everyone's Well-being*, London: Allen Lane.

Williams, R. (1959), *Culture and Society: 1780–1950*, Harmondsworth: Penguin.

Williams, R. (2000), *Lost Icons*, Edinburgh: T and T Clark.

Wilson, J. (2007), *The Performance of Practice*, London: Karnac.

Wimberley, A. E. S. and E. L. Parker (eds), (2010), *In Search of Wisdom: Faith Formation in the Black Church*, Nashville: Abingdon Press.

Winnicott, D. (1980/2002), *Playing and Reality*, Hove: Brunner-Routledge.

Winston, J. (1998), *Drama, Narrative and Moral Education: Exploring Traditional Tales in the Primary Years*, London: Falmer.

Wood, E. A. (2014), 'Free Choice and Free Play in Early Childhood Education: Troubling the Discourse', *International Journal of Early Years Education*, 22 (1): 4–18.

Woodhead, L., C. Partridge and H. Kawanami (eds), (2016), *Religions in the Modern World: Traditions and Transformations* (3rd Ed.), London: Routledge.

Woods, P. and B. Jeffrey (2002), 'The Reconstruction of Primary Teachers' Identities', *British Journal of Sociology of Education*, 23 (1): 89–106.

Woodward, K. (2002), *Understanding Identity*, London: Hodder.

Wright, C. (2013), 'Understanding Black Academic Attainment', *Education Inquiry*, 4 (1): 87–102.

Yelland N. and S. Grieshaber (1998), '"Blurring the Edges" in N. Yelland', *Gender in Early Childhood*, 1–11, London: Routledge.

Young, R. M. (1994), *Mental Space*, London: Process Press.

Yust, K.-M. (2017), 'Cultivating Christians: North American Family Cultures and Religious Identity Formation', *International Journal of Children's Spirituality*, 22 (3–4): 260–73.

# Index

ability  125, 140, 143, 183, 192
   beliefs about  125 (*see also* growth mindset)
abstract ideas  86, 91, 101, 104, 119, 146, 165
abuse  60, 78, 135, 138
acceptability  26, 70, 117, 118
'accomplishment of natural growth'  45, 156
accountability  61, 122, 201
   collective  123
achievements, level of children's  7, 13, 28, 42, 44, 121, 200
activity/ies  76, 96, 126, 134, 163, 174
   meaningful  6, 76, 174
   practical  177, 192
ADHD (Attention Deficit Hyperactivity Disorder)  38
adolescence  1, 4, 7, 42, 78, 157, 159, 190–1, 201
adults, availability of  137, 157
advertising  57–8, 85, 191
affiliation  43, 48, 56, 77, 126
   religious  8, 48–50, 67, 109, 188
affirmation  54, 84
agency  12, 55–6, 95, 99, 121, 125, 130, 151, 153, 186, 193
   sense of  13, 18, 72, 84, 88, 94, 97, 108, 110, 114–15, 124, 140, 158, 173–4, 78–9, 189, 192, 195, 201
   transfer of  95, 119, 121, 195
Alexander, Robin  23, 24, 52, 61, 67, 139, 171, 178, 199
altruism  48, 116
ambiguity  103, 149
ambition  40, 68–9, 142
analogies  78, 149, 179
anonymity  57
anxiety  36, 43, 57, 78, 81, 98, 114, 151, 181
   containment of  113, 119, 178, 192
appearance  20, 36, 38, 144, 194

apprenticeship  12, 95, 130–1, 151–3, 181, 195, 198
approval  54, 111, 116–17, 125, 139, 194
art  48, 166, 175, 198
arts, the  21, 23, 106–8, 198
   marginalization of  61–2, 64–5, 106, 201
   role of  96, 107, 177
aspirations  119, 141, 156, 199, 200
assessment  61, 182–4
   collective  185
   formative  64, 183
   holistic approach to  164, 182–4, 201
   summative  64
assumptions  3, 5, 7, 11, 13, 21, 43, 72, 82, 116, 143–6, 170, 183–4, 188, 196
   cultural  6, 10, 25, 83, 94, 185
attachment  77, 81–2
   models of  81, 114, 117, 156, 191
   theory  81
attainment  40, 46, 142, 166, 199
attention  58, 117, 119, 148, 158, 164, 181, 190
   centre of  53, 84, 197
attitudes  5, 23, 27, 35, 126, 196
   towards children  47–8, 187
attunement  81, 116, 137–8, 179, 200
authority  12, 130, 135, 157, 179, 200
   deference to  8, 56, 58
   opposition to  37
autonomy  50, 55

babies  2, 80–1, 156
backgrounds  3, 13, 21, 28–9, 34, 43, 51, 109, 112, 120, 122, 126, 134, 136, 138, 143–4, 149, 160, 164, 166, 169, 172, 176, 180, 183–4, 193, 195, 199
   advantaged  124, 193
   chaotic  121, 198
   disadvantaged  4, 28, 33, 38, 40–1, 43, 46, 62, 75, 88, 91, 159, 175–6, 187–9, 193–4, 198

balance   136, 148, 174
barriers   10, 29, 46, 113, 133, 141, 143–4, 171, 183, 195
'basics'   61, 170, *see also* Curriculum 1
becoming   29, 30, 190
behaviour
   children's   32, 36–9, 42, 44, 54, 62, 117–18, 122, 140–1, 153, 155, 174, 181, 193
   management of   30, 62, 117, 153
behaviours   4–5, 18, 35–7, 39, 57, 66, 68, 76, 115–16, 122, 140–1, 157, 170
beliefs   3, 4, 24, 43, 48, 72, 104, 109, 116, 130, 136, 170
belonging   2, 5, 24, 30–2
   sense of   4, 13, 29, 30, 51, 70, 111, 113, 115, 126, 129, 133–4, 154, 172, 189, 201
bias
   confirmation   142–4
   unconscious   142, 144, 188, 196, 199
bigotry   177, 196
*Bildung*   177
boundaries   6, 121, 130, 153, 157, 177, 194
boys   35–9, 42, 92, 99, 124, 145, 147, 157, 163, 192–3
brain   77–8, 90, 119
brittleness   84, 108, 165, 188, 191, 193
Bruner, Jerome   18, 62, 136, 151, 170–1, 176, 182
bullying   57, 123, 145
   cyber   112

calibration   87
capital
   bonding   7
   bridging   7, 126, 166, 194
   cultural   33, 154, 175–6, 194, 198
   social   46, 88
care   111, 129
   children's need for   80, 113, 172, 192
   for others   113, 145, 193
categorization   35, 39, 77, 79, 112
celebrity   32, 59, 85, 134
challenge   56, 111, 113, 127, 130, 133, 138, 139, 157, 174, 192–3
change   6, 65, 188–9
   capacity for   170
   climate   56

constant   13, 187, 189
   social and cultural   9, 187, 201
character   17–18, 30, 66
characteristics   66, 86, 192, *see also* qualities
childcare   36, 164
childhood
   early   2, 191
   imaginative space of   136–7
   lens of   1, 179
   'scholarisation' of   54, 97, 156
   views of   52–3, 77, 130, 154
'child-within'   135, 182
choice   32, 46, 48, 59, 83, 119, 121, 130, 191
   and consequence   59, 62, 117–19, 123, 153
   limiting   121–2, 153
Christian   48–9, 165
citizenship, global   9, 66–7, 109–10, 123, 189, 198
class, social   4–5, 20–3, 28, 43, 99, 112, 167, 171, 183, 188, 196
   link to status   43–4, 46
   meanings of the term   43
   middle-   22, 43–7, 54, 119, 120, 154, 156, 197
   working-   22, 37, 43–7, 75, 120, 124, 156
classroom   178, 181
   climates   171, 179
   as 'dilemmatic space'   178, 201
   dynamics of the primary   181
clothes   10, 26, 59, 120, 156
cognition   61, 66, 154
   link to emotion   61, 76, 78, 90, 101, 122
'cog-wheeling'   135
coherence   21, 51
   search for   85
collaboration   101, 121, 123, 154, 195
colonialism   6, 22
colour
   'blindness'   144, 196
   persons of   28, 59, 175
   skin   42, 112, 143
communities   22, 56, 120, 151, 189
   faith   49, 50, 151, 164–6
   learning   121, 186

local   26, 32, 151, 190
  migrant   41
community of practice   152, 194
comparison   181, 191
compassion   116, 148
competition, inter-personal   36, 65, 101, 118, 167, *see also* rivalry
competitiveness   167, 173-4, 181, 188, 199
complexity   108, 149, 185, 195
compliance   64, 142, 149
compulsion   118
concepts   9, 17, 39, 58, 68, 90, 107-9, *see also* abstract ideas
concerns
  adults'   40, 44, 56-7, 62, 160
  children's   117, 133, 138, 141, 157, 160-1, 197
'concerted cultivation'   45, 54, 92, 119, 156, 197
confidence   8, 69, 124, 148-9
conflict   2, 48, 123
conformity   121, 170
conscience   116
consistency   62, 130, 157
consumerism   53, 58, 134, 137, 196
context   18-20, 28-9, 67, 76, 88, 95-6, 114, 117, 119, 124, 136, 151-2, 170, 177, 183
  social and cultural   4, 12, 65, 67, 72, 111
control   12, 23, 88-9, 99, 105, 118-19, 136, 146, 152, 178, 182, 195
  children's sense of   52, 95, 113-14, 140
conversation   77, 140, 163
cooperation   96, 98, 101, 116, 127, 166-7, 180, 185, 199, *see also* teamwork
courage   18, 104, 170
'creatives'   166
creativity   12, 63, 93-7, 101, 108, 127, 130, 149, 179, 192-3
  definitions of   94-5
critical thinking   58, 69, 108, 177, 193
criticism   87, 140
cues   81, 83-4
  interpretation of   138
  visual   181
culture
  changing nature of   27, 94
  children's knowledge of other   57, 106, 189

of compliance   64
consumerist   58-9
'high'   21-2, 176, 198
'low'/ popular   22, 176
macro-   4, 58, 109, 165, 188, 190
meanings of the word   3, 22-3
micro-   3-5, 12, 32, 51, 141, 171, 189-90
as normative   6, 23, 26, 188
performance   58
of schools   41, 169, 174
signifiers of   24-6
as space(s)   3, 11, 24, 26
sub-   5
transmission of   171
youth   27
curiosity   95, 98, 104, 108, 127, 179, 193
curriculum   61-2, 170, 173
  broad and balanced   63, 170, 173, 176, 198, 200
  formal   173
  hidden   173
  inclusive   173-4
  informal   173
'Curriculum 1'   61-2, *see also* 'basics'
'Curriculum 2'   61-2

data   64, 182
defensiveness   65, 96
deference   8, 58, 68
democracy   25, 107, 125, 136, 201
deprivation   78, 82
  cultural   41
development
  aesthetic   17, 96
  cultural   9, 17, 94, 96, 176
  emotional   17, 63-4, 79, 96, 154
  mental   17, 81
  moral   17, 176
  non-linearity of   11, 190
  physical   17, 81
  SMSC   64, 176, 192
  social   17, 63-4, 79, 154, 176
  spiritual   17, 176
  stages of   76, 190
  of the whole child   17, 65, 107, 154, 198
dialogue   91, 140, 198
diet   78, 158, 192

difference    7, 109, 126, 130, 166, 175, 180, 185, 198
differentiation    64, 77
difficulties    20, 35–6, 40, 42, 51, 57, 60, 98, 113, 130, 138, 164–5, 193, 197
   emotional and behavioural    37, 44, 62
dilemmas    7, 130, 157, 178
disability    17, 27, 29, 34, 40, 59, 63, 112, 175, 187
disapproval    139, 153
discipline
   external    118, 166
   self-    118
disciplines, subject    96, 106, 108, 171, 173–4, 177, *see also* subjects, school
discovery    179
discrimination    9, 28, 42, 48, 51, 59–60, 112, 122, 143, 187, 192, 195–6, 201
discussion    36, 45, 91, 119, 158, 178–80, 197
disorders
   anxiety-related    57
   behaviour/ conduct-related    57
dispositions    12, 18, 66, 112, 116–17, 124, 129, 133, 148, 173, 189, 197, 201
divergence    95, 100, 170, 184
diversity    4, 94, 67, 104, 145, 149, 175, 188, 194, 197
   cultural/social    6, 7, 29, 43, 56, 67, 93–4, 171, 174
   ethnic    29, 43
   linguistic    56
   religious    8, 49, 56
drama    98, 101, 108, 166–7, 177

education    11, 43, 178
   academic    62
   aims of    62, 64, 141, 169–70, 198
   parental interest in    44–6, 165
   physical    63
   vocational    62
effort    41, 54, 72, 123, 125
egocentricity    126
embarrassment    33, 79, 159, 181, 190
embodiment    86, 88–9

emotion    36, 54, 66, 76, 79, 81, 89, 103–4, 113, 115–16, 138–9, 167, 181–2
   denial of    18, 36, 125, 147
   link to cognition    61, 76, 78, 90, 101, 122
emotional intensity    78, 98, 160, 162, 164
emotional repertoire    36, 89, 163, 193
empathy    7, 69, 104, 113, 121, 125–6, 138, 148, 193
engagement    72, 78, 116, 174–5, 178
Engel, Susan    36, 76, 79, 83, 84, 85, 90, 95, 99, 100, 102, 113–14, 149, 179, 185
enjoyment    22, 94, 99, 100, 102, 104, 110, 116, 130, 134–5, 158, 164, 166–8, 176, 192
entertainment    22, 27, 100–1
enthusiasm    69, 127, 148
entitlement    62, 177
   sense of    120, 124, 158, 193
environments    12, 20, 24, 72, 95, 109, 110, 119, 134, 141, 164, 197, 199
   home    46, 156, 165
   inclusive    12, 110–13, 122–3, 125, 133, 141, 144–6, 172
equipping children    65, 112, 125, 130, 137
Erikson, Erik    30, 54, 85, 135
ethnicity    39–42, 99, 120, 166, 183, *see also* race
evaluation    18, 181
example, learning by    12, 37, 72, 78, 85, 117, 129, 140, 146, 148, 159, 182, *see also* role models
excitability    80
exclusion    5, 6, 29, 33, 37, 51, 80, 100, 112, 122, 192
executive function    119, *see also* regulation, self-
exercise    78
expectations    4, 9, 20, 28, 51, 70, 72, 120–2, 129, 133, 139, 146, 154–6, 160, 164, 168–9, 194
   adult    13, 35, 46, 53, 135, 141–2, 191, 193, 197
   clash of    120, 154, 197
   class-based    43, 82, 167, 191
   gender-based    36–8, 82, 162, 191
   low    41, 166, 180, 188, 199, 200
   'race'-based    82, 191

experience, early   4, 76, 80
experience, prior   88, 134
experiences
   broad range of   12, 92, 96, 107, 125, 127, 157, 193–4, 198
   shared   171
exploration   179
externalizing   36, 42

facilitation   63, 152, 200
failure   98, 153
fairness   25, 68, 148, 167
faith, religious   6, 34, 48–50, 68, 103
familiarity   94–5, 113–14
family   5, 26, 32, 56, 77, 151, 160
   child's place in the   34, 159–60
   extended   56, 83, 159–60, 162
fashion   1, 27, 32, 59, 134
fathers   60, 159
fear   33, 98, 104, 116, 118, 139, 153
features, external   18, 26
feedback   72, 84, 86–7, 152
   from adults   139, 146
   to adults   179
   non-verbal   87, 139
   verbal   87
feelings   17, 33, 78, 89, 97–9, 101, 105–6, 113, 126–7, 138, 140, 190, 197
femininity   36–9
   models of   39
firmness   148, 200
flexibility   7, 69, 106, 121, 125, 130, 148, 153, 157, 178, 186, 194, 200
flourishing   113, 116, 134, 189
foundations for ethics   50
fragmentation   4, 30, 56
freedom   45, 54, 99, 136, 177
friends   5, 32, 180
   family   159, 162–3
   imaginary   113, 191
futility   46

games   53, 168
   computer   58
Geertz, Clifford   11, 23, 25, 133
gender   4–5, 20, 28, 34–8, 77, 112, 171, 188, 199
   'blindness'   144, 196
generalization   24, 133, 143

generosity   18, 86
geography   106, 109
girls   35–8, 58, 99, 124, 145, 147, 157, 163
globalization   22, 51–2, 188
goals   139
   performance   140
   process   140
grandparents   160–3
gratification   58, 116
groups   11, 23, 31, 55, 112, 120, 153, 185
   disadvantaged   28, 57, 86, 102, 144, 186–7
   friendship   32, 157
   informal   111
   voluntary   133, 151, 164, 166, 168
growth   3, 21, 192
growth mindset   125, 140, 170–1
guidance   72, 84, 95, 120, 130, 139, 155, 195
guilt   79, 118

habit/ habituation   22, 78, 84, 86, 116, 181
happiness   5, 32, 58, 116, 155, 190
Hargreaves, Andy   58, 68
haven   111, 113, 133, 192
health
   mental   40, 43, 48, 56–7, 78, 134, 155, 170, 192
   physical   40, 43, 56–7, 78, 134, 155, 170, 192
helplessness, learned   137
heritage, cultural   29, 31, 108, 175
hierarchy
   cultural   31, 41
   of identities   21
   of needs   30, 113
history   108–9, 175
holistic approach   72, 130–2, 134, 151–5, 186, 192–3, 195, 198
home   44, 120, 133
   influence of the   151, 156, 190, 195
homophobia   31, 60, 122
honesty   67–8, 139
honour, family   117, 149
hope, *see* optimism
hopelessness, sense of   47
horizons, cultural   7, 57, 16, 194
horizons of possibility   141, 145, 173

humanities, the   23, 106–8, 198
  marginalization of   61–2, 64–5, 106, 201
  role of   177
humiliation   47, 139
humility   68–9, 148–9, 182
humour   27, 53, 149
husbandry   23–4
Hyde, Brendan   18, 59, 100

identities
  conflicting   51, 188
  construction of   13, 30, 72, 84, 86, 91–2, 99, 114, 120, 129, 147, 153, 159, 189, 191, 194–5, 200
  family   169
  fluid   20, 57, 170
  fragile   36, 84, 191
  genderized   42, 190
  local   32
  metaphors of emerging   12, 71–2
  multiple   2, 8, 19, 129, 170, 188
  negotiation of   3, 13, 20, 45, 54, 72, 111, 134, 136, 159, 195, 201
  racialized   42, 190
  situational   20, 117, 124, 167
  substantive   20, 87, 124, 139
identity   65, 80, 151
  coherent   12, 20–1, 60, 189, 198
  collective/group   2, 17, 21, 27, 166
  different elements of   17, 20, 173
  emerging   184
  essentialist/fixed view of   11, 76, 183
  hybridised   19
  hyphenated   19
  intersection of factors affecting   3, 17, 51, 188
  markers of   3, 10, 26, 134
  narrative(s) of   3, 13, 19, 31, 91, 102, 153
  national   2, 86, 108
  personal   2, 4, 5, 67
  religious   50, 86, 165
  robust, but flexible   1, 7, 12, 51, 60, 69, 71–2, 110, 123, 129, 146–7, 173, 187, 189, 195, 200
  'roots' of   1, 136
  'routes' into   136
  sense of   3, 102
  signifiers of   10, 26, 31, 39, 47

illustrations   78
image   38, 49, 85–6, 89–90, 159, 165, 175, 179, 190–1
  body   58–9
imagination   12, 93, 95, 97, 100, 193
imitation   77, 83, 85, 129, 152
immediacy   58, 190
impressionability, young
  children's   28, 117
impulsiveness   38, 80, 193
incentive   111, *see also* rewards
inclusion/ inclusiveness   5, 7, 99, 100, 112, 166, 175, 198
independence   18, 53–4, 58, 95, 158, 189
individual   17, 19, 55, 193
individualism   59, 65, 188, 191
inequality   41, 56, 57
infantilizing   53, 105, 137, 158
inferiority   40–1
influence   12, 101, 136
inhibition   80
innocence   52, 130
insecurity   30, 59, 72, 189, 192
instruction   25, 53–4, 63–4, 179
intelligence   41, 125, 192
  artificial   51, 190
  multiple   170
interaction, social   75, 80, 84, 135
interdependence   19, 30, 67, 109
interests, shared   32, 36
internalizing   42, 37, 82, 104, 156, 194
internet   5, 57
inter-subjectivity   79, 156
intolerance, religious   6, 48
intuition   127
Islam   48, 171
isolation   32
*izzat*   117, 149

Jackson, Philip   87, 139, 148, 173, 181, 197
Jenkins, Richard   2, 19, 76, 77, 83
jokes   31, 79, 120, 149
Judaism   48–9, 171
judgement   105, 156, 172
  adult   148, 156, 198
  children's   79, 107, 121, 153
  professional   63–4, 182, 201
justice   7, 67

kindness  28, 47, 68, 79, 123, 137
knowledge  7, 61, 130, 170, 174–5
   canonical  174
   core  62
   funds of  75, 174–5, 183, 186, 198
   pedagogical content  183
   personal/inter-personal  61, 85, 88, 170
   procedural  61, 85, 87–8, 170, 192
   propositional  61–2, 170, 177
   tacit  85, 88

labelling  38, 183
Lancy, David  52, 54, 55, 56, 99, 100, 125, 134, 158, 176
language  4, 9, 21, 24, 44–5, 88–90, 112, 124, 140, 175
   body  139
   difficulties in using the right  9–10
   English as an additional  40, 185
   home  21, 172, 185, 188
   spoken  89, 91
Lareau, Annette  45, 119, 155
lead, taking the  152–3
learning
   embodied  86, 88–9
   by example (*see* example, learning by)
   informal  197
   intergenerational  197
   processes  83–4, 189, 190
   rote  62, 88
   scaffolding of  137, 155
   tacit  78, 83–4, 175, 190
listening  83, 138, 140, 146, 152, 179
literacy  7, 28, 40, 44, 63, 177, 200
   cultural  62
literature  48, 108, 175, 198
loneliness  57, 134
love  134, 157, 172, 189

manipulation  101, 127
marginalization of groups  6, 28, 31
masculinity  36–9, 167
   models of  38–9, 147, 156, 188
materialism  13, 59, 196
maxims  121, 139, 153, 193, *see also* rules
meaning, children's search for  47, 65, 79
media  4, 5, 27–8, 48, 58–9, 151, 157, 190
   social  57–8
meme  87, 129

memory  19, 78, 88, 103
   collective  47
   working  80
men  22, 28, 35–6, 60, 147, 159, 175, 188
mentoring  152
messages, mixed  119–20, 139, 151, 189, 197
metacognition  98
metaphor  78, 149, 179
milestones  6, 159
mind  77–9, 86
mirror neurons  85
mirror stage  85
misconceptions  179, 183
mistakes, making  148
modesty  68, 149
morality  67, 118
mothers  81–2, 159
motivation  33, 48, 78, 99, 112, 115–18, 153, 175, 189
   extrinsic  118, 166
   intrinsic  13, 115, 118, 133, 148, 153, 178, 192–3
music  27, 48, 166, 175, 198
Muslim  28, 48–50

name-calling  123, 145
narcissism  59, 126, 191
narrative(s)  8, 29, 68, 77, 90, 101, 104, 134, 141, 159, 161, 176
natural world  67, 168
needs  134, 136, 178, 180, 192–3
   emotional  81, 113
   physical  81, 113
   special educational  40, 63, 184
neglect  60, 138
Noddings, Nel  113, 172
norms  5, 7, 9, 24, 121, 146
numeracy  7, 63, 200
nurture  3, 12, 24, 112, 127
Nussbaum, Martha  79, 98, 103, 107, 113, 122, 127

obedience  36, 118
observing  77, 85, 88, 96, 108, *see also* watching
open-mindedness  69, 136
opportunities  56, 186, 192
optimism  94, 125, 148, 159, 197, 201
'othering'  28–9, 31, 79, 123, 126

outcomes  28, 36, 40–1, 54, 60, 94, 100, 140, 144, 188
  measurable  63–4
outsider  26, 31, 42, 50–1
overprotection  53, 125, 137, 158, 188, *see also* protection

pain  89, 95, 98, 116, 137, 154
  emotional  98
parents/carers  60, 142, 162, 184–5
  specific role of  155–60
participation  29, 120, 194, 201
  guided  12, 121, 130
passivity  59, 100, 178
patience  104, 148, 198
patriarchy  6
patriotism  68, 86
patterns  4, 81, 83, 87
pedagogy  61, 63, 178
  need for a wide repertoire of  179
peer group  3, 32, 77, 99, 111, 117, 151, 166, 190
percept  90, 175
perceptions  4, 17–18, 191
performance  46, 101, 167, 200
performativity  63–4, 173, 180, 201
persistence  93, 140, 146, 167, 174
person  19, 20, 52, 96, 170, 173, 195, 199
  cultured  3, 22–3, 106
  educated  22, 64, 106, 169
  whole  3, 12–13, 17, 107, 129, 153, 201
persona  101, 127
personality  17, 97
perspectives, different  107, 109, 126, 136, 141, 160, 163, 175, 177
pets  113, 158
place, sense of  70, 109
planning, teachers'  185
play  53, 97–101, 110, 134, 156, 158, 177, 179, 192
  as an activity  97, 100
  adult involvement in  100
  class and  99
  different types of  97
  gender and  99, 100
  learning through  63–4
  as a process  97–8, 100
  pseudo-  100
  stages of  98–9
  suspicion of  53, 97

playfulness  95, 100, 148–9
popularity  20, 38
possessions  56–8, 134, 158
potential  110, 141
poverty  28, 43, 46, 51, *see also* class
  of aspirations  143
  of experiences  143
  of relationships  46, 143
power  12, 28, 43, 99, 112, 130, 140, 158, 172
  abuse of  100, 145
  asymmetry of  130, 139, 149, 172, 200
powerlessness  52, 130
practice  78, 84, 86, 194
practices  5, 6, 87
  child-rearing  44–5
  cultural  43–5, 131, 136, 172, 200
  religious  48–50, 109, 149, 165
praise  84, 125, 139
pre-adolescence  2–4, 11, 20, 26, 32, 36, 38, 51, 58, 65, 77–8, 89, 100, 117, 137, 157–8, 162–3, 167, 190–1, 195
predictability  6, 78, 83, 108, 113–15, 130
prejudice  28, 142
pressures on children  36, 51, 159
pride  31, 79, 119
priorities  133, 136
privilege  10, 28
problem-solving  69, 94, 107, 121
professionals  164–5
programmes  63, 176
protection  53, 113, 130, 137, *see also* overprotection
punishment  18, 48, 54, 117–18
  corporal  8, 54
purpose  47, 65
puzzle  7, 130
  of predictability  83

qualities  18, 66, 146, 149, 156, 167, 183, *see also* characteristics
  adults'  130, 147–9, 182, 197–8, 200
  children's  12, 18, 20, 52, 66–9, 71, 72, 86–7, 104, 110, 112, 119–20, 123–5, 129, 170–1, 173, 183, 185, 189, 193, 195
questions  18, 21, 94–5, 102–3, 141, 155, 193
  complex  109, 177
  difficult  161

race 4–5, 28, 39–42, 147, 188, 196, see also ethnicity
racism 31, 42, 60, 112, 122, 166, 199
reassurance 139, 152, 155, 157
Reay, Diane 43, 47, 159, 176
reciprocity 68, 84, 86, 140, 156, 158, 189
references, cultural 29, 31–2
reflection 103, 121, 193
reflectiveness 68
regularity 78, 114–15, 146
regulation
   self- 38, 115–19, 152–3, 156, 167 (see also executive function)
relationships 25, 46, 76, 80–2, 98, 110, 114, 117, 120, 129, 137–41
   between adults and children 117, 130, 133–5, 151–2, 156–8, 199
   caring 169, 189
   continuity of 85, 151, 168
   reciprocal 86, 135
   of trust 12, 135, 151
   unpredictable 60, 172
religion 8, 18–19, 47–50, 67, 109, 117, 163, 175, 188, 196
representation, modes of 88–9, 96, 108, 127
resilience 18, 68, 93, 140, 146, 148, 154, 155, 170
   children's need for 125
   nature of 125
resourcefulness 68
respect 7, 58, 68, 135, 146, 148–9, 152, 192, 199
responsibilities 55, 120, 137
   adults' 54, 145, 168, 198
responsibility, children taking 55, 77, 115, 118, 121, 123, 145, 158
rewards 18, 41, 54, 78, 114, 117
   tangible 117, 153
rights 67
   children's 55–6, 97, 145
   participation 55
   protection 55
   provision 55
   and responsibilities 55, 120, 145
risk-taking 69, 95, 114, 151
ritual 49, 114–15, 158, 165

rivalry 116, 118, 123, 158, see also competition, inter-personal
Rogoff, Barbara 45, 55, 84, 121, 152, 156, 160
role models 59, 85, 86, 146, 152, 156, 164, 175, see also example
   need for diverse 147, 159, 197, 198, 200
routine 48, 78, 83, 114–15, 146, 158, 178
rules 99, 114, 166, see also maxims
   explicit 121, 181
   implicit 121, 167, 181

safety 95–6, 199
Salmon, Phillida 75, 84, 89, 169
sanctions 54, 118
schemata 87
school 5, 7, 28, 41, 46–7, 54, 61–5, 75, 130, 133, 169–74, 179, 195, 198–201
   supplementary 166
scripts 83
second nature 5, 25, 89, 120
secularization 49, 57, 67, 188
security 111, 115, 137, 157, 165
self-concept 78
self-esteem 8, 18, 20, 46, 57, 78–9, 87, 93, 113, 124, 139, 141, 151, 153–5, 159, 161, 166–7, 172, 174, 191, 192
self/selfhood 17–19, 80, 139
   narratives of 102
   understanding of 82
sensitivity 13, 60, 69, 87, 127, 139, 148, 161, 163, 185, 196, 198
   cultural 129, 164, 171–2, 175, 182
settings, formal 20, 45, 83, 85, 112, 120, 124, 149, 151
sexism 27, 60, 122, 166, 196, 122
sexualisation 36, 59
shame 21, 32–3, 46, 79, 116
showing how 152, 180
sibling 158, 160
'significant others' 82, 117, 164
similarity 7, 109, 126, 130, 180
skills 7, 61, 177
   decontextualised 63, 65, 173
   practical 6
   social 156

sleep   78, 134, 192
socialization   5, 8, 35, 37, 76, 120
   primary   3, 82, 156
   secondary   3, 82-3
space   92, 96, 101, 109, 114, 156, 158, 192, 194, 197
   'dilemmatic'   178
   hospitable   114, 145, 173
spirituality   18, 47, 59
sport   59, 167
stability   81, 156-7, 182
'standards agenda'   63, 201
status   21, 23, 26, 33, 35, 38, 43, 77, 152
stereotypes   5, 24, 122, 143, 145, 147, 157, 187, 196
stimulation   53, 99
stories   78, 90, 101-5, 110, 168, 175, 177, 179
stress   46, 78, 99, 114, 134, 151, 192
   effect of   114, 119
structure   12, 48, 83, 94, 121-2, 133, 145, 167-8, 178, 188, 194
subjects, school   61, 63-4, 176, 177, 198, *see also* disciplines
success   5, 13, 38, 41, 45-6, 58, 63-4, 124, 125, 141, 156, 169, 174, 196
   images of   59, 86, 134, 142, 159, 189-91
superiority   28, 40, 42
support   72, 82, 84, 120, 130, 139, 155-7, 195
support staff in schools   169, 185
survival   55, 116
sustainability   7, 67

talk
   adult   138, 152, 159, 161
   children's   12, 63, 89, 91, 98, 114, 120, 127, 156, 158, 161, 163
teacher, role of the   169, 173-4, 181-2, 199
teaching
   as an 'impossible profession'   181-2
   as a profession   172
teamwork   167, 174, 185, *see also* cooperation
teasing   79, 184
technology   57, 99
   availability of   57
   influence of   57-9, 190

television   27, 31, 158
telling   179
temperament   8, 11, 20, 76, 116, 134
tests   7, 54, 182
theory of mind   77-9, 121
thinking
   critical (*see* critical thinking)
   logical-scientific   62, 90
   narrative   62, 90
   sustained shared   123, 179
thought, children's   4, 80, 87
time   59, 92, 96, 108, 114, 152, 158, 192, 194, 197-8
'time-out'   54, 118
toddlers   2, 90, 156
toys   5, 18, 37, 99, 157, 175
tradition   6, 23, 29, 48-9, 72, 94, 102, 103, 174, 177
   religious   48-9, 103, 109, 165
transition   45, 120, 154-5, 197
trivialization   10, 59, 149
trust   86, 117, 126, 129, 148

uncertainty   65, 95, 149
   confident   182
unconscious   4, 11, 89, 106, 144, 181-2
UNCRC (United Nations Convention on the Rights of the Child)   52, 55, 97
underachievement   28, 42, 163, 200
understanding, children's   7, 17, 21, 61, 75, 77, 83, 91, 105-10, 121, 126, 145, 161, 176, 183, 189
unhappiness   57, 134
uniform   166, 168
unpredictability   108, 114
upbringing   35, 188

values   24, 43, 67, 94, 104, 112, 119-20, 130, 136, 147, 156, 160, 162, 171, 174, 193
   aspirational   67, 119
   descriptive   67
   hierarchy of   68
   lived   119
   universal   67, 68, 120
violence   27, 36, 137, 147
   domestic   60, 134
virtue ethics   18, 66, 130, 195

voice, children's   179
vulnerability   72, 98, 101, 137, 163

watching   83, 101, 138, 146, 152, 179,
    *see also* observing
ways of working   3, 47, 152
WEIRD (Western, educated,
    industrialized, rich
    democracies)   6, 54, 197

well-being   30, 116, 129, 134, 190
women   8, 28, 35–6, 59–60, 120, 147,
    159, 175
wonder   98
worship   165–6

xenophobia   57

Zone of Proximal Development   84, 179

Lightning Source UK Ltd.
Milton Keynes UK
UKHW010425070921
390095UK00004B/185